THE STORY OF LITERATURE

FROM ANTIQUITY TO THE PRESENT

© 2010 Tandem Verlag GmbH
h.f.ullmann is an imprint of Tandem Verlag GmbH

Editors: Ritu Malhotra & Gaurav Dikshit
Design: Supriya Sahai & Baishakhee Sengupta
DTP: Neeraj Nath, Ajmal Khan
Arrangement: e.fritz, berlin06
Project coordination: Daniel Fischer, Ulrike Reihn-Hamburger
Cover arrangement: e.fritz, berlin06
Cover design: Yvonne Schmitz
Overall responsibility for production:
h.f.ullmann publishing, Potsdam, Germany

Printed in China

ISBN 978-3-8331-5258-0

10 9 8 7 6 5 4 3 2 1
X IX VIII VII VI V IV III II I

If you would like to be informed about forthcoming h.f.ullmann titles, you can request our
newsletter by visiting our website (**www.ullmann-publishing.com**) or by emailing us at:
newsletter@ullmann-publishing.com.
h.f.ullmann, Birkenstraße 10, 14469 Potsdam

DANIEL ANDERSSON
MARIA LORD
MICHAEL MACAROON
CLARE PEEL
TARA STUBBS

THE STORY OF LITERATURE

FROM ANTIQUITY TO THE PRESENT

h.f.ullmann

CONTENTS

Chapter 1
ORIGINS AND ANTIQUITY
MYTHS, LEGENDS, AND EPICS

THE GREEK TRAGEDIANS, Study of *The Apotheosis of Homer,* 1827, Jean-Auguste-Dominique Ingres, oil on canvas, Louvre, Paris, France

Ingres' work of art, probably inspired by Raphael's *The School of Athens,* shows Homer surrounded by famous Western figures of literature and art. Sophocles and Aeschylus are seen here, who, along with Euripides, are the best-known Athenian tragic poets. Homer is the most influential author ever, whose epics *Iliad* and *Odyssey* form the base of the classical Western tradition.

FACING PAGE: Reconstruction of the Agora (main square) in Athens, the birthplace of Western literature.

The geographical origins of Western literature lie in areas as diverse as the Middle East, the Mediterranean, the central European forests, and the northwestern coasts, each of which produced a body of oral histories, myths, and legends, many of which were subsequently written down. They have been drawn on by writers since the emergence of a Western literate culture in ancient Greece. Stories have been used as entertainment, as origin myths (of the physical world, culture, or society), and as a way of preserving ideas and traditions.

Attesting to the power of such stories as an important component of human societies, for good or ill, many of these retain a grip on the modern world, whether as religious texts or as a corpus of ideas that give peoples and nations a series of myths through which they can define and identify themselves as a distinct group. Though these should be taken as myths—and even the idea of a Western literary tradition is "mythological" and hard to delineate—many of the stories that have shaped Western history stem from other

CUNEIFORM INSCRIPTION ON THE STONE OF TAK-KERSA, Assyria

cultures (such as the Bible), or were a consequence of trade or colonialism (for example, the constructions of the "other" through crusader narratives or collections such as *Arabian Nights*), or were exported or were brought by migrating peoples (as in the work of North American writers, some like Henry James who moved east across the Atlantic, or writers from a South Asian background, such as Salman Rushdie, who have spent their working lives in Europe). The boundaries of European, and even Western, literature have been porous, allowing for the exchange of ideas and narratives. Indeed, it is partly this ability to absorb and integrate literary influences that has defined the Western world as a cultural region.

MESOPOTAMIA AND EGYPT

Perhaps the earliest recorded narrative is the *Epic of Gilgamesh,* known to modern-day scholars through inscriptions on 11 cuneiform tablets from the reign of the Assyrian Ashurbanipal (*r. c.* 668–627 BC). However, elements of this Mesopotamian epic are thought to have been composed during the Sumerian kingdom in around 2000 BC. The central hero, Gilgamesh, may in fact have been based on a historical figure, a king of the city of Uruk, currently believed to have been situated on the banks of the Euphrates. The story itself is complicated and episodic, but all the sections are concerned with the exploits of Gilgamesh and can be summarized as follows: Gilgamesh and Enkidu fight, after which, as neither emerges victorious, they become friends. Together, Gilgamesh and Enkidu then defeat Humbaba while raiding wood from his lands. Gilgamesh rejects the advances of the goddess Ishtar (referred to as Inanna in the Assyrian text). Angered, she sends the Bull of Heaven to kill him, which is subsequently killed by Gilgamesh and Enkidu. As Gilgamesh is protected by the sun god Utu, Ishtar demands that Enkidu dies in his place. After Enkidu's death Gilgamesh searches for the secret of immortality and meets Utnapishtim, the only man to have achieved endless life, granted by the gods following his rescue of humankind during the devastating flood sent by the god Marduk. Gilgamesh realizes that he will never achieve true immortality and returns to Uruk.

A number of themes seen here run though many epics, including that of a heroic figure at the center of the narrative who overcomes many trials sent by the gods. Of particular

GILGAMESH, Layard relief

Gilgamesh was an ancient king of Uruk in Babylonia in about 2700 BC. Many stories and legends have been told about him; the *Epic of Gilgamesh* is the most complete version known. It is derived from 11 stone tablets in the Akkadian language, found in 1853 al Nineveh in the library of Ashurbanipal (who reigned as king of Assyria from about 668 to 627 BC).

interest in the Gilgamesh epic is the episode that deals with the flood, which is the earliest source for the same story (that of Noah) in the Book of Genesis in the Bible. The same myth also corresponds with the ancient Greek story of Zeus unleashing a flood to destroy humankind; Deucalion and his wife Pyrrha survive by building a huge boat, and repopulate the earth by throwing stones behind them, which turn into men and women. Some scholars believe that the passage where Gilgamesh searches for immortality shows parallels to Homer's *Odyssey* where Odysseus travels to the edge of the world and enters the underworld. While it is the best-known Sumerian/Assyrian text, *Gilgamesh* is not the only Mesopotamian epic that has survived. Other stories include *Enmerkar and the Lord of Aratta*, *Enmerkar and Ensukheshdanna*, and the *Epic of Shulgi*.

The flood also occurs as a significant theme in the mythology of ancient Egypt, this time related to the Nile annually bursting its banks and providing the Egyptians with fertile soils. The twin concepts of "dry" and "wet" run through many of the Egyptian creation myths, the dry associated with the male principle and the wet—in essence, fertility and creation—with the female.In addition, the falcon-headed sun god Ra, also considered the god of creation, is said in some accounts to have emerged from primordial flood waters. The most famous of the Egyptian myths, however, concerns the god Osiris, and is in many ways similarly linked to the Egyptian landscape, alluding to the unification of the kingdom. Osiris was the ruler of the world, but his brother Seth murdered him and took his place. Osiris's body was dismembered and scattered all over Egypt, only to be collected in secret by his wife and sister Isis. She reassembles his body, and before Osiris descends to become god of the underworld they have a son, Horus, who, like Ra, is also depicted with a falcon's head. A battle between Horus and Seth ensues during which, in most versions of the story, Seth is defeated and Horus subsequently takes his father's place as the god of the earth. A possible link with later Christian iconography might be made

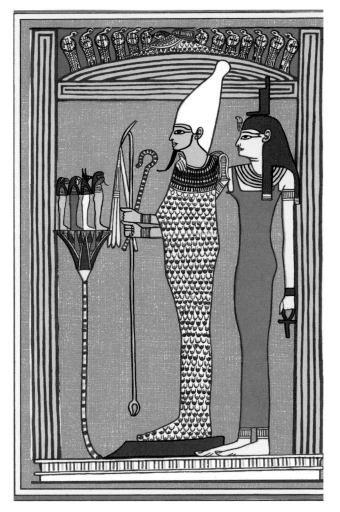

ISIS AND OSIRIS, AND THE CHILDREN OF HORUS

Osiris, the god of the dead and the ruler of the underworld, was one of the most important deities of ancient Egypt. Together with his consort Isis, he became popular in the first millennium BC when worship of the sun god was in relative decline. Various myths about him, Isis, and their son Horus are derived from allusions in the *Pyramid Texts* (c. 2400 BC), from New Kingdom source documents such as the *Shabaka Stone* and the *Contending of Horus and Seth*, and from the writings of Greek authors Plutarch and Diodorus Siculus. According to these myths, Osiris was the dead and resurrected king, who symbolized fertility and the renewal of life in the other world. In the Egyptian concept of divine kingship, the king in death was identified with Osiris, and his son and successor with Horus. Gradually, Osiris evolved from being the ruler of the underworld to the power that granted life to the dead. He was worshiped, along with other local underworld deities, in the temple of Abydos, in the hope of gaining rebirth in the next life.

between Isis nursing the infant Horus and the similar figure of Mary with the infant Christ. Aside from this, there is little else that filters through into general Western culture until the 18th and 19th centuries, when excavations began to bring to light the monuments and, after the decipherment of hieroglyphics in the 1820s, the written records of early Egypt. The region, like many other areas, was eventually to fall under the spell of the Hellenic world, first through the conquests of Alexander the Great (*r.* 336–323 BC) and subsequently under the Ptolemaic dynasty (*r.* 305–31 BC).

ALCAEUS AND SAPPHO

Sappho and Alcaeus (6th century BC), inhabitants of Mytilene on the island of Lesbos, wrote lyric poetry in 612–609 BC. While Sappho wrote love poetry, Alcaeus's themes were wine, war, and politics. Both were aristocrats and rumored to be lovers.

ANCIENT GREECE

While myths and legends from the Middle East (in the form of the Bible) were to have a decisive effect on the direction of Western literature after Christianity was established during the Middle Ages, before then—and, later, from the 17th and 18th centuries onward—a wholly different set of ideas and writings were to hold sway: that of the ancient Greeks. The scale of the influence of Greek thought, transmitted via the Romans and Arabs, on Western art and literature can scarcely be exaggerated, for from the Renaissance to the Enlightenment it vied with Christian scripture as the dominant cultural influence and laid the foundations for much of the philosophy and thought of the modern world.

The peculiar quality of Greek thought and writing that enabled it to cast such a clear and critical eye on the world may lie, in part, in the religious beliefs of the ancient Greeks. While other early societies, such as those in Egypt, Palestine, and the Middle East, were bound by rigid social structures, sanctioned by a religion in which there were strict and definable rules and modes of behavior, in Greece it was believed that there was a pantheon of deities—many of questionable moral virtue—who, while they occasionally meddled in human affairs and were keen on seducing mortals, generally remained detached from the everyday workings of the world and were not shown any strict allegiance by humans. This left thinkers and writers relatively free to conduct their own investigations into nature and human behavior, and privileged the aim of a dispassionate observance of the world, in

GREECE

c. 2100–1200 BC First the Minoans on Crete and then the Mycenaeans on the Peloponnese form Bronze Age kingdoms.

c. 1100–750 BC Dorians begin to establish city-states, including Athens and Sparta, on the Greek mainland.

c. 800 BC Homer and Hesiod write the *Iliad*, *Odyssey*, *Theogony* and *Works and Days*.

7th century BC Sappho writes poetry.

5th century BC The dramas of Aeschylus, Sophocles, Euripides, and Aristophanes.

490 BC The Athenians defeat the Persians at Marathon, marking the beginning of the ascent of Athens as a dominant power.

478 BC The naval Confederation of Delos is formed as a protection against further attacks from Persia.

443–429 BC The age of Pericles; the Acropolis in Athens is rebuilt and the Parthenon erected.

431–404 BC The Peloponnesian Wars; Athens capitulates and Sparta emerges as the strongest Greek city-state.

411 BC Aristophanes produces *Lysistrata*.

338 BC Philip of Macedonia takes control of all Greek city-states except Sparta, later incorporated into the Macedonia Empire by Philip's son Alexander.

320 BC Aristotle begins *Poetics*, a defense of poetry.

POLYPHEMUS THE CYCLOPS

In Homer's *Odyssey* (Book 9), Odysseus and his men take shelter in the cave of Polyphemus the Cyclops. The giant traps the Greeks by blocking the entrance of the cave with a huge stone and begins devouring them. Odysseus intoxicates Polyphemus with wine, and while the giant sleeps, pierces his eye with a burning stake. The blinded Cyclops tries to sink Odysseus' escaping ship with rocks, but fails in the attempt. Here he is seen hurling stones at Odysseus and his crew.

of Greek literature occur, therefore, later than the period in which Greece was starting to develop a distinctive identity. Two of the most important of these sources, however, do set their narratives in Mycenaean Greece (c. 1700–1250 BC) and introduce us to a world of figures who were to remain constant characters throughout Greek literature; these are the *Iliad* and the *Odyssey*.

Traditionally these two great epics—in many ways the founding texts of Western literature—have been ascribed to the writer Homer. Most scholars currently doubt whether he or she is the original author of the poems. It, however remains likely that a single figure around the 8th century BC collated existing oral epics on the same themes and produced the two texts known today. Both works are set during and after the Greek siege and victory over the city of Troy. A city-state, known as Troy VIIa, on the coast of present day Turkey, was destroyed between 1300 and 1200 BC, around the time of the collapse of the Mycenaean kingdoms in Greece, although there is considerable conjecture as to whether this was due to the war described by Homer. One way or another, the *Iliad,* in particular, was seen by the Greeks as the most important founding document of their civilization, narrating the unification of the Greek peoples for the first time against a common enemy and articulating concepts such as honor, bravery, and right action—important ideals in ancient Greece.

The story of the *Iliad* takes place against the siege of Troy by the Greeks under the legendary house of Atreus. The two sons

all its beauty and ugliness, above that of an imposed discourse that sought to limit narratives to devotion and obedience.

While there was undoubtedly some influence on the core of Greek literature from earlier and neighboring cultures (especially the Phoenicians, whose alphabet partly inspired the Greek and modern Roman scripts), no surviving sources remain to give us a clear idea of the literatures of peoples such as the Phoenicans and, until perhaps the decipherment of the Linear A script, the Minoans of Crete. The earliest sources of Atreus—Agamemnon, king of Mycenae, and Menelaus, king of Sparta—married the two sisters Clytemnestra and Helen. Helen was very beautiful and was awarded by Aphrodite to Paris, son of King Priam of Troy, after he had chosen her as the most beautiful of three goddesses. Paris abducted Helen and took her back to Troy, prompting Agamemnon and Menelaus to form an all-Greek army to retrieve her and punish the Trojans. It is at this point that the poem begins. With the Greek army camped outside the walls of Troy, their leader Agamemnon argues with the hero Achilles, who refuses to continue fighting. Following this, the poem describes the battles and the changing fortunes of the two sides, as well as the machinations of the gods in trying to gain advantage for their favored side. One

of the most famous narratives lies toward the end of the *Iliad*, in which Patroclus, Achilles' close friend, borrows the hero's armor but is killed by Hector, King Priam's son. This prompts Achilles to rejoin the fighting, subsequently beating back the Trojans, and eventually killing Hector, whose body he drags around the walls of Troy behind his chariot. The poem ends with Priam pleading for his son's body. Ultimately, Achilles relents and relinquishes Hector's body to the king.

In the continuation of the Trojan war narrative, Achilles is killed by Paris, who wounds him in his heel, his only vulnerable spot (hence the expression "Achilles heel"). The Trojans are subsequently defeated through a subterfuge by the Greeks;

THE TROJAN HORSE

The legends from the Trojan War, fought between the Greeks and Troy, were found throughout the Greek and Latin literature, the most notable being Homer's *Iliad* and *Odyssey*, and Virgil's *Aeneid*. When the Greeks were forced to withdraw from the 10-year war, they left behind the Trojan horse, with Greek soldiers concealed inside, who subsequently plundered Troy.

FACING PAGE: *ACHILLES DEFEATING HECTOR,* 1630–1632, Peter Paul Rubens, Oil on panel, private collection, Freiburg, Germany

During the Trojan War, Achilles slays Hector, the eldest son of King Priam of Troy and drags his body behind his chariot. At Priam's heartfelt request, Achilles relinquishes Hector's body. The *Iliad* ends with Hector's funeral. However, it makes no mention of the death of Achilles at the hands of Paris, though Achilles' funeral is mentioned in the *Odyssey*. The poet Arctinus, in his *Aethiopis*, takes forward the story of the *Iliad* and mentions that Achilles, having slain the Ethiopian king Memnon and the Amazon Penthesilea, was himself killed by Priam's younger son Paris, whose arrow was guided by Apollo and pierced Achilles' heel, the only vulnerable part in his body.

they leave a supposed offering of a large wooden horse that contains hidden Greek soldiers, who emerge at night and lay waste to the city. This incident is described in Homer's second great poem, the *Odyssey*, which primarily focuses on the wanderings of the Greek hero Odysseus, who becomes lost on his way back to his home island of Ithaca from the war against Troy. During his travels Odysseus is shipwrecked, fights the Polyphemus Cyclops, escapes from the witch Circe, evades the dangers of Scylla and Charybdis, and is imprisoned by the nymph Calypso. When he finally reaches Ithaca, he finds that his wife Penelope is about to choose a husband from a

number of suitors who have been importuning her (as he has by this time been away for 10 years, Odysseus is thought to be dead). With the help of his son Telemachus and the old faithful servant Eumeus, Odysseus kills the suitors and regains his wife and lands.

Although the *Iliad* and *Odyssey* are the earliest surviving Western literary texts, known not only through the original Greek but also in celebrated translations by notable literary figures, including Alexander Pope and Samuel Butler, other poems exist from the same period, such as those by the poet

HERODOTUS READS THE *HISTORIES* TO A LARGE CROWD, Late 19th century engraving by Heinrich Leutemann

Herodotus wrote about the wars between Greece and Persia (499–479 BC) in the *Histories*. Divided into nine books in its surviving form, the *Histories* also describes the growth and organization of the Persian Empire.

Hesiod. He is known as a figure with more certainty than Homer from slight references to events in Hesiod's own life within his two surviving poems, the *Theogony* and *Works and Days*. Valuable in their own right and because of the influence they had on later writers such as Virgil and Milton, the two poems also contain valuable evidence concerning the beliefs and lives of the early Archaic Greeks. The first work, the *Theogony*, outlines the origins of, and relationships between,

the Olympian deities of ancient Greece—a vital source in understanding its religion—while *Works and Days* describes rural life and agriculture.

Lying chronologically between Hesiod and the later writers of Classical Greece (from the 5th century BC onward) is the female poet Sappho (mid-7th century BC), who was born on the island of Lesbos. Her surviving works are a series of 12 love poems, mostly known from fragments, this possibly makes her the first lyric poet. The desired object in the poems is a woman, leading many to conjecture that she was a lesbian (indeed the word itself, derived from the island of her birth, refers to Sappho).

While these works of ancient Greek poets, especially Homer and Hesiod, provided many clues to classicists and archeologists piecing together the history of ancient Greece, two writers in particular consciously set out to record the events of their own time and immediate past: Herodotus (*c.* 484–425 BC) and Thucydides (*c.* 460–395 BC). Herodotus is known as the "father of history," the first writer to record and evaluate the evidence and sources for events that actually happened, having as his aim a true record of events. His work, *Histories*, describes the events leading up to and the attempted Persian invasion of Greece by Xerxes in 480 BC. In this masterful and wide-ranging account, Herodotus outlines the earlier histories of both Athens (the dominant city-state within the Greek army) and Persia, deals with the earlier invasion of Greece by Xerxes' father Darius, and includes valuable information from his own travels to distant lands such as Egypt. Earlier texts that survive from ancient Greece are either poems (as with Homer and Sappho) or, with Aeschylus, drama. The *Histories* is the earliest surviving work of prose of Western literature—although fragments remain of earlier prose writers of histories (or, more likely, hagiographies) of city-states, such as Hecataeus of Miletus (*fl. c.* 500 BC).

THE CHORUS OF *ANTIGONE*

Antigone, the daughter of King Oedipus, defies the order of her uncle King Creon and buries her brother Polyneices secretly. For this, she is immured in a cave, where she hangs herself. The chorus, an integral part of the play, provides insightful commentary on the actions of the characters.

A SCENE FROM *BIRDS* BY ARISTOPHANES

Regarded as a comedy of fantasy, *Birds* is perceived by some scholars as a political satire on Athenians ill-fated expedition in 415-413 BC to conquer Syracuse in Sicily. The actors in this performance are wearing masks as was the normal practice on the Athenian stage.

For all his reliance on verified sources and his highly readable prose, Herodotus is not, however, a truly dispassionate observer—his sympathies lie clearly with the Greek side. The slightly later figure of Thucydides might hold a better claim to being the "father of history" in a modern sense. In his great work *The History of the Peloponnesian War*, an account of the conflict between Athens and Sparta that wracked ancient Greece between 431 and 404 BC, he brings a scientific approach to the presentation of his evidence and sources. Where Herodotus introduced legends, travelogs, and intimations of divine intent into his text, Thucydides is more direct and factual, declining to make moral judgments or unsupported speculations, even if as a result *The History of the Peloponnesian War* is less readable and engaging than Herodotus's Histories. The period of history following that of Thucydides was recorded by Xenophon (c. 430–352 BC) in his *Hellenica*. More importantly, however, he is noted for his biography of Cyrus of Persia (the *Cyropedia*). This fictionalized account was the first in what would become a tradition of imaginative biographical writing and shows the early beginnings of a genre that was eventually to become the novel.

While legend claims that the first actor was the 6th-century singer Thespis and the first writer of tragedies his pupil Phrynichus (*fl.* 511 BC), the earliest Greek dramatist whose work still survives is Aeschylus (525–456 BC). The first Greek tragedies, of which none remain, are thought to have consisted of one actor whose words and actions were commented on by a chorus that stood as a group at the back of the stage. This convention was retained by Aeschylus but, aside from his impressive skill as a dramatist, his importance lies in introducing more than one actor to the stage at the same time, thus allowing characters to directly interact with each other. Interestingly, his first surviving play, *The Persians* (472 BC), drew directly on his own experiences at the battle of Salamis, predating Herodotus's writings on the same theme.

Aeschylus wrote over 70 plays, of which seven still exist. These are *The Suppliants*, *The Persians*, *Seven Against Thebes*, *Prometheus Bound*, and the *Oresteia* trilogy (perhaps his greatest achievement), comprising *Agamemnon*, *The Choephori* (also known as *The Libation Bearers*), and *The Eumenides*. The narrative follows the events that befall the house of Agamemnon on his return from the Trojan war. In his absence, Agamemnon's wife Clytemnestra has taken as a lover Aegisthus (Agamemnon's uncle, who was robbed of the throne by his brother Atreus), and when Agamemnon returns to Mycenae, Clytemnestra murders him. In *The Choephori*, Orestes, Agamemnon's son, returns to Mycenae to avenge his father's death. He kills both Clytemnestra and Aegisthus, but for the terrible crime of killing his mother he is pursued by the Furies as he flees to the shrine of Apollo at Delphi. *The Eumenides* tells of Orestes' appearance before the oracle at Delphi and his plea to the gods to release him from the Furies. Apollo defends Orestes to the goddess Athena, who absolves Orestes from his crime and releases the Furies from their charge of pursuing those guilty of matricide and parricide. Aside from the debate throughout the trilogy about "right action," the final play can be seen as the conclusion of a

Act III. MEDEA. *Scene I.*

Thornthwaite sculp

M.ʳˢ SIDDONS as MEDEA.

MEDEA, Actress Sarah Siddons as Medea, 1792

Medea, one of Euripides' best-known plays, is the story of the ruthless revenge of a wronged woman. In this dark tragedy, Medea, having been betrayed by her husband, slaughters their children to punish him.

passage from darkness to light, as an allegory of the rise of a democratic Classical Athens out of the age of the dictators, or as the triumph of the Olympian gods over the older and crueler Dionysian world represented by the Furies.

The 5th century BC was the age of Periclean Classical Athens. Besides Aeschylus, the city saw the emergence of three other

SOPHOCLES,
Lateran Museum,
Rome, Italy

A famous Athenian tragic poet, Sophocles is best known for his plays *Ajax*, *Antigone*, and *Oedipus*. In many ways, he changed the way tragedies were enacted on stages. He raised the number of actors from two to three and enlarged the size of the chorus from 12 to 15 members. This allowed the dramatist to increase the number of characters and depict more complex situations. His plays were more about relations between humans rather than between humans and gods. Another innovation was his use of large painted panels. He also abandoned the Aeschylean style of a connected trilogy and completed the story in a single play.

Although these do trace the story of Oedipus—who kills his father and unknowingly marries his mother, and who was later to lend his name to one of Freud's theories of psychoanalysis—there is no evidence that they were originally meant to be grouped together, and it is thought they were written many years apart.

Euripides, by contrast, while also prolific and no doubt aware of the dramatic developments explored by Aeschylus and Sophocles, has a larger corpus of works (possibly 19 plays, although the authorship for one of these is disputed). A number of them—notably *Medea*, *The Bacchae* and *The Trojan Women*—are still part of the theatrical repertoire, having been reintroduced through late-19th- and 20th-century translations. While Aeschylus and Sophocles were greatly concerned with the mythology and legendary history that underpins much of their work, Euripides has a dramatic urgency that still appeals to modern audiences and readers through his greater concentration on the individual characters of his *dramatic personae*. In the hands of Euripides, these become real, living people whose actions are neither wholly good or bad but tinged with shades of gray, and so awaken our sympathy.

exceptional dramatists. These are Sophocles (496–406 BC), Euripides (c. 485–406 BC), and the younger Aristophanes (c. 448–380 BC). Like Aeschylus, Sophocles is said to have also written a large number of plays—thought to be around 120 in number—of which only seven have survived. Sophocles was possibly even more influential than Aeschylus, and very highly regarded during his lifetime, and his writing and insights into the human condition influenced writers as diverse as Milton, Yeats, and Freud. His surviving plays include *Ajax*, *Elektra*, *Philoctetes*, and *The Women of Trachis*. However, again like Aeschylus, his most famous work is the so-called *Theben Trilogy*: *Oedipus Rex*, *Oedipus at Colonus*, and *Antigone*.

While these three great dramatists—Aeschylus, Sophocles, and Euripides—are all writers of tragedy, Aristophanes is a very different, though equally important, figure. Although there was a strong tradition of satire and comedic writing in Athens, the 11 plays we know of Aristophanes are the only surviving examples (the others are known from second-hand reports) and include *The Wasps*, *The Frogs*, *Lysistrata*, and *Ecclesiazusae*. Like modern satire, his plays attack and ridicule prominent individuals in public life and, as such, are a valuable historical source on life in contemporary Athens as well as amusing dramas. Aristophanes' humor was not always at the expense of politicians and statesmen—Euripides also makes several appearances in his plays.

Aristophanes died in 380 BC, by which time the temporal power of Athens was beginning to wane, and with it the city's cultural dominance. However, the 5th and 4th centuries BC saw Athens emerge as the center of philosophical discourse with an extraordinary lineage of thinkers and teachers making the city their home, including Zeno (c. 490–430 BC), Socrates (c. 470–399 BC), Plato (c. 428–348 BC), and Aristotle (384–322 BC), the latter being the teacher of Alexander the Great. With the rise of the Macedonian Empire under Philip II (r. 359–336 BC) and Alexander the Great (r. 336–323 BC) the demise of Classical Greece was complete, although the new Hellenic kingdoms produced little to match that of the 5th-century Athens.

ROME TO BYZANTIUM

In 168 BC, Macedonian Greece was subsumed into the burgeoning Roman Republic (c. 509–27 BC), now the dominant power in southern Europe. As in so many other areas, from music to architecture, Rome aped the achievements of the earlier Greeks in its literature. This does not denigrate the many superb, and often lively, writers, poets, and dramatists of Rome

but rather points to the overwhelming legacy bequeathed to the Western literary tradition by the Greeks.

Little survives of the earliest Latin writers but works remain by the two most important figures, the comic dramatists Plautus (c. 254–184 BC) and Terence (c. 190/180–159 BC). Both writers looked to the plays of the Greeks and many of their works are reinterpretations of Greek plays for a Roman audience. However, the comic narratives they looked to were not the biting political satires of Aristophanes but the later works of Hellenic writers of "New Comedy," such as Menander (c. 342–292 BC), which were devoid of political and social comment. As Greek literature tended to be more obscure than Latin writing until a wider dissemination of the texts in the 19th century, dramatists such as Plautus and Terence were important sources for later writers seeking to learn about classical comedy.

If the 5th century BC was a "golden age" for the Athenians, then the 1st century BC was a similar period for Rome. Up until the fall of the Republic and the birth of the Roman Empire under Augustus in 27 BC, 1st century Rome saw the emergence

THE TRIUMPH OF JULIUS CAESAR,
Paolo Uccello, 100–44 BC, Tempera on panel,
Musée des Arts Décoratifs, Paris, France

ROME

c. 750 BC Rome is founded.

509–265 BC The Early Republic.

c. 200 BC Plautus and Terence create Roman drama based on Greek originals.

168 BC Rome conquers Macedonia and takes control of the Hellenistic kingdoms of Syria and Egypt.

1st century BC The Golden Age of Rome sees the writings of Virgil, Horace, Ovid, and Cicero.

45 BC Julius Caesar becomes the sole ruler of the Roman Republic. He writes *The Gallic War*, an account of his suppression of the Gauls.

27 BC Emperor Augustus assumes power as the Senate-approved Princeps. Livy begins writing *The History of Rome*.

54 BC Nero becomes the emperor of Rome.

19 BC Virgil dies, leaving *Aeneid* incomplete.

AD 79 Vesuvius erupts and destroys Pompeii and Herculaneum.

AD 161–80 Marcus Aurelius becomes the emperor of Rome.

313 Constantine's Edict of Milan ensures religious freedom for Christians.

330 Byzantium is renamed Constantinople and from 395 becomes the capital of the Eastern Roman Empire.

OVID

The Roman poet of elegiac couplets is known for his technical accomplishment of adapting the Latin language to dactylic Greek meters. His hexameters in the mythological *Metamorphoses* are a superb medium for the fast narrative.

VIRGIL, *The Georgics*, 1469, Bibliothéque Municipale, Dijon, France

Virgil, regarded as the greatest poet of Rome, is best known for *Aeneid*, which, taking its cue from the Trojan War, tells the story of Rome's legendary founder Aeneas.

of some of the most important figures of Western literature. Towering above all of them is Virgil (70–19 BC). Not only were his works to help in creating a mythological justification for the Roman state, but they were also to have an immense influence on later writers. Following Hesiod, he made a substantial contribution to the genre of pastoral poetry in his *Eclogues* and *Georgics*, while his greatest, and most substantial work, the *Aeneid*, took its cue from Homer. Virgil traces therein the end of the Trojan war from the viewpoint of the Trojans and describes the flight of Aeneas via Carthage—where he conducts a doomed love affair with its queen, Dido—to Italy where, with the grace of the gods, he founds the city of Rome. By merging the foundation of Rome with the revered canon of the Greeks—even if the Romans thus claimed to stem from the losing side—was particularly welcomed with the fall of the Republic and the need of the emperors to justify their dictatorial position. Both Shakespeare and Milton were influenced by Virgil, but his most celebrated appearance in later literature is as the guide in Dante's *Divina Commedia*.

Virgil was not, of course, the only poet of the period to make his mark on future generations. The works of Catullus (c. 84–54 BC), Horace (65–8 BC), and Ovid (43–18 BC) all display a typically Roman breadth of style and genre, often accompanied by a satirical attitude and keen eye for observation. Catullus was perhaps the most diverse of this trio, producing love poetry,

satirical epigrams (a form that achieved great popularity in Rome), and elegiac verse. Horace is best known for his odes, a form based on earlier Greek lyric poetry and to a sub-genre of which, in the Horatian ode, he gave his name. The youngest of the three, Ovid, was almost as versatile as Catullus, although he is best known for his elegiac love poetry, some of it erotic, and the mythological narratives of his *Metamorphoses*. Stories from this collection achieved a certain popularity during the

CICERO DENOUNCES CATILINE, 1882–88, Fresco by Cesare Maccari, Villa Madama, Rome, Italy

Famous orator and statesman of ancient Rome, Cicero was elected Consul, the highest office in Rome, in 64 BC. He thwarted a conspiracy by Senator Catiline to seize power, and denounced him in the Senate in a series of now-famous orations that forced Catiline to flee. A staunch supporter of the Republic, Cicero was forced into political retirement when Julius Caesar consolidated his power in 48 BC. During this time he wrote his famous essays.

late 19th century and prompted revised versions by a number of authors. Indeed, it inspired the title of Kafka's nightmarish short novel *The Metamorphosis* (*Die Verwandlung*).

Shortly after Ovid, one writer was to produce both essays and dramas: Seneca (*c.* 4 BC–AD 65). A philosopher and politician like Cicero (see below), Seneca wrote philosophical essays outlining the main ideas of Stoicism, and in one he mounted a justification for his espousal of Stoic ideas in the face of his immense personal wealth and comfort. Unlike the works of many of the earlier Roman dramatists and poets, Seneca's nine surviving plays are tragedies, dealing with themes from Greek mythology. It is thought that these highly colorful and gory texts were not meant to be actually performed but instead read aloud at intimate gatherings.

As a republic, the workings of Rome's political system gave rise to much public debate and oratory, particularly in the prosecution of criminal cases or in debates over the on-going wars and power struggles within the political class. The greatest exponent of rhetoric and the discussion of ethics of the time was Cicero (106–43 BC), and many of his own speeches have been recorded. A brilliant orator, he spent his life immersed in the volatile politics of Rome, occasionally condemned to exile. His writings and ideas were to be influential throughout the Middle Ages and Renaissance, and from them it is possible to reconstruct much of the Roman political history of the 1st century BC. Cicero opposed Julius Caesar (100–44 BC) in the general's efforts to take over the Senate and his opponent was to become a rival in literature as well as politics. Caesar's accounts of his military campaigns are not only brilliantly written but are also valuable as first-hand accounts of the peoples and lands of Gaul and Germania.

If Caesar's *Commentaries* provide a contemporary version of events, the foremost historian of the age, Livy (59–17 BC),

PLINY THE ELDER, frontispiece to the *Naturalis Historiae*

The *Naturalis Historiae*, comprising 37 "books," is the first encyclopedic work of general knowledge. Though lacking in accuracy, the encyclopedia was an authority on scientific information up to the Middle Ages.

around them. Martial wrote over 1,500 epigrams which were to achieve considerable popularity after their translation during the 17th century, while Juvenal was similarly popular with writers of the 17th and 18th centuries for his 16 satires on the various foibles of Imperial Rome.

In prose, the 1st century AD was perhaps better served. One of the first natural histories was written by Pliny the Elder (AD 23–79), an immense work that—like the later Encyclopédistes in France, where Pliny's influence was particularly strong—sought to assemble knowledge. The *Natural History* covers subjects as diverse as agriculture, architecture, mining, and textiles. Pliny's nephew (known as Pliny the Younger, AD 62–112) is remembered for his account of the eruption of Vesuvius and the destruction of Pompeii and Herculaneum. It was not only in Rome that there were notable literary endeavors: in Greece, under Roman rule since 168 BC, Plutarch (c. AD 50–125) became the most prominent biographer and essayist of his day. In one of his most famous works, *Parallel Lives*, figures from Greek and Roman history are opposed in pairs to draw attention to their relative faults and virtues. Among his biographies are the *Life of Alexander* and the *Life of Pyrrhus*. As an essayist he is best known for his *Moral Essays,* which cover a great deal of antiquity's philosophical debates and codes of behavior.

sought to record the entire history of Rome up until the first decade AD. Of the 142 books that were said to have encompassed this huge work only 35 remain, but from these, many passages have been taken up by later writers, providing the inspiration for a number of works. The later historian Tacitus (c. AD 55–115) was, through his *Annals* and *Histories*, to provide even more magisterial accounts of the empire's history and in his *Germania* was to give a more balanced description of the peoples of Germany. This latter work counts as one of the first attempts at ethnography and is a seminal source on the early history of northern Europe.

The fall of the Republic seems to have dampened the ardor of Rome's poets and engendered a greater contempt for its society and rulers. The 1st century AD saw two masters of satire turn their jaundiced eyes on Rome, Martial (c. AD 40–104) and Juvenal (c. AD 60–136). Their biting and frequently scatological writings pour scorn on the decadence of the society they saw

The so-called Silver Age of Rome (that of the pagan empire) was brought to an end with the emperor Constantine's Edict of Milan of 313, granting freedom of worship to Christians, and in 395 the division of the empire and the rise of Constantinople and Byzantium in the east. With the adoption of Christianity as the official state religion, the literary world that had hitherto existed waned and disappeared, replaced by the writings of the Church Fathers and the Bible as the most prominent literary influences at the beginning of the Middle Ages.

SCANDINAVIAN AND GERMANIC MYTHOLOGY

THOR FISHING FOR THE SERPENT OF MIDGARD, From *The Boat of the Giant Hymir*, Pen and ink on paper, Royal Library Copenhagen, Denmark.

The Germanic-speaking peoples of northern Europe—those of Germany, Scandinavia, and, to a certain extent, England—can point to a rich body of literature and mythology that pre-dates the imposition of Christianity on their lands. The pantheon of Germanic and Norse deities (often known by slightly different names in Scandinavia and Germany) is largely known to us from the *Snorra Edda* by the great Icelandic writer Snorri Sturluson (1178–1241). In this he re-tells a number of Norse myths through a masterly demonstration of the different types of Norse verse meters. Another 12th-century collection, known as the *Elder Edda*, also describes the history of the Norse deities as well as the epics of a number of Germanic and Norse heroes.

Notable among the deities is Odin/Wotan (the Norse and Germanic forms of his name), the most powerful of the gods, who resides in the mythical hall of Valhalla among the heroes of the dead, brought there by the Valkyries from the field of battle. He is especially associated with the protection of the Volsungs, the heroes of the Germanic epic the *Nibelungenlied*. This 13th-century poem derives much of its material from the *Eddur*, via the *Völsunga Saga*, and tells in part the story of Sigmund and his son Sigurd (Siegfried), Sigurd's love for Brynhild, his tricked marriage with Gudrun of the Niblungs, and Sigurd's death at the hands of Hagen. This, perhaps the greatest of the German epics, formed the basis for

Richard Wagner's opera cycle *Der Ring des Nibelungen*.

Other gods and goddess included Thor/Donnar, the god of thunder. While Wotan was to reign supreme in Germany, Thor was thought of as the most powerful deity in parts of Scandinavia. He is identified by his miraculous hammer—by which he produces the thunder and lightening—and represents the ideal hero. The goddess Frigg/Frija/Freya is sometimes distinguished as two separate goddesses, but each is seen as the wife of Odin/Wotan. Loki, a god of fire and trickery, seems to have lent some of his attributes to Christian conceptions of Satan and is one of the most important Norse/Germanic deities, not least

BRUNNHILDE AND VALKYRIES

Act Three : Brunnhilde instructs her Valkyries to save Siglind.

as it is due to his actions that the end of the world comes about, the Ragnarök or Götterdämmerung, as it is devoured by the wolf Fenrir and the fire giants. Besides these major deities, there are numerous lesser gods and goddesses, trolls and sprites, and heroes and spirits, many associated with aspects of the landscape, that permeated the Norse and German world.

Completely culturally and linguistically separate from the Germanic world, Finland too has its myths and legends that informed its pre-Christian world view. These are contained in the *Kalevala*, a body of oral lore and narratives that was first written down in the 19th century. It is believed that many of the stories it contains are of considerable antiquity.

The Sagas

Perhaps the most well-known and best-loved of the Norse epics are the sagas ("story" in Old Norse). These Icelandic and Norwegian narratives fall into three main types: heroic sagas, royal sagas, and family sagas. The first includes the *Völsunga Saga*, source for the *Nibelungenlied*, as well as the *Sturlunga Saga* that includes heroic figures from the near-historical past. Of the royal—or historic—sagas one of the greatest is the compilation by Snorri Sturluson of the stories of the kings of Norway up to 1177, the *Heimskringla*. The royal sagas are generally written in skaldic verse, a complex set of rules of rhyme, alliteration, and meter that was practised by Norse poets during the 10th and 11th centuries.

The majority of the sagas, however, are those of the "family" type. These are the stories of the settlement and subsequent history of Iceland, and the families that descended from the first settlers. They show the development of Icelandic society from one of disparate settlers into a whole with centralized laws, customs, and government. Forming, in part, a genealogy it is from these that we know much of early

OLAF AND OLD WOMAN, Laxdaela Saga, Legend dated *c.* 956. Olaf Peacock, in Ireland, assures the old woman on his knee that her foster daughter Melkorka is fine in Iceland, giving her a familiar knife and belt.

BIRDS INSTRUCT SIGURD

Part of the epic *Nibelungenlied*. Sigurd (or Siegfried), having tasted dragon's blood, can understand the birds who give him helpful instructions.

Icelandic history, and even today many Icelandic families can use elements contained within the sagas to trace back their past. Of these sagas the two most famous are the *Laxdaela Saga*, about the loves and fortunes of one of the most powerful of Icelandic families, and the *Njáls Saga*. This tells the story of Gunnarr, a brave hero who eventually dies in a fight caused by a feud set off by his wife Hallgerr. Njáll, of the title, is the loyal friend of Gunnarr. The Eyrbyggja and Grettis sagas are also family tales, but also contain stories of trolls, the dead, and other supernatural happenings. Some of the family sagas contain *lausavísur* (occasional) and love poems written in skaldic verse.

CELTIC MYTH AND LEGEND

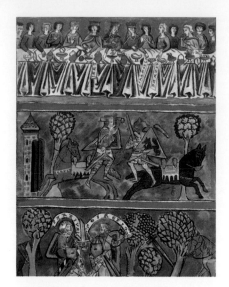

THREE SCENES FROM PARZIFAL

Facsimile from a 13th century manuscript of Eschenbach's epic poem, *Parzifal*. Bibliotheque des Arts Décoratifs, Paris, France.

To talk of the Celtic world as a generalized idea that encapsulates all the peoples rather loosely—settlers in the Central Alps, Scots, Irish, Welsh, Cornish, Breton, Basque, and early-Britons—is problematic. Little now links all these groups and many scholars are now circumspect about ascribing them all a similar cultural past. In addition, the archeological evidence, much of it dating from Roman incursions into the Celtic world, is hard to link to the surviving records we have of Celtic myth and legend. The surviving written sources from the world of Celts overwhelming come from Wales and, especially, Ireland. These survive as both poetry and prose, and the earliest manuscripts date back to the 8th century, although they record stories that have their origins much earlier.

The two sets of surviving tales, the Irish and Welsh, have much in common and tend to support each other, giving at least some evidence of a broadly common culture between these two areas and peoples. Both sets of mythologies were often recorded by Christian monks and so there is undoubtedly some re-working of the myths to bring them more into line with Christian thought, and no doubt to be self-justifying on the part of early missionaries. The Irish sources tend to record more details of the religious beliefs of these early peoples, contained in the *Books of Leinster, the Dun Cow, Ballymote*, and the *Yellow Book of Lecan*. However, one of the most important sources of all is the *Lebor Gabála*, or *Book of Conquests*. This tells the history of Ireland through a series of myths, and how successive waves of invaders and peoples brought new technologies (such as forging gold) and changed the pattern of the landscape before the arrival of the mythological ancestors of the present Irish, the Sons of Mil.

Of these invasions one of the most significant, the one that predated the arrival of the Sons of Mil, were the Tuatha Dé Danann, who may be equated wth the deities of the Celtic, at least Irish, pantheon. Foremost among these deities were Dagda and Lugh, to whom the Irish did not seem to ascribe a fixed, and unique, set of attributes but rather a series of powers, and most especially stories. Dagda is associated with life, death, and fertility. He is said to have dragged a huge club that carried the power of life and death, as well as at a certain festival having to eat a ferocious amount of porridge before having sex with a daughter of the ruling family, thus pointing to his role in human fertility. Lugh, by contrast, was known for his great learning,

CÚ CHULAINN

Cú Chulainn is an Irish mythological hero who appears in the stories of the Ulster Cycle, as well as in Scottish and Manx folklore. Here he is setting out for the fort of Emain Macha in a battle frenzy.

MACHA CURSES ULSTER MAN

The divine queen Macha, a key figure in the Ulster Cycle, curses the men of Ulster because they once insulted her prowess.

Mabinogion, and those deities and heroes mentioned in the Irish sources. The *Mabinogion* consists of four stories, brought together from two manuscripts, the *White Book of Rhydderch* (1300–1325) and the *Red Book of Hergest* (1375–1425). The stories deal with: Pwyll, father of Pryderi; Branwen, daughter of Llyr; Manawyddan, son of Llyr; and the death of Pryderi. Manawyddan and Llyr correspond to the Irish hero-gods Manannán and Lir, but the children of Llyr as a group seem to be more particularly British. Notable among these was Bran, the brother of Manawyddan. If Manawyddan had the terrifying fortress made of bones, Bran was the keeper of a magic cauldron that could bring the dead back to life.

Another family that, while they bear some resemblance to the Irish deities, are only encountered in the Welsh texts are the Children of Don. Among these are Gwydion,

having something in common with Dagda and Lugh, and the smith and brewer Govannnan, who seems to be the equivalent of the Irish Gobniu. Two deities, however, that seem to have no parallel within the Irish myths are the goddess Arianrod and her son Llew, both of whom were occasionally associated with stellar constellations.

As well as these pantheons of deities there was also a tradition of the hero, of which the Arthur legend may be part. If Arthur was the main hero figure of the Britons, then in Irish mythology by far the most important hero was Cúchulainn. One version of his story has him descended from the god Lugh, and, having killed the fierce guard dog of Culann the smith at the age of seven, he is made to guard the kingdom of Ulster against the other four provinces of Ireland during the great Cattle Raid of Cooley, during which he died a hero's death.

legend recounting that he was a warrior, poet, smith, genealogist, and magician. Irish goddesses were a major trinity of Danu, Anu, and Brigit, all associated with the fertility of the ground besides having more complex identities of their own. A further goddess, Macha, was both a warrior and associated with childbirth. The most terrifying of the Irish goddesses of battle, however, was the Morrigan, who could appear in different guises.

The mythological history of the Welsh seems to more overlain with Christian additions but often a direct correspondence can be made between figures mentioned in the main text to have survived, the

THE KNIGHTS ESCLABOR AND ARPHASAR OFFER THEIR SERVICES TO KING ARTHUR

Arthur is an important cultural figure in early Celtic sources from Wales, Cornwall, Lowland Scotland, Brittany, and Cumbria. He appears in various roles—as leader, warrior, chieftain, hero and champion against Anglo-Saxons, to name a few.

Chapter 2
THE MIDDLE AGES
CHURCH AND CHIVALRY

CHAUCER READING *THE CANTERBURY TALES* TO EDWARD III AND HIS COURT, at Sheen Castle in Surrey, England

Written in the 1380s, *The Canterbury Tales* is about a group of pilgrims who agree to tell stories while they travel together to Canterbury, the seat of the English Church and the site of the shrine dedicated to Thomas Beckett. It is a cross section of the medieval society—feudal, ecclesiastical, and urban. Chaucer's interest in middle class characters, such as a cook, carpenter, miller, priest, lawyer, merchant, clerk, and physician, reflects the rise of the middle class in the 14th century.

FACING PAGE: Head of Charlemagne (742–814), Tournai workshop (tapestry), Musée des Beaux-Arts, Dijon, France

Once the Roman empire had effectively ceased to exist as a single entity—split between the West centered on Rome and the East that revolved around Constantinople formerly known as Byzantium—power in Europe became more dispersed. This coincided with the adoption of Christianity across large parts of the continent—an on-going process that was not to be complete until the early years of the second millennium AD, as missionaries took Christianity to the farthest corners of Europe. The power that the Church was to exert over large parts of Europe's cultural life was to be immense—in the visual arts, music, and literature—bequeathing large parts of the continent a single narrative, that of the Bible, through which writers, poets, and chronologists were to interpret the world. However, this pan-European narrative was also to exist in a world that was more fractured than the relative stability of the Roman Empire. To a greater extent than before, the beginnings of national literatures thus arose and a gradual increase in writing in the local vernacular became noticeable, slowly replacing the pan-European convention of Latin as the preferred medium of literary expression (further evidence of the power of the Church). Again, this was a process that would continue well into the second millennium AD. The overlap between the Middle Ages and the succeeding Renaissance was considerable—the works of the English author Geoffrey Chaucer (1343–1400), or his friend John Gower (1330–1408), are a good case in point, straddling two world views—with the medieval esthetic gradually fading over a period of some 200 years.

As with other areas of cultural endeavor, our picture of the literatures of the first half of the first millennium AD is patchy as the peoples of Europe struggled to reorganize and reorientate themselves in the wake of the Roman collapse. It would, however, be a mistake to consider this a period of the Dark Ages merely as so few texts have survived. For those that remain indicate a lively tradition of bardic and epic recitation. These texts were only written down at a much later date, often on the geographical periphery of the continent and from those areas that were outside of the Roman sphere of influence. Examples of these

JOHN GOWER, author of the *Mirroir de l'Omme, Vox Clamantis,* and *Confessio Amantis*.

regional nationalisms—the beginnings of national myths—and also overlaid a pattern of ideal behavior, in particular romantic love, which combined both Christian morality and the social codes and structures of the time.

MONASTICISM, BIBLICAL COMMENTARY, AND THE LIVES OF THE SAINTS

Many surviving literary texts from the Middle Ages come from the libraries of the great monasteries of the time. Monasticism was one of the great innovations of Christianity, arising in the deserts and mountains of Egypt and the Sinai, around the third and fourth centuries AD. This retreat into religious seclusion was in large part an attempt to adhere more closely to the precepts derived from the Bible by the early church fathers. These precepts came from a close reading of the Biblical texts and were propagated by the preservation and dissemination of the Biblical narrative, and its derived teachings. The technology of the time meant that the duplication, or replacement, of texts was an intensive and time-consuming activity, one that was perhaps only possible in a secluded community, where such a specialization was supported by a closely-knit group of like-minded colleagues. It is not surprising, therefore, given the restricted access to literacy and the act of writing itself, that most literary works of the Middle Ages come from the pens of ecclesiastical figures. The monks of the scriptoriums of the medieval monastery diligently copied, recopied, and often beautifully decorated texts.

include the Icelandic sagas, the Germanic *Nibelungenlied* and the Welsh *Mabinogion*. Stemming from bodies of traditional lore, they are a vital source—as are the histories of wars in these regions by Roman commanders—in discovering more about the lives of the peoples of northwestern Europe during their pre-Christian periods. More straightforward, indigenous, and ethnographic accounts, such as that of Pliny, do not exist for these peoples.

More than this, the Middle Ages saw the rise of not only religious commentaries and the start of a biographical tradition recounting the lives of saints and ecclesiastical figures, as well as re-enactments of Biblical narratives through religious dramas. In addition, there emerged a reinterpretation of legend intertwined with contemporary history, yielding narratives that both reinforced a rising sense of large-scale

597 St Augustine is sent by Rome to convert the British. For the next century, Roman Christianity (Catholicism) spreads throughout Anglo-Saxon and Celtic Britain.

632–733 Muslim expansion and conquests in Arabia, Syria, Palestine, Mesopotamia, Egypt, North Africa, Persia, northwestern India, and Iberia.

750 The first great English epic poem, *Beowulf*, is written in Old English.

800 Charlemagne (French king) is crowned Emperor of the Holy Roman Empire.

962–1806 Holy Roman Empire of western and central Europe.

1096–1291 Western Christians undertake the Crusades, a series of religiously-motivated military campaigns, to recapture the Holy Land from the Muslims.

1225 *Parzival*, a major medieval German epic poem attributed to the poet Wolfram von Eschenbach, is written in the Middle High German language.

1273 Thomas Aquinas writes *Summa Theologica*.

14th century Earliest King Arthur tales are recorded in *Mabinogion*.

1307 Dante Alighieri publishes his *Divina Commedia*.

1337–1453 Hundred Years' War, a series of military campaigns between England and France.

1346–1351 Bubonic plague (Black Death) kills one-third of the European population.

1375 *Sir Gawain* and the *Green Knight* appear in Middle English.

1386 Geoffrey Chaucer completes the *Canterbury Tales*.

1436-1440 Gutenberg invents a printing machine that uses movable type.

1455–1487 War of the Roses.

1484 Thomas Malory publishes *Le Morte d'Arthur*.

After Constantine granted Christians freedom of worship, Christian texts soon followed, of which the earliest date back to the rule of Constantine himself. St Athanasius (296–373), bishop of Alexandria, wrote several works including one on the life of St Anthony of Egypt. In addition, the Athanasian Creed has been attributed to him. Shortly thereafter, St Augustine of Hippo (354–430) wrote an account of his own early life, but most importantly a work entitled *De Civitae Dei* (413–427) that was later used to oppose the arguments of the Scholastics. Of the early church fathers, one of the most prolific writers was St Gregory I (540–604), who was responsible for significantly reorganizing the monastic system.

One of the earliest surviving monastic texts from the British Isles on the life of a individual saint is that on St Columba, thought to have been written by St Adomnan (625–704), who was the Abbot of the monastery of Iona. Besides the monastery at Iona, one of the other great British centers of the time was Canterbury. Under the influence and tutelage of Theodore of Canterbury, a school of writing and thinking established itself, giving rise to a body of Anglo-Latin literature, epitomized by writers such as St Aldhelm (639–709). Of his surviving works, perhaps the most remarkable are the series of Latin riddles, contained in a letter to the king of Northumberland, Aldfrith.

Alcuin (735–804), a major figure and thinker of the Carolingian Renaissance, came from the court of Charlemagne (742–814). Although this first Holy Roman Emperor was himself illiterate (signing his documents with three small dots), Charlemagne was keen to promote a culture of scholarly endeavor at his

CHARLEMAGNE WITH ALCUIN

Alcuin spent much of his early life in Yorkshire England. In 781 he met Charlemagne in Italy and accepted his invitation to become head of the Palace School at the court of Charlemagne in Aachen, Germany, where he remained in the 780s and 790s. He wrote many theological and dogmatic treatises, as well as a few grammatical works, and a number of poems. He is considered among the most important architects of the Carolingian Renaissance.

court, extending considerable patronage to writers and philosophers. Under Charlemagne's rule Alcuin established a system of education and wrote a number of works on grammar and philosophy. However, it was not only in continental Europe that inspirational rulers were to promote scholarly works. In England, King Alfred ("the Great"; 848–899) was not only a scholarly man himself (translating the *Historia Adversus Paganos*) but also perceived a need to reinvigorate learning in the country after what he felt was a period of decline.

Similar biographical texts hail from the monasteries of France. One of the most notable is that of Abbo of Fleury (945–1004), who produced a work on the lives of the saints. The Benedictines of Fleury were responsible for re-establishing a strict form of monastic rule and this was brought to England in the 10th century by St Aethelwold (908–984) when he became the bishop of Winchester. He translated the rules of St Benedict, and was also the teacher of one of the most important, and prolific, writers of Old English, Aelfric (955–1010). Besides being a great Biblical translator and one of the most learned men of his day (also writing a Latin grammar), he is best known for his *Lives of the Saints* (993–998). The later monk and chronicler Matthew Paris (*d.* 1259) not only wrote a notable history, the *Chronica Majora*, but also the *Vitae Abbatum S. Albani*, a history of the abbots of the abbey of St Albans.

Peter Abelard (1079–1142), a teacher at Notre Dame and St Geneviève in Paris, was one of the major figures, and often seen as the instigator of Scholasticism, a rational theology that proved to be a radical departure from the theology that had prevailed in the Catholic church so far. Condemned as a heretic in 1142 at the Council of Sens, his *Sic et Non* was a very influential text, but perhaps Abelard's greatest literary legacy is his letters to the niece of the canon of Notre Dame, Héloïse, his student. Their love epitomizes the hopeless romantic attachment favored in medieval literature and prompted later writers to uphold the couple as a supreme example of an all-encompassing but distant dedication. Famously, in order to protect himself from falling into a state of sin through the breaking of his vow of chastity, Abelard castrated himself.

At the Council of Sens, Abelard was opposed by St Bernard, taking his cue from the writings of St Augustine of Hippo whose ideas formed one of the most often-used defenses against

THOMAS AQUINAS

Aquinas was an immensely influential philosopher and theologian in the Scholastic tradition. He developed in great detail a synthesis of Christianity and Aristotelian philosophy that became the official doctrine of Roman Catholic theology in 1879. His best-known works are the *Summa Theologica* and the *Summa Contra Gentiles*, the former representing the most complete statement of his philosophical system.

the Scholastics. However, Scholasticism was to remain one of the most influential theologies throughout the remaining centuries of the Middle Ages. Taking a logical approach to the teachings of the Bible, and also drawing on the writings of Greek philosophers, especially Aristotle, it was given a systematic basis through the extensive discussions of the works of Aristotle, written by the Domenican Albertus Magnus (1206–1280). As a philosophical movement it reached its peak in the writings of Thomas Aquinas (1225–1274), especially his *Summa Theologica*. Aquinas, a Domenican friar from Italy, studied under Albertus Magnus. As a writer, he wielded enormous influence and paved the way for the writings of Dante, especially the *Divina Commedia*. The Scholastic movement saw its final flowering in the works of William of Ockham (1285–1349) in the 14th century.

The Augustines were also concerned with the place of reason within Christianity and their most important exponent of this philosophical position was St Anselm (1033–1109). Originally from Aosta in Italy, he moved to Normandy and was then appointed as the Archbishop of Canterbury. Among his works are the *Monologion* and the *Proslogion*, the latter being particularly influential for its philosophical defense of the existence of God. Reason and logic were also the driving ideals behind one of the first translations of the Bible into the vernacular by John Wycliffe (1330–1384), whose attacks on the excesses of the church predate those of Luther by several centuries.

RELIGIOUS DRAMAS

Religious plays that enact the episodes of the Bible were common across Europe from the 13th to 15th centuries. A number of these still survive and are performed regularly, such as the German *Obergammerau Passion*. Broadly known as "Mystery Plays" they take their name from the word for

PREPARING FOR A MYSTERY PLAY, 16th century, Holland

their actors, "mestier" (from the French *métier*, meaning "trade"). The forerunner of the mystery play can be found in Anglo-French literature (the language used by some after the conquest of England by Normandy in 1066), especially the religious drama the *Mystère d'Adam* (mid-12th century) deals with themes that became commonplace later on, such as the expulsion of Adam and Eve from the Garden of Eden and the story of Cain and Abel.

Four English cycles have survived, from York, Chester, Wakefield, and one from an anonymous source, and it seems as though almost all towns had their own cycle. Each trade guild would be given the task of performing the plays annually for important religious celebrations, in particular that of Corpus Christi. The often multiple authors appear to have been local and often included amusing episodes that throw light on the lives of ordinary people. While secular elements had long been present as part of religious dramas, as comic interludes, it would take a while before a truly secular play appeared in English. *Fulgens and Lucrece* was written by Henry Medwall (*fl.* 1486) and it heralds the arrival of the ideas of the Renaissance in drama.

HISTORY AND LEGEND

Some of the surviving early bardic materials give insight into the history of western Europe, especially the British Isles, that might otherwise have been lost. For example, the poem "Y Gododdin" (thought to have been composed by a bard known as Aneirin in the 6th century, the earliest manuscript of which dates from the 13th century) recounts the story of the battle of Catreath.

Along with this bardic tradition, a considerable body of histories by Anglo-Latin authors surfaced over time. The most notable of these include Bede (673–735), Eadmer (early-12th century), the Benedictine monk Geoffrey of Monmouth (*d.* 1155), noted for his Arthur narrative, as well as William of Malmesbury (1095–1143), and Henry of Huntingdon (1084–1155). Of this group, Bede, a monk who spent most of his life at the Monastery of St Paul, at Jarrow in Northumberland, remains the most famous and reliable. His *Historia Eccelsiastica Genti Anglorum* (731) is one of the principal sources for early English history. Bede was also responsible for a large number of Biblical commentaries and made one of the first attempts at a natural history, after Pliny, with his *De Natura Rerum*.

Histories, however, were not restricted to those scholars working in Latin. One of the most important sources for the history of the pre-conquest British Isles was written in English and the manuscripts are collectively known as the *Anglo-Saxon Chronicles*. Telling the story of England from around the 5th century onward, it is conjectured that King Alfred may have ordered part of the manuscript, even though the last entries

date from 1154. Besides histories, some scholars also wrote geographies and natural histories of various parts of the British Isles. Giraldus Cambrensis (1146–1220) produced the *Itinerarium Cambriae* and the *Topographia Hibernica*, geographic histories of Wales and Ireland respectively. A similar source for Welsh history is the *Annales Cambriae*, dating from the 10th century and containing some evidence for the historical background to the story of King Arthur.

Perhaps the most famous and important figure of all medieval, secular, and quasi-historical narratives, Arthur crops up in a number of histories. While to contemporary readers the idea of Arthur is now interwoven with the adventures of the Knights of the Round Table and the search for the Holy Grail, it is likely that Arthur was a British chieftain of the 5th or 6th century. Indeed, some basis for the story of a king who fights and dies in an epic battle exists. The major source for the tale comes from Geoffrey of Monmouth but the eventual form is the product of a number of different variations and adaptations, many of which progressively added new elements, which in their turn became almost more important than the original narrative.

The best-known version of the Arthur epic in English is that by Thomas Malory (*d.* 1471), the *Morte d'Arthur*, and it appears that much of Malory's version was taken from the French sources. The story had proved extremely popular with French writers of chivalrous courtly verse, most especially Chrétien de Troyes (*fl.* 1170–1190). His version of the stories of Perceval (Parsifal) and the search for the Grail, Lancelot, and Yvain (Gawain) did much to promote the popularity of the individual stories of the knights of King Arthur's court, relegating the story of Arthur in some versions to an almost introductory role.

According to Geoffrey of Monmouth, Arthur was the son of Uther Pendragon, the king of Britain, and Igraine, who had been captured by the king with the help of the sorcerer Merlin.

Arthurian literature thrived during the Middle Ages, culminating in *Le Morte d'Arthur*, Thomas Malory's retelling of the entire legend in a single work in English in the late 15th century. Malory based his book on the various previous romance versions, in particular the Vulgate Cycle, and appears to have aimed at creating a comprehensive and authoritative collection of Arthurian stories.

One of the most fascinating characters in the whole corpus of Arthurian legend, the most complete story of Merlin's life is told in Geoffrey of Monmouth's *Vita Merlini* (1150). Besides being advisor to Arthur when he becomes king, among the tasks that are credited to Merlin is the creation of the stone-circle at Stonehenge. Important sequences in the legend tell of Arthur fathering Modred with his half-sister Morgawse and of his marriage to Guinevere. His death at the battle of Camlan (Camelford) and the carriage of his body to the island of Avalon is the concluding section of the narrative, although some authors such as Malory have Arthur escape death to return to rule over Britain.

Although the Arthur legend may be the best-known—and most influential—of the British legendary narratives, one of the finest works from the British Isles from the early Middle Ages is the epic poem *Beowulf*. Thought to have been composed around the 8th century, it tells of the eponymous hero who fights and kills the monsters, Grendel and his mother. Much later, once Beowulf has become king, he fights a dragon, and, during the course of this battle, the hero also dies. It is possible that some elements in the story have some basis in history, but on a wider level it belongs to the broader sphere of Germanic, Norse, and British mythology.

One equally important piece of writing in slightly later Middle English is William Langland's (1330–1386) *Piers Plowman*. This long poem consists of religious visions of a plowman called Will as he falls asleep on the Malvern Hills. Other regional narratives from a later date also exist. These include romances such as the 14th-century *Tale of Gamelyn* or the legend of the outlaw Robin Hood, whose story can be found in manuscripts from the 15th century onward.

CHIVALRY AND COURTLY LOVE

If the church formed one important source of literary endeavor during the Middle Ages, another was provided by the far more secular environment of the various European courts. Particularly in Northern and Central France, Provence, and Germany the courts employed often itinerant poets and singers, who recited epics on the themes of chivalry and courtly love. Their different names—*minnesinger* (Germany), *troubadours* (Provence), and *trouvères* (France)—hide an essentially similar function and mode of performance. A slightly different group were the *jongleurs*, poets from outside the court system but whose works—although sometimes verging on the more scandalous aspects of romantic attraction—bear great similarities with those poets at court. That certain *jongleurs* were aware that the tales of courtly love at times touched on the absurd can be seen in the gentle 13th-century pastiche *Aucassin et Nicolette* that parodies the conventions of the genre.

BEOWULF KILLS GRENDEL

Known as one of the most important works of Anglo-Saxon literature, the Old English heroic poem *Beowulf*, boasts 3,182 lines. Of unknown authorship, this lengthy work was recorded in the Nowell Codex manuscript sometime between the 8th and early 11th century. The hero Beowulf fights three battles in the poem. Shown here, Beowulf shears off Grendel's head and kills him, the bone sticking from Grendel's severed arm from a previous encounter still being visible.

ROMAN DE LA ROSE, c. 1400

The *Roman de la Rose*, or *Story of the Rose*, is an allegorical poem of chivalric love from the 15th century, illustrated with 92 brilliant miniatures. The poem was composed in France at the height of the age of chivalry and courtly love by Guillaume de Lorris and Jean de Meun. The illustration shows a dance in the Garden of Pleasure.

ROBIN HOOD AND LITTLE JOHN

This is the first unpromising encounter between Robin Hood and Little John, when Little John throws Robin off the bridge into the river. The oldest references to Robin Hood are not historical records, or ballads recounting his exploits, but hints and allusions found in various works from medieval times. He is an archetypal figure of English folklore who became a part of the popular culture.

Perhaps the greatest, and certainly most influential, disposition on courtly love was written by the French cleric Andreas Capellanus (*fl.* late-12th century). Greatly influenced by the writings of Ovid, he systematically explores the nature, procurement, retention, and loss of love in his *De Arte Honeste Amandi*. The concept of courtly love is posited to have a parallel to the feudal society from which it grew, the lover's adoration of a high and distant lady likened to the relationship between a feudal lord and vassal. This idea was first taken up by the troubadours of Provence (who include Arnaut Daniel, *fl.* 1180–1200; Guiraut de Borneil, 1165–1212; and Bernart de Ventadorn, *fl.* 1140 1175), from where it spread north and east to the courts of France and Germany. One of the most famous of the French romances and one that was to be highly influential, is the 13th-century *Roman de la Rose*, where the rose of the title represents ideal love.

klingesor vo vngerlant.

13TH CENTURY SINGING CONTEST

Landgraf Hermann von Thüringen and wife Sophia preside over a singing contest featuring such illustrious minnesingers as Wolfram von Eschenbach and Walther von der Vogelweide. While Eschenbach is best known for his *Parzival*, sometimes regarded as the greatest of all German epics from that time, Vogelweide is famous for his poems of enduring immediacy, such as the popular "*Under der linden*."

---

the great French medieval poets is generally held to be Charles duc d'Orléans (1394–1465), who, besides attracting many poets to his court, composed numerous works of his own.

The *trouvères* were not necessarily restricted to the courts of France—Benoît de Saint-Maure, one of the most prominent *trouvère* of the 12th century, known for his *Roman de Troie*, was employed at the English court of Henry II, although England remained outside of the main sphere of the *troubadours'* influence. In Germany, however, the *minnesingers*, such as the great Wolfram von Eschenbach (1170–1220) in his *Parzifal* (1205) and Walther von Vogelweide (1170–1230), not only took on board the conventions of courtly romance, but also introduced ideas of the epic into their poems.

ARABIC INFLUENCE

The Middle Ages came to a close with the rise of the ideas of Renaissance, at first in Florence in Italy and then throughout Europe. Much of the knowledge that was essential for the "rebirth" of Classical ideas and ideals was not, however, preserved in Europe. A great deal of Classical learning and philosophy, especially that of the ancient Greeks, was carefully nurtured by the Arabs, in their heartland of the Middle East and also in the Levant, North Africa, and Spain. Knowledge of the writings of Aristotle, so important to the thinking of writers such as Abelard and Aquinas, could, to a large extent, be traced back to the great scholar Abu al-Walid Muhammad bin Ahmad bin Rushd, also known as Averroës (1126–1198), from Cordoba,

Of all the forms associated with these courtly poets, 12th-century Old French *chansons de geste* are the most coherent as a group. Taking their themes from historical figures, especially that of Charlemagne and the 12 paladins (knights) of his court, culminating in the masterly *Chanson de Roland*, they form a body of some of the most imaginative and exquisitely written literature of the later Middle Ages. A high point of this courtly love, chivalry, and legend in French poetry came at the court of Marie de Champagne, particularly through the works of Chrétien de Troyes based on the Arthur legend. The last of in Spain. Besides earning a mention in Chaucer's *Canterbury Tales* and Dante's *Divina Commedia,* he was most influential for his commentaries on Aristotle. While the works of Averroës spread through Europe by generally peaceful means, another major form of contact between the Christian and Muslim worlds came through the crusades. This series of wars designed to "liberate" the holy places of Christendom brought Western knights into contact with great places of learning in the Muslim world. In addition to philosophy, the Islamic world was also to be influential on the conventions of courtly love through the writings of the Persian Abu-'Ali al-Husayn bin Sina, or Avicenna (980–1037), who also makes an appearance in the works of Chaucer and Dante. Besides writing on love, he also greatly affected the Scholastics through his commentary on Aristotle.

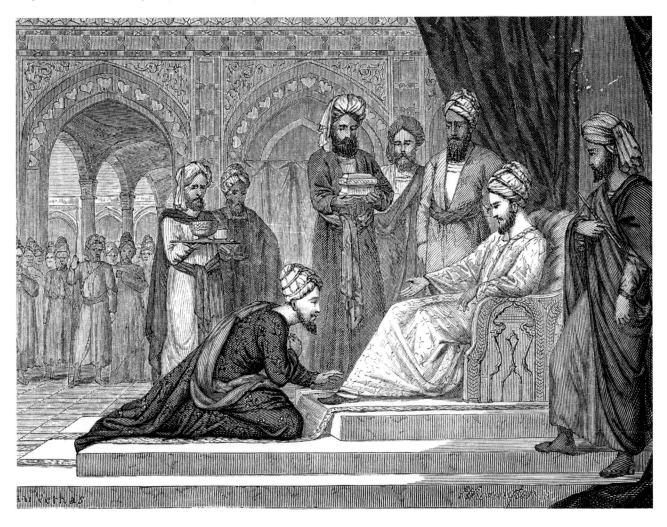

AVICENNA

Here, the Governor of Isfahan receives Ibn Sina, known in the West as Avicenna.

Chapter 3
RENAISSANCE
HUMANISM, NATIONALISM, RELIGIOUS REFORM

Textbooks are fond of signposts, but history, like a bad driver, tends to ignore them. The two most famous poets of the 14th century, Dante Alighieri (1265-1321) and Francesco Petrarch (1304-1374), are excellent examples of this. Many people have seen Dante as the pinnacle of the "spirit" of the Christian Middle Ages, whereas Petrarch is the embodiment of the Renaissance. They were, however, near contemporaries.

HUMANISM

The Renaissance was home to a cultural movement that was obsessed with the recovery and imitation of the Roman, and (a little later) Greek, past. That cultural movement is called "humanism" and those who practised it "humanists"––which is wholly unrelated to current usage of the word, pertaining to ethical conduct and the search for objective truth, unhampered by faith and mysticism. Humanism was associated in its earlier stages with Italy (though Petrarch spent much of his time in Southern France). Italy's monasteries had more manuscripts of ancient Latin literature than anywhere else in Europe, more architectural ruins from the Roman empire. Its society, too, was not the feudal pattern of master and serf that characterized much of the rest of Europe. Its society was more urban than anywhere else in Europe, thus allowing for the expansion of a commercial class or "bourgeoisie" and for greater wealth. The world of olives, of vines, of familiar mountains and rivers described in the texts of Cicero, Virgil, and Livy were far less alien and remote to a 14th century Italian than to, say, an inhabitant of Scotland.

The cult of antiquity did not restrict itself to literature: for instance, the Florentine Niccolo Niccoli (1364-1437) wore togas and recreated Roman meals. Anything that made the Roman past more alive, after what was increasingly seen as the "dark period" of the Middle Ages, was celebrated. The works of Petrarch are filled with such metaphors of darkness and light applied to history. As a poet, Petrarch is most famous for his beautiful *Canzoniere*. These are 366 poems, endless variations on the theme of his love for Laura. There are two important aspects of this immensely influential sequence of poems. One is the high degree of psychological realism: they are filled with convincing details that broke new ground in the analysis of the relation

1335 Petrarch writes poems to Laura, including *Sonnets* (published 1360).

1338–1453 Hundred Years' War.

1349–1353 Giovanni Boccaccio's *Decameron* is in progress.

1348–1350 The Black Death.

1387–1399 Geoffrey Chaucer writes *The Canterbury Tales*; he dies in 1400.

1453 Constantinople falls to the Turks.

1474 William Caxton prints the first book in English.

1492 Columbus discovers America; Spanish conquest of Granada

1494 Sebastian Brandt publishes *The Ship of Fools* in German language.

1516 Desiderius Erasmus's edition of the New Testament of the Bible. First publication of Ariosto's *Orlando Furioso*.

1517 Martin Luther nails his 95 Theses to the door of the Castle Church in Wittenberg.

1519 Charles I of Spain becomes Holy Roman emperor.

1527 Rome is sacked by the French.

1528 Baldassare Castiglione publishes *The Courtier*; he dies the following year.

1534 François Rabelais completes *Gargantua and Pantagruel*.

1534 Henry VIII breaks with Rome and becomes head of the Church of England.

1547 Francis I dies; Henry II accedes to the French throne.

1549 England declares war on France.

1551 First English translation of Thomas More's *Utopia* is published; More is executed for high treason by Henry VIII in 1535.

1559 First official index of forbidden books issued by Pope Paul IV.

1563 Council of Trent concludes.

1581 Torquato Tasso publishes *La Gerusalemme liberata*.

1588 Montaigne's publishes his autobiographical *Essais*.

1588 England defeats Spain's invincible Armada.

1596 Edmund Spenser publishes *The Faerie Queene* (Books 1–6) as well as the *Mutabilitie Cantos*.

A SCENE FROM *DECAMERON*

Based on humorous French tales popular throughout the Middle Ages, the *Decameron* is about seven women and three men who, hoping to escape the Black Plague of 1348, retreat to the hills of Fiesole above Florence, where for ten days they tell each other stories dealing with such topics as love, intelligence, and human will, before returning to the city.

between body, soul, and the emotions. He is particularly insistent on the contradictoriness of desire and the impossibility of pinning it down. Here is a passage from his Sonnet 134:"I find no peace, and all my war is done; I fear and hope; I burn and freeze like ice; I fly above the wind, yet can I not arise; And nought I have, and all the world I seize on; That looseth nor locketh holdeth me in prison; And holdeth me not, yet can I 'scape nowise; Nor letteth me live nor die at my device; And yet of death it giveth none occasion."

Other prose genres began to flourish in the newly self-confident Italian language. Petrarch's friend, Giovanni Boccaccio (1313–1375) perhaps represents the most famous and amusing exponent of some of these. Boccaccio was less self-conscious about the recovery of the ancient past in his writings than the obsessive Petrarch, but he was instrumental, for example, in providing assistance to Barlaam of Calabria in his translations from Greek literature: a humanist project. For all such enthusiasms, it was

a work that, at least at first reading, feels more medieval than humanist, which had more lasting impact: the *Decameron*, a collection of short stories, or perhaps, a novel that consists of unrelated stories. The opening describes the effects of plague. The Black Death has come to Florence, and so the main protagonists, of whom there are ten, seek health in the countryside and solace in storytelling. Medieval culture was fond of seeing, in T. S. Eliot's memorable phrase, "the skull beneath the skin," and death is always an uninvited guest at the table of Boccaccio's fictions. We should remember that he had lost both his father and step-mother to the plague. On the surface, the stories are highly secular, often erotic tales of sudden reversals of fortune, lovers' amusements and implausible coincidences. A popular theme of the medieval erotic imagination was the sexual transgressions of the clergy, and so the connection between love, sin, and death was easily made. Take for example the story of Ferondo. Having consumed a 14th-century equivalent of Haitian zombie powder, Ferondo is buried. Ferondo's wife, meanwhile, has an affair with senior priest. This priest later removes Ferondo from his tomb and imprisons him, convincing the poor man he is in Purgatory. Eventually, Ferondo is resurrected, but raises a child that was in fact fathered by the priest. Connections between sex, death, and religion were everywhere.

Boccaccio's works soon spread all over Europe. One English author influenced by this morning star of the Renaissance was Geoffrey Chaucer (1343–1400), whose *Canterbury Tales* owe much to the Italian writer, in their combination of storytelling, earthy humor, and lingering concerns with religion and death. We are accustomed to thinking of Chaucer as a "medieval" writer, but he was more in touch with developments in both French and Italian literature than England would be for another hundred years. He would not have called himself a humanist, but he is certainly more of a recognizably European writer than Shakespeare.

Humanism and its attempt to study and imitate the culture of antiquity were a fashionable enthusiasm of a minority, with little firm foundation in the universities, or in popular culture. Erasmus was to change all that. Desiderius Erasmus (1469–1536) was born in the Low Countries, the bastard son of a priest. After he lost his parents to the plague in 1483, he was educated in a monastery at Steyn, though he soon chafed at the intellectual and personal constraints he found there. Erasmus never held a formal permanent position inside a university. He was, nonetheless, passionately committed to the intellectual and the scholarly life. He therefore soon realized the importance of the printing press as a tool by which he could support himself financially as well as set his educational program based on Latin and Greek literature on a firmer and better-publicized footing. He was the first scholar to appreciate and exploit to the full the resources of professional authorship and the creation of an Erasmus "brand." Some of these works were works of religious satire, such as the *Praise of Folly*, a light but damning satire on both religious and intellectual conservatism. Other productions of his pen had a more direct effect on the progress of literature. Perhaps the most important was his *De copia* (*Foundations of the abundant style*), a handbook of style that he wrote in 1511. This book was to profoundly influence the Renaissance fondness for elaboration. The book consists of a series of illustrations (that would have been easily adapted and copied in the schoolroom, as Erasmus knew) for how to take one simple thought or phrase (such as "Good morning" or "I have received your letter") and how to use all the techniques of rhetoric to examine this single thought or phrase from many perspectives to slightly alter the tone, style, or meaning. Erasmus had read, and republished, a similar, although less popular work by the Italian humanist Lorenzo Valla (1405–1457): the *Elegances*.

After Erasmus (and Valla), the Renaissance schoolboy (if he had any kind of sensitivity to language at all) was sure to have a much greater command of tone, nuance, and style than his medieval predecessor. Perhaps more negatively, he would also indulge in a taste for elaborateness that appears excessive to the 21st-century ear In any piece of Renaissance prose such as the chivalrous romance of Sir Philip Sidney (the *Old Arcadia*), there is the sheer pleasure of infinite variation of tone

DESIDERIUS ERASMUS,
Holbein miniature

and phraseology, which can be attributed to the influence of Erasmus.

De copia was a great success and became the foundation of many schoolrooms through the 16th century. It was, however, left to Philipp Melanchthon (1497–1560) to finally embed the enthusiasms of humanism into a fully-fledged and rounded educational program for the Protestant universities. Melanchthon was a close associate of the reformer Martin Luther, but whereas Luther's message of spiritual renewal found only a minor role for educational reform, Melanchthon attempted to integrate the religious concerns of the Reformation into the educational ideals of humanism. He taught at the university of Wittenberg, but many other universities in the German-speaking lands sprang up, inspired by the need for a new education to assist the new religious doctrine. Erasmus's works, especially *De copia*, were usually included in these new universities' statutes. So influential was Melanchthon that he became known as *Praceptor Germaniae* ("Germany's Teacher").

In many ways, one can thus speak of an international Renaissance: the printing press and a common educational pattern meant that, especially in the works written in Latin, but also in the various vernaculars of Europe, there were more common features of style and reference than had been the case in medieval Europe. Naturally, there were exceptions: Spain began to carve a more individual path, and slowly, in other lands dominated by Catholicism, the education program of the Roman Catholic religious order (founded in 1547), the Jesuits, would, to an extent, modify the Erasmian-Melanchthonian one. But these were mainly differences of degree.

REFORMATION

This emphasis on humanism's shared literary and educational identities, however, should not lead us to underemphasize the importance of the divisions of the Reformation. Martin Luther's (1483-1546) attack on the excesses, the grasping materiality and artificiality of the Catholic church was, of course, a religious attack. The church had become corrupt and had lost the ability and authority to undertake its basic function of the welfare of the souls of the faithful. Luther did not compose literature in the sense of poems and romances, though he wrote some biting satires on the Catholic church. There was, however, a literary aspect to the Reformation which cannot be emphasized enough: the reading of the Bible and the translation of the Bible out of the Latin into the language of the people. Throughout the Middle Ages, the Catholic church never encouraged believers to read the Bible. Such reading was not, after all, essential to salvation. Instead, the rituals of the church, especially the sacrament of the holy mass, were believed to be far more important. Furthermore, since Saint Jerome had been commissioned in 382 to translate the Bible into Latin, this version was slowly accepted as the only version permissible. It

was called the Vulgate. Naturally most people in the Middle Ages could not read Latin, and so were dependent on stories recycled by priests or on images in stained glass windows (what Gregory the Great famously referred to as "the Bible of the Poor"). If, however, the Bible was so important to mankind, why (some began to ask) did the church not allow it to be translated and read by all? Luther was not the first to translate the Bible into the

PRE-REFORMATION

Circa 1382, John Wyclif (1324 - 1384) sends his band of traveling preachers or 'Lollards' out into the world with his English translation of the Vulgate Bible. He was condemned as a heretic.

REFORMATION, *c.* 1382

Martin Luther (1483-1546) writing on the church door at Wittenberg in 1517. Woodcut, 16th century.

language of the people. National consciousness and anti-clerical feeling often coincided with the production of vernacular Bibles. John Wyclif (1324–1384) is a good example of this. In addition to critically opposing some aspects of the church, he translated most of the New Testament into vernacula English. His ideas found a ready adherent in the Bohemian theologian Jan Hus (1372–1415), who also played a canonical role in the evolution of the Czech language. Both figures were adopted as part of an emphasis on a "national" as opposed to "papal international" religious and linguistic tradition.

In the early years of the 16th century, the national consciousness of German as a literary language was still highly undeveloped. Luther was to change that. Sequestered in Wartburg Castle in 1521-1522 as an attempt to protect him from the growing storm that had been brewing over the dissemination of his radical anti-Catholic religious ideas. While in this castle, he began the project of translating the Bible. It was eventually published in 1534. The work was instantaneously hailed as a masterpiece,

and was profoundly influential. Not only did it kickstart the creation of a far more self-confidently and linguistically innovative German, the very phrases that Luther used to translate the Latin became ingrained in the language, so that even today, German speakers quote Luther without knowing it. The influence of the literary, the linguistic, and the religious were intimately connected for this early period of German Renaissance literature.

England is a good example of how the tension between local and European powers played out. When King Henry VIII (1491–1547) ascended the thone in 1509, he proved himself an intelligent man, who was interested in theological affairs. Aided by his humanist chancellor (and friend of Erasmus), Sir Thomas More (1478–1535), he even wrote in 1521 a defense of the Catholic concept that there should be seven sacraments against the Lutheran heresy that there were merely two: *Assertio septem sacramentorum.* The Pope at the time, the cultivated Leo X, rewarded Henry with an honorific title: Defender of the Faith, which the English monarch continues to

SIR THOMAS MORE

Sir Thomas More is famous for his book *Utopia* and for his martyrdom. As Chancellor to Henry VIII, he refused to sanction Henry's divorce of Queen Catherine, for which he was imprisoned, tried, and executed.

bear to this day. Henry was not, however, a particularly deep or consistent thinker. His defense of orthodoxy was also borne out of fear of social rebellion, while his intellectual opposition to the Lutheran Reformation was bolstered by such people as More and Cardinal Wolsey.

Henry was frustrated by the church's refusal to sanction a divorce from his wife. Eventually, through a series of acts of Parliament in the early 1530s, Henry declared himself, and England, independent of the Church of Rome. The royal coffers soon swelled by the state's looting of the wealth of the monasteries. Although there would be refinements to the idea of a Church of England and to boundaries of England, the events of Henry VIII's reformation meant that the pattern was created for a newly self-confident nation state, with a thirst for self-definition to mark itself as different from the Catholic church. One Act of 1534 actually starts with the words: "This realm of England is an Empire." The stage was set for expansion, not only colonial, but also linguistic. The next hundred years were to see more words added to the English dictionary than any other period in British history. So began a period of unparalleled experiment and innovation in literature, a period that saw English slowly emerge as a viable alternative to Latin for works of the highest seriousness and international standing.

ENGLAND

If you asked a Frenchman or a Spaniard in 1550 to name a famous work of recent English literature, they would probably have mentioned Sir Thomas More's *Utopia* of 1516. This was a playful fantasy, whose tone and seriousness are difficult to pin down, just as in the comic satires of the Greek writer Lucian, whom More and Erasmus translated. This half-serious, half-playful genre was much beloved by humanists, but it remains very hard to interpret. Certainly, More would have

UTOPIA
More described an idealized, imaginary commonwealth in his *Utopia*, which was first published in Latin in 1516.

been surprised to discover that the learned Vasco di Quiroga actually set up a society in New Spain (Mexico) using his little English book as a blueprint.

In one sense, however, *Utopia* was not really English at all. It was conceived and written in Latin. All across Europe, long after Dante and Boccaccio had proved how supple and articulate Italian could be; the various vernaculars were busy defending their merits against Latin. One reason for this revolution was simultaneously technological and financial: the invention of the printing press. England's newly self-confident sense of nationhood, found by breaking with Rome, worked with the technology available to create a national literature.

An important example of this trend is Edmund Spenser (1552-1599). England had long had national myths (for example, the tale of King Arthur), but it had no national epic. Spenser set about to fill this gap. In his *Faerie Queene*, he took the Romance tradition and integrated it into a set of national contemporary concerns. Spenser was born in London and educated at

books (out of a projected twenty four) took as its theme a given virtue. This virtue was then illustrated by a knight's adventures through "Faerie Land" (ruled over by a thinly disguised Queen Elizabeth, Henry VIII's Protestant daughter).

Spenser's epic was, then, a sort of Arthurian Virgil. This created an interesting problem. Literature is sometimes serious, rarely solemn, often playful. There is just something about the way we speak of "enjoying" literature or "taking pleasure" in it that makes playfulness a common feature of much literary creation. One form of such pleasure is the pleasure of storytelling; the pleasures of suspense and relaxation. When children or defendants in court are asked to tell their stories, we usually ask them to "begin at the beginning;" but Spenser's "romance" or "Arthurian" epic does no such thing. Knights seem to be forever wandering around, getting lost in pathless forests, battling dragons, taking detours which end in more detours and digressions. Spenser is sometimes like one of his errant knights, lost in the sheer pleasure of storytelling excess.

For all his hopes, Spenser did not become England's national poet. The national poet would turn out to be a dramatist. Drama

Pembroke College, Cambridge. In the 1570s he served in Ireland, where England had for some years been engaged in aggressive colonial action. In his 1590s pamphlet ("A view of the present state of Ireland"), Spenser argued that the only way to subdue Ireland was through brutal eradication of its culture. This concern with the forceful imposition of "peace" emerges strongly in his epic poem. Just as England should colonize Ireland, so Spenser colonized all previous poetic registers to create his own authoritative summary of tradition. Spenser took Virgil as his model, starting with some pastoral poems (*The Shepherd's Calendar*) in 1579 (modeled on Virgil's *Eclogues*), and moving on to the *Faerie Queene* (1590 and 1596). Spenser strove to merge poetic and political authority so as to speak as England's national poet. Therefore his language looks back as much to Geoffrey Chaucer as it does to the linguistic innovations of the humanist poetics around him. Each of the six was the most distinctive product of the English Renaissance, in particular tragedy. There had been medieval morality plays, usually performed at set times of the year, and with a very limited range of themes and stock characters, all religious. Readers of the ancient classics increased considerably in the 16th century and with them the awareness that other forms of drama were possible. In particular, the bold characterization and bloody revenge plots of the works of the younger Seneca were influential. Tragedy raised difficult questions for a Christian audience—for how could true tragedy be possible if God is in heaven, if the righteous are to be rewarded and the wicked punished? Thomas Norton wrote the first true English tragedy in 1561 (*Gorboduc*), directly modeled on Seneca.

The old morality plays had been tied to the rhythms of the Catholic church. They had also been tied to particular provinces of England (there were the York plays, the Lincoln plays and so on). Now London was newly dominant and the Catholic church had been swept away. Although the earliest plays, such as Gorboduc, were written only for a very small audience (rather like the Latin dramas that were being performed at Oxford and Cambridge), a more popular theater was on its way. The theaters of London began to function as a sort of social space wherein which ideas, debate and entertainment could mingle (though often with an increasing degree of state surveillance). The theater (where boys and men played female roles, free speech reigned, and brothels abounded) was an object of suspicion for many.

Christopher Marlowe (1564-1593) seemed to personify these tensions. Born to a shoemaker in Canterbury, Marlowe attended Cambridge University, where he may have worked as some kind of covert government agent. Rumors of homosexuality and Catholicism accompanied him throughout his career. Marlowe was quick to see the financial and literary possibilities that writing for the stage allowed. He had thought of himself first as a poet and it was his skill to combine a poet's delight in the sensuous power of words with an increasingly controlled approach to dramatic construction. His own works show a progressive deepening of characterization and tragic power. His story of the necromantic magician, *The Tragicall History of Doctor Faustus*, shows his powers at full stretch. Faust made a pact with the devil so that he could achieve all worldly power and knowledge. Whereas the humanists sought to come to an intimate knowledge of the ancient world through books, Faust's magic allows him to physically conjure and kiss Helen of Troy. "Was this the face that launched a thousand ships/ and burnt the topless towers of Ilium?" Helen was not merely an erotic fantasy, however, she was also responsible for the conflict that set in motion the very first work of ancient literature, Homer's Iliad. Marlowe thus seemed to have outdone dead humanists, for he overreached all knowledge with his combination of poetry and action—going beyond anything previous humanist drama had offered. This combination was one which his most famous successor, William Shakespeare, developed to new heights.

DOCTOR FAUSTUS

Actors Michael Goodliffe and Paul Daneman as Mephistophilis and Doctor Faustus in Christopher Marlowe's 'Doctor Faustus' at the Old Vic, 1961. The play was based on the story of Faust, who sold his soul to the devil in return for power and knowledge.

WILLIAM SHAKESPEARE

William Shakespeare (1564–1616) was born in Stratford upon Avon. We know that he married Anne Hathaway in 1582. By 1592, he had attracted notice as a poet and actor on the theatrical scene in London. His professional dealings with the theater were successful and he retired in 1613 a wealthy man. His earliest plays appeared in print in 1594, and a "first folio" of his works appeared in 1623 (seven years after his death and there is some confusion over which of the various texts are "authentic"). Although best known for his plays, Shakespeare turned to the printing of poetry to make some money in 1593 and 1594, when the theaters were closed for fear of plague. He also wrote somewhat more personal poetry, in the shape of the *Sonnets*, poems about desire and loss addressed variously to a young man and a "dark lady" (whose identities have given rise to endless speculation).

Shakespeare started writing light comedies and historical dramas. The former had plots drawn from, among others, the ancient Roman writer Plautus. These deal with the standard comic themes of mixed up identities and sudden implausible recognitions. These include works such as *A Comedy of Errors*. In the 1590s defining and characterizing England and Englishness became quite popular, particularly in the wake of the new self-confidence gained by England's surprise victory over world power Spain in the battle of the Armada in 1588. England's humanist fondness for history was slowly transferring itself from an interest in the Roman past to the medieval past of England. It was clear, after all, that England had had a past before the year zero of the Reformation. One such early play of Shakespeare was *Richard III*. The main concern in the early history plays is with the causes and consequences of failed monarchy. People have disagreed whether this is to be viewed as a justification for or a critique of the last years of the Tudor dynasty under Elizabeth.

The next period of Shakespeare's career saw him write what are usually thought of as the greatest tragedies in the English language: *Hamlet*, *Othello*, *King Lear*, and *Macbeth*. The same persistent interest in identity that surfaced in his early comic

writings reappeared in these later works. Shakespeare asks "What is it to be human," "How are we connected to those around us," and "How much can one man make the world in his image?" Shakespeare ended his career with the writing of more gentle "tragi-comedies," such as *Cymberline* and *The Tempest*.

HAMLET AND HORATIO IN THE CEMETERY, 1859

The story of the eternal procrastinator, Hamlet, Prince of Denmark, was the first of Shakespeare's four great tragedies: *Hamlet, Othello, King Lear, Macbeth*.

FRANCE

The state that we know today as France had not yet come into being. At the beginning of the 16th century, French borders were hardly clearly defined; the Eastern frontier with the German states was particularly vague. There was furthermore no common language: in the south, even educated people spoke "langue d'oc," with the northern areas speaking "langue d'oïl," which is closer to modern-day French. Legal customs varied from place to place, and the first serious attempt to create a unified legal system was under Louise XII (on the throne from 1498 to 1515). As with many other states, the story of cultural development in 16th-century France is connected to an unusual degree with the growth in national consciousness and the growth in the patronage possibilities afforded by princes. The evidence from court payrolls makes it clear that the 16th century slowly but significantly saw an increase in the size of the court: for example, under Louis XII in 1500, there were 100 court artisans; in 1544, under Francis I, there were 160.

The influence of the classical idiom in art and architecture was powerful in Francis's program to remodel his palace at Fontainebleau. A popular abridgment, however, of the work of the Roman architect Vitruvius had been published in French in 1526 by Diego di Sagredo. This spawned a large number of palaces in the 1530s and 1540s: Chantilly, La Rochefoucauld, Chateaubriand. Similar patronage, on a less lavish scale, began to be available for literature. Marguerite of Navarre (a small kingdom on the borders of the Spanish Pyrenees) with strong humanist and reformist sympathies had a disproportionately significant role. Clément Marot (1496-1544) was the most important court poet of this early stage of the French "courtly Renaissance." Reacting against what he came to see as the unsubtle allegories of the poets immediately before him, Marot quickly became an enthusiast of the humanist movement. He wrote light-hearted, sensitive verse letters, but he became

CLÉMENT MAROT

Marot was one of the greatest poets of the French Renaissance. He spent the greater part of his life in court service, and his Protestant sympathies led to his arrest or exile on several occasions. He developed the *rondeau* and *ballade*, and introduced many new forms into French poetry, including the elegy, the eclogue, epigram, epithalamium, and the Petrarchan sonnet.

progressively more identified with the new evangelical movements of the reformers of the German-speaking lands, as had his patron Marguerite Angoulème of Navarre (wife to Henry II). The powerful linguistic appeal of the Bible, increasingly read in the vernacular —following the first translation into French by the evangelical humanist Jacques Lefèvre d'Étaples (1455-1536)—was one of the most important inspirations for the new literature of 16th-century France. Literature had always dealt with religious themes but the highly technical language of Latin theology did not easily slip into poetry. For all those reformers for whom the Bible and not medieval philosophers was the new centerpiece of their theology, the language and rhythms of Holy Scripture found a much readier route into the poetry (and later drama) of the French Renaissance.

Another figure associated with the court was the satirist François Rabelais (1494-1553). In 1520 he became a Franciscan monk, but he crossed swords with his superiors over his desire to learn Greek in order to read Scripture in the original. He then transferred to the Benedictine order. From 1528 to 1530 he was at the University of Paris, but then enrolled in a medical course at the University of Montpellier. He moved to Lyons, which was a great publishing center, where he worked for a

printer of humanist works, Sebastianus Gryphius. One of his works, the satire *Pantagruel*, was publicly condemned by the University of Paris in 1533. He found a new patron in Joachim Du Bellay, Bishop of Paris, with whom he traveled to Rome in 1534. By 1537, he had close connections with Francis I. Restless, multi-talented and endlessly hungry for new knowledge and new perspectives, Rabelais' learning was considerable, but it was genius to integrate the obscene profusion and fecundity of satire with a more searching intellectual critique. There is a persistent sense in Rabelais's works that no system, no educational program, no discipline is enough to satisfy the appetites of life. His most successful satire, *Gargantua*, was published in 1534. It is the bizarre story of the life of a giant: Gargantua. It is essential to the book that Gargantua is of huge physical size (his first meal consisted of seventeen thousand

FRANÇOIS RABELAIS A Renaissance monk, physician, and scholar, Rabelais has for centuries been acclaimed for his *Gargantua and Pantagruel*, a multi-volume narrative full of comedy, satire, myth, and humanism.

BELOW:
FEEDING THE BABY GARGANTUA

From Rabelais' *Gargantua and Pantagruel,* published between 1532 and 1564 as four novels brimming with gross burlesque and profound satire.

DICE OFFERING A BANQUET TO FRANCUS, IN THE PRESENCE OF HYANTE AND CLIMENE

La Franciade, which Pierre de Ronsard (1524-1585) intended to be the national epic in the style of Virgil's *Aeneid*, was abandoned after the death of Charles IX. The four completed books were published in 1572. (Oil on canvas, Louvre, Paris, France).

LEFT: PIERRE RONSARD AND THE PLÉIADE Ronsard was the leader of the "Pléiade," a group of 16th-century French poets.

nine hundred and thirteen cows from the town of Pontille), but it is often hard to explain quite why. Rabelais's sheer pleasure in the consumption of words and ideas is rather like Gargantua's own vast hunger. Reading Rabelais in the original French is a dizzying and difficult process: he invented hundreds of new words and drew words from the most elevated and obscene registers. It is as if Rabelais simply cannot contain his pleasure in piling up new words, bizarre linguistic explosions of tone and style and fantastical characters. Not for Rabelais the perfection of verbal anorexia. Phrases agglutinate one to the other with endless "thens" and "ands," rather than in the carefully elaborate syntax of traditional literary French.

Rabelais, as we have seen, was closely involved with the printing industry, not only publishing his own "literary" works and doing editorial work for Grpyhius, but also publishing translations of medical works in the early 1530s. The role of printing and the pains and pleasures of professional authorship came early to

France: In 1480 only nine French towns had printing presses, by 1500 this number had risen to 40. The close association between humanism and the new industry created some uncomfortable problems of self-definition for one group of mid-century poets. If humanism related in some ways to the new worlds of technology and international brand-management of educational reforms movements and popular scholarship, it was also the rhythmical and metrical subtleties of Horace's lyric, the obscure mythology of Propertius, and the learned commentaries on poetic texts by the Italian humanists. It was this deliberately elite self-presentation that inspired a group of mid-century poets known as the Pléiade, who would meet regularly in the Hotel Baif, a stunning house in Paris built in the latest style and decorated with Greek inscriptions over the doorways.

The leader of this group (seven in number, named after the seven stars of the Pleiades constellation) was Pierre de Ronsard (1524-1585), although the leading academic in the group was Jean Dorat (1508-1588). Dorat was an enthusiast of some of the more unusual and marginal poets of antiquity such as Pindar, Theocritus, and the epigrammatists of the Greek anthology, with their rich vocabularies and verse forms. Greek was the new Latin, and one of the group even wrote a treatise explaining the linguistic conformity of French with ancient Greek! The emphasis on the creation of a subtle and detailed language was the focus of what has come to be seen as the manifesto of the group: Joachim du Bellay's *Deffence et illustration de la langue française* (1549). As so frequently in this period, linguistic and poetic reform went hand in hand. The first part of the treatise argues that French does not have the resources of Greek and Latin, but in the second part du Bellay shows how poetry (and here, of course, he meant the poetry of his friends from the Pléiade) would overcome the deficiencies of the language and renew and restore the excellence that French could, in principle if not in fact, attain. Linguistic innovation has long been seen as central to the creation of the new ways of feeling and thinking that literature, especially poetry, can bring: for du Bellay, such innovation was to be formed by careful study of ancient Greek and Latin. Ronsard, usually deemed the finest poet of the French Renaissance, combines this interest in the retrospective revolution of humanism with a heightened interest in nature. He wrote much from the *Horatian Odes* of 1550 to his unfinished epic, the *Françiade*. His eye ranged widely and restlessly: behind his elaborate surface structures of sound and rhythm are perpetual metaphors of movement and time, ageing and loss. Water, wind, and wheel are all symbols of his own restless poetic creativity and the difficulty of fixing experience in a set form, against the ever present time and death, and yet the knowledge that poetry can make one as immortal as the heavens. The Irish poet W. B. Yeats picked up this theme when he chose to translate the *Ronsard's Sonnets pour Hélène*, which asks Helen to read the poem when she is old and gray, and "bending down beside

**JOACHIM DU BELLAY
(c. 1525-1560)**

Bellay, in true Renaissance spirit, exhorted the raising of French language to the standard of ancient Greek, and argued that French poetry was the best medium to achieve this noble goal.

the glowing bars, [to] murmur, a little sadly, how love fled and paced upon the mountains overhead, and hid his face amid a crowd of stars."

Mid-16th-century France was, however, home to other voices than the Pléiade. There was another group of poets, sometimes called the School of Lyon. In 1555, Louise Labé (1526-1566) published her *Œuvres*. She was born into a family of ropemakers, and her works shows that she read widely in the lyric poetry of the period. She did not share the enthusiasm of the Pléiade poets for the close connection between scholarship and poetry; she was, in any case, less educated than any other member of that circle. Her interest lay in bringing a new twist to the (seemingly endless) variations of Petrarchan love lyric. For example, her twenty-first and twenty-third sonnets take the tradition of the *blason* (a way of enumerating each part of the female beloved's body) and then wonders what sort of devotion this dismemberment signifies and what would the female equivalent for a male beloved might be, thereby drawing critical attention to the traditions of Petrarchan gender politics.

A more prolific figure was Maurice Scève (1501-1564), who also hailed from Lyon, that intellectual counterweight to Parisian

JEAN CALVIN (1509-1564)
Founder of the Reformed faith of Calvinism, Jean Calvin had to flee to Switzerland to escape persecution in his native country, France. But his religion spread rapidly among French intellectuals and the merchant class.

there in the 1530s, Calvinism soon became influential among the merchant classes and the intellectuals in France. The new religion spread rapidly. By the Edict of Chateaubriand (1551), however, King Henry II enacted brutal suppression of the Calvinists (also known as Huguenots). It provided the legal basis for the burning and other forms of state-sponsored murder of dissenters. His death allowed the even more extreme Charles IX (behind whom was his powerful and scheming mother, Catherine de Medici) to continue these policies, alienating and repressing the Huguenots. The culmination of this was the famous bloodbath of St. Bartholomew Day's Massacre (1572), where thousands of Protestants were slaughtered. From 1562 until 1598, France was torn apart by civil war. The

dominance. Scève was a learned writer, and was interested in providing conundrums and riddles for his readers. In this he was endebted to the tradition of the emblem book, where a classical motto was illustrated with an accompanying image, and then the image "explained" with further poetry, thus forming a kind of symbolic vocabulary into matters of philosophical or cosmological significance which Scève could then manipulate. He published his *Délie* in 1544, a series of complex emblem poems, and though rather different from Pléiade poetics, the work showed a similar concern with elaborate surface structure. While masking as love poems, they instead pose riddles that Dèlie, who is not a real person, can help resolve, functioning as a sort of magic key. She is a cosmological principle of Platonic Love, which illuminates the folding darkness of these Chinese boxes.

France had not experienced a full-scale Reformation, in the way that Britain had. Religious tensions, however, became increasingly apparent as the century wore on. By 1540, Francis I had, after some earlier vacillation, come down on the side of the Catholic church. The great systematic theologian of the Reformed faith, Jean Calvin, was French and, although he had fled to Geneva to establish a "pure" Protestant church

PORTRAIT OF MICHEL EYQUEM DE MONTAIGNE (1533-92)

Regarded as the father of the literary essay, Montaigne, in his monumental autobiographical *Essais*, composed one of the most captivating and intimate self-portraits ever written. He became famous for his style of merging serious intellectual speculation with casual anecdotes, and autobiography. French School, Oil on canvas, Private collection.

open-ended international humanism, with its faith in networks of learning and literature, its educational program to produce wise princes informed by a shared desire for religious renewal, had fallen apart. The most interesting , readable, and influential of the responses to the civil wars was one of the most oblique: the *Essais* by Montaigne.

Michel Eyquem de Montaigne (1533-1592) was born to wealthy, landowning parents in Bordeaux. His father schooled his son in the latest humanist fashion: the child was brought up speaking Latin and not French. He studied law at the University of Toulouse, and began a career as a lawyer. In 1570, however, he shut himself away in a citadel with his library, where he began to compose a series of meditations on life, ideas, and literature. These were published in 1580, though Montaigne would continue to expand on them. These jewels of literature exerted an unprecedented influence on writers and philosophers alike, from René Descartes to Friedrich Nietzsche.

Montaigne's stated aim was to understand himself: at one level, the *Essais* are revealing autobiographical observations, full of a patient psychological acuity about his own habits, foibles, and drives that was hitherto unknown in the history of literature. On another level, since Montaigne was a man who spent much time with philosophy, his attempt to understand himself could be seen as an attempt to understand what anyone can know of themselves. He notes how we deceive ourselves, and the difficulty of being certain of our knowledge. Montaigne remained a politically enfranchised landowner all his life. His retreat from public life, however, and his taking refuge in the private virtues of self-restraint and friendship were as influential, just as they were influenced by the horrors of war. Petrarch commented as he walked down Mount Ventoux that the only true journey is that inward into the soul; Montaigne is a last stage of this Renaissance journey.

PIETRO ARETINO

The works of Italian playwright, poet, and satirist Pietro Aretino exploited to the full the market that the printing press had opened up. He is often called the inventor of modern literary pornography.

BELOW: BALDASSARE CASTIGLIONE

Castiglione's *The Courtier* was a chief vehicle in spreading Italian humanism into England and France.

PIERRE ARETIN.

RUGGIERO RESCUING ANGELICA Ariosto's masterpiece, *Orlando Furioso*, is the tale of the madness that grips Orlando when his beloved Angelica elopes with a Saracen knight.

LUDOVICO ARIOSTO
The epic writer of the Italian Renaissance, Ariosto showed great skill with narrative, which won him such eminent fans as the scientist Galileo.

ITALY

Italy continued to be a rich source of literary inventiveness throughout the 16th century. Although the country was wracked by wars, and even though Rome itself was sacked in 1527 by the troops of Charles V, it is impossible to speak of any dimming of creative energies. The new emphasis on the cultural achievements of the aristocracy was summed up in the hugely influential work *The Courtier* by Baldassare Castiglione (1478-1529). This series of graceful dialogues playfully gave a template to all of Europe of how cultural capital was essential in consolidating and legitimating the power of the noble and, by default, literary supporters. Pietro Aretino (1492-1556) carved a career of many parts, including poetry and pornography, exploiting to the full the markets for sophisticated sensationalism that the printing press offered.

It was, however, in the field of epic that the most substantial achievements of the late Italian Renaissance were found. Ludovico Ariosto (1474-1533) was born in northern Italy, and

was educated in law and the Latin classics. Ariosto started by writing poetry and some comedies, though he was not successful in obtaining any lasting or well-paid position at the hands of his supposed patron, Ippolito d'Este (in Ferrara). His masterwork, *Orlando Furioso*, was first published in 1516, and then subsequently reworked twice, finally being republished in 1532. The action of the poem is notionally set in the time of Charlemagne, in particular the battles with the Islamic Saracens. The sprawling highly episodic nature of the poem makes any plot summary difficult, but its central topics are Orlando's crazed passion for the pagan Angelica. A good flavor of the plotting style, however, can be given: after Angelica saves a wounded Saracen knight, Medoro, she falls in love with him, and they subsequently elope to China. Orlando goes mad on hearing this news, persuing a one-man scorched-earth policy throughout Europe. An English knight travels to Ethiopia on a legendary animal, the hippogriff, and then uses the handy expedient of Elijah's chariot to fly to the moon. On the moon he recovers Orlando's sanity, bottles it and returns it to Orlando, restoring the lovelorn knight to peace and normality.

The two distinguishing features of Ariosto's style almost pull in opposite directions. On the one hand, there is his love of sudden interruption of the story to tell another anecdote and on the other is the easy, unruffled sense of narrative fertility. Ariosto seems so packed full of ideas and stories that the tone and smooth telling of tales never falters. This was what the Italian scientist Galileo so loved about Ariosto. By contrast, Galileo said of Torquato Tasso (1544-1595) that he seemed just to take one idea and spin it out so it hardly contained any strength; endless variations on the same theme were given because Tasso, Galileo continued, had not the slightest degree of Ariosto's originality and depths of resources. Tasso, the other great epic writer of the Italian Renaissance, is certainly a very different writer from Ariosto. Tasso's subject matter is cut from the same cloth as that of Ariosto: the first crusade and the clashes between East and West. Reading Tasso is to live in a very different world. Whereas plot, and its interruptions, seem to be the driving forces of Ariosto, Tasso's *Gerusalemme Liberata*'s (1574) concern is with the portrayal and the heightening of emotion, with strange contrasts of tones and an almost neurotic appreciation of detail. His characters, rather like Virgil's Aeneas, are forever conflicted between emotion and duty, and there is a perpetual sense of things unsaid, bubbling away beneath the surface. Tasso had himself been educated by the new Catholic religious order, the Jesuits, and his unusually strong religious fervor (rooted in the mid-century movement of Catholic reform) is also seen in some of the intense, but difficult to articulate, inward lives of his characters. It is these characteristics that have led some people to compare Tasso to the movements in art which were opposed to the classical simplicity of Michelangelo and sought to replace it with more self-consciously artificial poses and lighting effects, a movement associated with such figures as Bronzino and Vasari.

Over in the Iberian peninsula, another national epic was being written by Luiz Vez de Camoens (1524-1580), Portugal's most

LA GERUSALEMME LIBERATA

Torquato Tasso's greatest achievement, the work aimed to surpass Homer and Virgil and provide Italy with a national epic poem.

TORQUATO TASSO (1544-1595)

Tasso incarcerated in a madhouse. Tasso's characters, rather like Virgil's Aeneas, are forever conflicted between emotion and duty, and there is a perpetual sense of things unsaid.

THE DEPARTURE OF AENEAS AND DIDO'S DEATH
A 1469 painting depicting an episode from Virgil's *The Aeneid*.
Bibliothèque Municipale, Dijon, France.

LUIZ VAZ DE CAMOENS Portugal's most famous Renaissance poet,
Camoens' *Lusiads* revolved around Vasco da Gama's colonial expeditions,
with its narrative style influenced by Latin epics such as Virgil's *Aeneid*.

famous Renaissance poet. He was educated by Domicans and Jesuits and appears to have studied at the University of Coimbra. Following a period during which he traveled to the Indies, he published the *Lusiads* in 1572. Its action concerns Vasco da Gama's colonial expeditions. Camoens was a careful reader of Virgil's *Aeneid*, though the work is more concerned with the glories and less with the price of empire than was Virgil's poem. The narrative style owes more to Latin epic than to the romance epics of Ariosto and Tasso, and for this reason, may be seen as a slightly L'Adone backward-looking work.

If Tasso represented some hints of the profound changes in taste that were come to be known as "Baroque," then it is Giambattista Marino (1569–1625) whose name is most associated with this

shift. Marino was born into a well-educated family of lawyers. His father had destined him for law, and like so many literary figures of the Renaissance from Petrarch on, he had refused to adopt this career. The beginning of the 17th century saw him move to Rome, then Turin and finally to Paris in 1615. His two most important works are *Le Rime* (1602) and *L'Adone* (1623). "The purpose of the poet," declared Marino, "was the marvelous." The creation of the marvelous was to create dizzyingly complex, stunning surface textures that exist in bizarre proximity to some powerfully simple emotional descriptions. This represented, in many ways, an end point of the Erasmian concern for variation, coupled with the Senecan taste for the pithy saying. The stage was set for the elaborations of Baroque, and the subsequent reaction in favor of the plain style.

Chapter 4
BAROQUE
DRAMA AND GRANDEUR

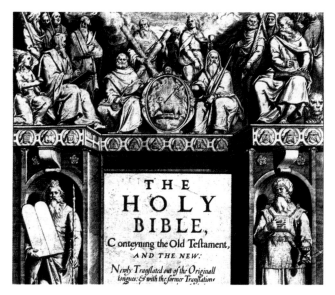

The Reformation broke the idea of universal loyalty to the universal Catholic Church. This was an important stage on the road to the creation of national consciousness and state formation and often resulted in the need for a new literature in that nation's own language. There were, of course, other factors. At the end of the Middle Ages, war was something that could be waged by almost any local lord or baron. New technology changed all that. By 1550, if not before, war had become so expensive that only the leaders (whether princes, emperors, or kings) of states could afford to engage in it. This had profound consequences. The old notion of the aristocracy as the men who led in battle had become obsolete. Humanist educational ideals and an increase in the centrality of the court, with its possibility for artistic patronage, slowly replaced the ideal of the military leader with that of the cultural leader. In the Middle Ages, there was no expectation that a king be particularly learned, though occasionally some were. Now literature and learning became part of the apparatus by which the aristocracy considered themselves superior to others.

SPAIN

Spain in the earlier part of the 15th century had been a backwater of Europe. For most of the Middle Ages, it was in fact a Muslim territory, where the three monotheistic religions coexisted relatively peacefully. Slowly from 1400 to 1600, Spain transformed itself from backwater to the greatest empire on earth at the time, with massive inflows of silver bullion from the New World, a newly self-confident language, and, in Cervantes, one of the greatest authors of world literature. The turning point was the marriage in 1469 of Ferdinand and Isabella, which united Castile and Aragon, and which became a template for the unification of the Iberian peninsula: one land, one church, one language. In 1492, Spain expelled its Jews. In that same year, following a long siege, the last Muslim territory in the south, Granada, was reconquered for Spain. Following the battle of Alcantara in 1580, Portugal was annexed to its more powerful neighbor. Spain, bounded by the Pyrenees in the north and the Pillars of Hercules in the south, had always made sense as a geographical unity. Now it began to unify itself religiously and linguistically as well. In 1492, Antonio de Nebrija published the first grammar of the Spanish language; "language and power," he wrote, "go hand in hand." In Renaissance literature, it is unfortunate that the increases in energies devoted to vernacular literature often accompanied a rise in nationalist fervor, although specifying the precise relationship between the two is difficult.

The most visible aspect of Spain's transformation was its empire. It began to expand into the New World, with the famous voyage of Christopher Columbus, landing for the first time in 1492 on what is today part of the Bahamas. Charles V, who ruled from 1516 to 1556 strove to consciously transpose the notion of the Roman Empire into a Christian–Spanish context. His son, Philip II, consolidated the imperial propaganda. The Roman Empire was not, of course, merely a political entity; it needed ideological, linguistic, and literary support as well. All of which Spain would need too.

As Spain began to flex its muscles on the international stage, so the intellectual and cultural life became simultaneously more vigorous and more narrow in its perspectives. Whereas in the earlier part of the 16th century, there had been some

influence of the more tolerant humanist outlook of Erasmus, soon Erasmus' works were banned. For example, Hebrew, since it was the language of the Jewish heretics, was only taught at one university in Spain (Salamanca). Foreign travel became increasingly subject to constraint, though trade flourished. This did not mean that Spanish culture was intellectually impoverished. What it did mean was that Spanish literature developed to a large extent out of previous Spanish works. The scene was set for a brilliant insularity. Spain went its own way, to a larger extent than some other national literatures. An excellent example of this independence is provided by the development of the novel.

If Cervantes humorously asked serious questions about doubting the stories we tell ourselves, then another branch of Spanish literature was moving at breakneck speed in the opposite direction: the exploration of the deepest and most intimate forms of inner certainty. Fortress Spain was the only country in Europe to be almost unaffected by the Reformation. Religious literature also, therefore, developed, like secular literature, along its own lines. The 16th and 17th centuries are remarkable for the creation of a distinctive and extreme brand of spirituality, though

DON QUIXOTE

The romance tradition of knights, getting lost in forests, castles, and love intrigues, slowly evolved into the novel in the Renaissance. The man most responsible for this transformation was a Spaniard. By the end of the 16th century, Spain had created an important tradition of "picaresque" romances, inaugurated by *Lazarillo de Tormes*, published anonymously in 1554. Picaresque fiction started a new tradition of the creation of character for its own sake. The main protagonist, who is often a social underdog, tends to be the sort of person to whom things just happen. He is the opposite of the traditional epic hero, such as Aeneas, who has a mission, and whose mission imposes a dreadful cost on the relationships of those around him. Everything must be subordinated to a higher purpose, and that imposes a strict standard on such things as digressions and the "pointless" pleasures of wandering after maidens in woods. It was the genius of Miguel de Cervantes (1547–616) to take this picaresque tradition of random comic incident and engage with larger concerns through a more coherent plot and with a more coherent backdrop of ethical concerns, and persistent questions about the status of truth and falsehood in literature. For this reason he may be viewed as the father of the novel.

Cervantes was born near Madrid, and though his works prove him a man of wide learning and deep culture, it is unclear whether he in fact attended a university. His own life suggests a certain impulsiveness and idealism: he fell in love with a barmaid, yet her parents barred him from marrying her, became a soldier in the Spanish army, and spent time in imprisoned captivity. He had no fixed base for much of his early life, and, like the hero of his novel, wandered around from town to town. In 1605, he published the first part of *Don Quixote* (the second part was published in 1613, and there is a fair amount of plot inconsistencies both within books and between books). Don Quixote is a knight addicted to the ideals of romance and chivalry, but whose lack of worldliness prevents him from seeing how the fictions of chivalry, and of his own identity, are useless for his own situation, as an impoverished and old-fashioned misfit. Earthy and pragmatic realism is supplied by his faithful companion, Sancho Panza. Sometimes Quixote is a teller of tales, sometimes he gets involved in the action himself, but Quixote is not a mere excuse for Cervantes's fondness for narrative digressions and for comic set pieces. All of the actions and stories discreetly reveal something about his character, a character whom Cervantes wants us to believe in and to love.

MIGUEL DE CERVANTES

Cervantes's influence on the Spanish language has been so great that Spanish is often called *la lengua de Cervantes* (the language of Cervantes).

Cervantes was not only interested in his protagonist. There are many characters from the lower orders of the society in his novel, who are important characters in their own right and do not serve as mere counterpoints to the nobles. Rather like Shakespeare and Tolstoy, Cervantes appears as much concerned to create a world in which the reader can fully participate, though he is keen that we critically assess the dependence of Don Quixote's—and indeed of all—identity on previous literature.

The importance of fiction, and hence of literature, to our sense of self is central to the book's plot. Cervantes suggests that his tale is based on that of precious historical manuscript by a Moorish scholar (Cide Hamete Benengeli), but this is itself a fiction. Whereas in the earlier parts of the book, characters attempt to persuade Quixote to see how futile his chivalrous behavior is in contemporary circumstances, by the end of the book Quixote begins to sink into depression as he realizes that life is indeed not a series of old-fashioned quests: at this point, his friends try to turn Quixote back into the out-of-synch idealist he once was. If literature is deceiving, perhaps it's better to be deceived. A direct, and even more dizzyingly complex descendent of Don Quixote can be found in the 1965 Spanish film, the *Saragossa Manuscript*, which highlights issues relating to truth, fiction, and identity, while set among tales of love and knights from Renaissance Spain. Indeed, so influential has *Don Quixote* been that it has been translated into more languages than any other book, with the exception of the Bible.

this literature was soon influential in other countries, including Protestant countries like England. Key figures were St John of the Cross (1542–1591) and St. Teresa of Avila (1515–1582).

Lope de Vega (1562–1635) was a representative of the last days of the Renaissance and its humanist culture. Whereas Cervantes mingled popular narratives with philosophical questions in a new genre—the novel—and whereas the mystics such as Teresa of Avila looked back to medieval traditions, Lope de Vega was more firmly rooted in the academic culture of humanism. If the humanist project was one of recovery, one had to start asking, what should we not recover? Born in Madrid, he was educated in a Jesuit academy and then in the University of Alcala. Although of a religious temperament, he relished a more active life—he even participated in the ill-starred Armada expedition against England. De Vega was no less energetic when it came to the

SAINT TERESA OF AVILA (1515 - 1582)
St Teresa of Avila was a Carmelite nun and a Spanish mystic. Here (top left) she is depicted enraptured in contemplation of the sacred heart of Jesus : her own heart is bleeding due to being pierced by an arrow.

production of literature—several books of religious poetry, a pastoral romance, historical writing in verse, and over 450 plays have survived. What was extraordinary about de Vega's dramatic works was their desire to include everything. Before de Vega, Spanish drama had certain thematic and stylistic limitations. By contrast, de Vega's hunger to make the drama a sort of "total art" (as Wagner would later do with his ideas on opera) meant that new verse forms, new subject matters, historical paraphrase, learned jokes, satirical indignation, and religious feeling were combined in what seemed like an endless font of creativity. His humanism was not merely a humanism of the past, but it was eager to embrace the Italian literate culture of the time, which also saw itself as rooted in the past and yet (as with the operas of Monteverdi) was growing ever more elaborate.

The question of which ancient world and what sort of Latin to recover had long worried humanists. As they discovered more and more texts from the ancient world, the question of which ones were the best to imitate became more pressing. This worry generated the obsession with style that is so distinctive a feature of the humanist project. The sort of prose style that had been upheld for generations as "correct" was that of Cicero, but by the end of the 16th century, new models, such as the dense and witty prose of Seneca, or the elaborate and rich works of Apuleius, had begun to be in fashion. These stylistic disputes soon spilled over from Latin into the various vernacular languages. In Spain, the most famous tussle over what sort of style was the most fluent and supple for poetry was between Francisco de Quevedo (1580–1645) and Luis de Gongora (1561–1627). Both had reacted against the domination of a clear, early 16th-century rich but lucid Ciceronian form of Castilian, but in very different ways. Gongora was a staunch advocate of Culteranismo, a Baroque style akin to that of Giambattista

LUIS DE GONGORA

Marino, full of complicated metaphors and strange word order. Quevedo, by contrast, was associated with the attempt to make a smooth and simple-seeming surface spread out multiple layers of meaning and association, icebergs concealing strange conceptual depths: Conceptismo. The unified humanist culture, along with its dreams of a peaceable republic of letters, had come to an end.

FRANCE

If Spain moved slowly into a period of decline after the glories of Emperor Philip II, France's commitment to prosperity, power, and peace after the grueling 16th-century wars of religion created a culture of considerable depth and sophistication in the 17th century. It was, however, a period of massive centralization: political, cultural, and linguistic. No figure better sums up this new spirit than Cardinal Richelieu (1585–1642). Armand Jean du Plessis de Richelieu was born to minor

CARDINAL RICHELIEU, By Philippe de Champaigne, Musée des Beaux-Arts, Rouen, France

This great politician and statesman was a patron of arts. He founded the Académie française, the learned society of matters pertaining to the French language. He built a theater in his Paris residence and formed a company of five authors (Corneille, Boisrobert, Colletet, L'Estoille, and Rotrou) to write dramas under his direction.

Parisian nobility and rose rapidly through the ranks of the church. By the 1620s he had become a chief minister of state and a cardinal of the Roman Catholic Church. Richelieu was keenly aware of the threat to his country's peace posed by an overly mighty Habsburg empire. He therefore set about making France as internally strong as possible. The king's word was to be law, aided by the power of the Catholic, but national, church. He wiped out the power of the independent nobility. The court became the undisputed center of all new cultural patronage. To further emphasize the notion of French unity, Richelieu gave his formal imprimatur to L'Académie française, a body of academics to oversee what would count as "correct" usage of the French language and who would promote French literature. Richelieu offered generous patronage to writers, the most famous thereof was the dramatist Corneille. Paris was

made the literary, political, and academic center of French life, and it has remained so ever since.

Drama lagged behind the other arts in France—the century before Richelieu did not consider drama a particularly esteemed genre. As in England, the first plays to break out of the religious or mystery play mold were humanist plays. These were usually translations or adaptations (sometimes via an Italian intermediary) of ancient comedies or tragedies. Pierre de Larivey (1550–1612) was a key figure in this early stage of the French drama. What began to happen at the end of the 16th century was an influx of new dramatic styles from Italy that were not based on ancient models and began to point forward to new "mixed" modes of dramatic experimentation: the *commedia dell'arte*, the pastoral and the court ballet combined with the earlier humanist plays to create a much richer (and often more visual or musical) sort of theatrical experience. Pathos, bizarre situations, strange tales of knights and ladies from the romance tradition, musical interludes, and a better awareness of the mechanics of stagecraft were all hallmarks of this new fertility of dramatic imagination at the turn of the 17th century.

This bizarre, multi-sourced fertility of the drama would not survive the century. As drama became a more academically respectable part of literature, so a body of rules grew up, which were supposed to govern how literature should be written. L'Académie française viewed itself as the judge and jury of whether or not plays had conformed to these rules, derived from theoretical writings on the newly fashionable text of Aristotle, the *Poetics*. Pierre Corneille (1606–1684) is a good example of how a practicing playwright interacted with the neo-Aristotelian tradition. Corneille came from Rouen where he received a traditional education at the hands of the Jesuits. Failing in the legal career for which his father had destined him, he moved to Paris in 1629 to write for the stage. He rapidly established himself as a successful author, winning the attention of Richelieu, who selected Corneille to be a crucial part of another of the Cardinal's centralizing schemes of propaganda. Richelieu, however, demanded too controlling a hand in the products of Corneille's imagination, and the two men went their separate ways. When in 1637, Corneille's new play *Le Cid* played to huge audiences, L'Académie française stepped in to criticize. The play failed, so L'Académie held, on numerous grounds. It did not respect the Aristotelian theory of plot-construction. Furthermore, it had immoral tendencies. In an important contribution to the theory of drama (his 1659 *Trois discours sur le poème dramatique*), Corneille subtly explored the relationship of rules to imagination. Corneille composed little in the last decade of his life, but the author who most built on Corneille's achievements was Jean Racine (1639–1699). Like Corneille, Racine was educated by Jesuits, destined for a career in law and came to Paris to write for the stage. Racine, however, was more concerned with the surface texture of his writing than his Rouen rival and his plays, particularly *Phèdre* (1677), and he displays a carefully-wrought elegance and simplicity. Even more so than Corneille, there is the sense of a powerful directive and controlling intelligence at work in Racine, a control that only heightens the tragic powerlessness of his characters.

There was, however, far more to the 17th century than mere drama. This was the century in which French prose reached new heights of subtlety and power. Blaise Pascal (1623–1662) represents one strand of this new development. He was born in the Auvergne and was a child prodigy in mathematics. Through a chance incident, he befriended two of his father's doctors, both of whom were part of a new religious sect, known as Jansenism. Jansenists looked back to St Augustine, and may, in many respects, be compared to the Lutheran emphasis on St Augustine's views on humans' sinfulness and their helplessness to save themselves. Jansenists have much in common, indeed, with the tradition of German mysticism on which Luther himself drew. They looked with

ABOVE: JEAN RACINE

RIGHT: *PHÈDRE,*
By Jean Racine, Featuring Sarah Bernhardt

Based on Greek tragedy, this dramatic tragedy was first performed in 1677.

LEFT: BLAISE PASCAL, Engraving from *Gallery of Portraits*, 1833

Pascal's polemical letters titled *The Provincial Letters*, a defense of the Jansenists against attacks by the Jesuits, marked the beginning of modern French prose.

RIGHT: 'THE WOLF AS A SHEPHERD,' From the Fables by La Fontaine, Color litho. Bibliothéque Nationale, Paris, France

horror at the Jesuit tradition of "casuistry." This was a form of moral discourse that, to its critics, looked as though it could, given the right circumstances, justify any sin. Pascal wrote his *Provincial Letters* in 1656 and 1657 to attack the practice. These letters have been seen as the highpoint of 17th-century French prose. They move effortlessly and elegantly between ridicule, satire, and philosophical argument.

Jean de la Fontaine (1621–1695) shows an equal but very different mastery of the French language. He was born in the Champagne region of France, and after abortive careers in both the law and the Church, he moved to Paris to make his name in literature. In some ways, Fontaine may be seen as another last excavator of the inheritance of antiquity—his first literary accomplishment, indeed, was an adaptation of the Roman comedian Terence. The model, however, for his masterpiece was not the grand writers of epic and tragedy such as Virgil and Euripides. Instead, he chose the ex-slave Aesop, whose little fables of animal behavior had been mostly seen as diversions

or good teaching tools for children (although Horace famously included a version of the town mouse and the country mouse fable in his *Satires*). La Fontaine wrote in a period of self-conscious sophistication and ideals of encyclopedic learning; his skill was to make the fables all things to all men. Not only are the tales immaculately constructed in a beautifully supple and yet simple French, they also display the great gift of knowing how to tell a tale. Their surface texture is more beguilingly self-conscious as an art work than the tales of Boccaccio. His tales are, furthermore, wiser and more profound in their psychology than any of the previous fabulists, though he owes a great deal to the cynical aphorist La Rochefoucauld (1613–1680).

Jean-Baptiste Poquelin (1622–1673) is better known by his stage name—Molière. He was born in Paris to a relatively well-off family. He was, however, not to follow the expected route for such a scion. Unlike the other great figures of the 17th century, Jean-Baptiste was not (or at least not primarily) a man soaked in antiquity and theological dispute, who tried to express the

humanist inheritance through his literary gifts. He was, above all things, a man of the theater. He received a good general education from a Jesuit academy, but soon set his sights on the stage, spending many years as a jobbing actor. His talent for stagecraft and for dramatic action surpassed all who had gone before him, though his skill as a craftsman of language did not match that of Racine. His plotting is superb, his often comically gloomy view of human nature and self-deception were ideal for the strange reversals of fortune that his plays demonstrate. Molière managed to complete the rehabilitation of the stage, and in particular of comedy, as a literary and commercial vehicle that could float free of the prejudices of the ancient world, social class, and of L'Académie française. In this he is a fitting end to a century of French literature that sought to make France its own world, owing nothing to anyone, supreme over all.

TOP: ITALIAN AND FRENCH COMEDIANS PLAYING IN MOLIÈRE'S FARCES, 1670, attributed to Verio, Oil on canvas

RIGHT: STATUE OF MOLIÈRE, ROMAN REGULAR

Molière was the greatest writer of the neoclassical comedy. He wrote as many as 11 farces in his early career. He worked closely with an Italian theatrical troupe The influence of the troupe's *commedia dell'arte* is evident throughout Molière's plays.

GERMANY

A glance at a map of 17th-century Germany shows dozens of petty kingdoms, principalities, and free cities. If Spain was geographically sound, Germany's borders were always more fluid. Bohemia and Moravia, some of the hinterland with France, Switzerland, areas on either side of the river Elbe were all influenced by German culture and sometimes in close political connection with any one or other of their neighbors. This patchwork of political loyalties and differing religious attachments, all living cheek by jowl one with another, had several consequences. The most significant was the slow emergence of the notion of the German state, unified by a single language.

In the early 17th century, a rough unity was provided, it is true, by the Holy Roman Empire. The Holy Roman Empire, however, was (at least in comparison to the Spanish empire) administratively and culturally a much more convenient amalgam rather than a guiding ideology. It was, in fact, neither holy, Roman, nor an empire. The emperor at the turn of the 17th century, Rudolph II (1552–1612), seemed to embody much of the ideal of the Renaissance prince—with strong centralizing tendencies and a pronounced love of literary and scientific culture. These would have functioned as a tool to further integrate his realm. He decided, however, to move his court to Prague, and, toward the end of his life became increasingly distant from affairs of state. This allowed Germany to remain what people today would call a "multi-polar" world.

Czech, German, and Latin were therefore all important in the eastern parts of the Holy Roman Empire. More than anywhere else, the German-speaking lands exhibited a kind of linguistic schizophrenia. Their literary personality was split between a sophisticated humanist Latin culture and, by comparison an underdeveloped German one. This was not merely because a

SEBASTIAN BRANT

Best known for his 1494 satirical poem *The Ship of Fools*, Brant was the most famous German writer before Johannes Wolfgang von Goethe. The poem is a tale of a shipload of 110 people bound for Narragonia, a "fool's paradise." Illustrated with dramatic wood-cuts, it satirizes the vices and follies of the time.

unified grammar (such as that by Nebrija for Spain) was slow in coming. So strong an association was there between Luther, the German language, and his translation of the Bible that German Catholics tended to write (to a greater extent than in, for example, England) their "literary" works in Latin. Indeed, the Latin writings (both Protestant and Catholic of the 16th century) are in the vanguard of European humanist culture. Conrad Celtis (1459–1508) expressed a proud awareness of the growing contribution of Germany to the recovery of the ancient world, writing many fluent letters and poems in the antique style. Petrus Lotichius (1528–1560) wrote several books of poetry in subtle and careful imitation of the ancient Roman elegists—Ovid, Propertius, and Tibullus. The Protestant humanist educational revolution of Philipp Melanchthon, and the universities that took his works as their model, placed this sort of work on a much firmer footing. The Jesuit educational model (a sort of Catholic parallel to the success of Melanchthon) was securely rooted in many parts of southern Germany by the end of the century—and Jesuit culture, with its greater emphasis on elaboration, whether verbal, visual, or musical—thus smoothing the path to the fashion for the Baroque in that area.

THE SHIP OF FOOLS, *c.* 1550, Glückschafft Schiff, Zurich, Switzerland,

Brant's satirical poem launched a new literary genre known as "fool's literature," and there were imitations of Brant's style and theme all over Europe.

It was a popular medium and written in clear German. This, however, only served to increase the distance (at least in the short term) between the learned Latin culture and the popular vernacular one. Probably the most famous work in the vernacular, before Luther's translation of the Bible, was Sebastian Brant's *Ship of Fools*. This influential satire was an immediate success and soon translated into other languages, including Latin. Brant (1458–1521) was not a voice of the people. He came from Alsace, and was associated with that town in the advance guard of humanism, Strasbourg. The book recounts the tale of a journey to fools' paradise, with a loose episodic structure designed to display the stupidity, ignorance, and vulgarity of mankind. The work provided an impetus to further experimentation, naturalizing other humanist Latin genres into German. The religious divisions of the Reformation, however, were not conducive.

Following the Peace of Augsburg (1555), which established an unstable peace between Protestants and Catholics, German literature remained a backward affair, with most writers committed to the aforementioned "linguistic schizophrenia" of Latin and German. Modifying Italian lyrics so they could adapt to the radically different language structures of German proved to be quite difficult, whereas the new fashion for a highly visual and conceptually complicated form of poetry seemed much easier. Martin Opitz von Boberfeld (1597–1639) strove to consolidate this fashion in Germany. Opitz was born in Lower Silesia, in what is today the southwest region of Poland. In 1618 he left to study at the University of Frankfurt, Germany. Language is the tool of literature; literary and linguistic developments are always intertwined. It is not surprising, therefore, to discover that Opitz's first book (*On the Contempt for the German Language*, 1618) was a book on how German could be made a proper vehicle for the expression of thought and literature. What Opitz sought to do was to establish a set of basic rules for what sort of language and what sort of form to use when expressing

The imitation of delicate music of Italian lyric poetry, however, with its complicated song-like rhythms and profusion of soft rhyming (such as in the works of shorter poems by Torquato Tasso) seemed to elude the Germans at this stage in the development of their literary language. Perhaps their energies were elsewhere; after all, the most lasting (and in some ways original) contribution of the 16th century to German and indeed world literature, was the hymn. The hymn can be considered a musical equivalent to the visual propaganda that Luther and his associates used so well. Its purpose was to be memorable—it aimed at the clarity of doctrine and expression.

MARTIN OPITZ VON BOBERFELD, Accompanied by friends and admirers on the title page of his poetical works.

Martin Opitz asserted the suitability of the German language for poetry and established the rules of German poetry.

different aspects of human experience. He therefore attempted to establish a purer form of German that would serve as the basis for expression across a number of different genres. One can compare this with a similar impetus attempted by the English writer, Samuel Daniel (1562–1619). Highly representative

of this worthy goal is Opitz's 1633 work, *Vesuvius*. Although he attempted an extremely strict domestication of certain neo-Latin rules, he remained interested in the distinctive characteristics of the German language—a language very different from the Romance languages of Italian, French, and Latin. It is entirely in accord with this nationalist recovery of the "true" German language that the last major work he completed was an edition of the linguistically archaic 11th-century German heroic poem: the *Annolied*. When the 19th-century German grammarians, the Grimm brothers (authors of the fairy tales of the same name) wrote approvingly that correct German was "direct, coarse, and spoken with no paper in front of the mouth," they were connecting to a long tradition of seeing a truly German linguistic past that had flourished since, and possibly even before, medieval times.

Opitz eventually settled in Gdansk, where he had secured a stable position at the court of Vladislav IV Vasa (1595–1648) and where he died from the plague in 1639. In Gdansk, he influenced the young poet Christian Hofmann von Hofmannswaldau (1617–1679). Hofmannswaldau was to expand the expressive ability of German. He also extended subject matter to include marked erotic content, with an interesting emphasis on

CHRISTIAN HOFMANN VON HOF-MANNSWALDAU

A friend of Martin Opitz and Andreas Gryphius, Hofmannswaldau became famous as a poet only after his death in 1679. Distinguished by unusual metaphors, skillful use of rhetoric, and bold eroticism, his style of poetry came to be known as galant.

ANDREAS GRYPHIUS

Gryphius was a lyric poet and dramatist of the German Baroque. As he grew up during the period of the Thirty Years' War, his lyrics focus on war and death, of which the best-known are the *Cemetery Thoughts*. He wrote both comedies and tragedies in the German vernacular.

female psychology (as in his *Heldenbriefe*). Whereas Opitz could be seen as a linguistic schizophrenic, with Latin always in the background, Hofmannswaldau is a fully German writer, however indebted he may have been to the Neo-Latin theorists of which Opitz was the channel. The third figure who was most responsible for the German Baroque also came from Silesia: Andreas Gryphius (1616–1664).

RELIGION AND LITERATURE IN EUROPE

Poland was a wise choice for writers requiring peace, for it had remained more or less unscathed than some other areas of Europe by the turbulent military and religious struggles that were going on in the early part of the 17th century. The uneasy balancing act of the Peace of Augsburg contained within it the seeds of its own destruction. It established the principle of *"cuius regio, eius religio,"* which meant the prince could choose the religion of his people. This had the undesirable consequence of making anyone who did not practice the religion of his

prince into a political subversive as well as a religious heretic. The resulting readily combustible tension partially accounts for the most important event of the 17th century: the Thirty Years' War (1618–1648), which began as a dispute over the religious freedoms of Protestants in Bohemia (the modern day Czech Republic). The Holy Roman Emperor, it was thought, had slowly eroded these freedoms. Soon a number of other grievances and nations were added, so that by 1630 nearly all of Central and Western Europe was involved.

The Thirty Years' War was the bloodiest conflict hitherto fought in Europe; millions of civilians were killed. By the time 1648 finally brought peace to a Europe exhausted by religious divisions, some writers began to look more critically at the relation between the court and the patronage system that financially supported them. Nothing changed overnight. Yet, the growth of a more popular media and genres, however, and the emergence of newspapers would alter how some writers viewed themselves and their audiences.

Poets have often thought of themselves as being in possession of a higher authority. Partly this is the mystery of creativity—it is very hard to say exactly where poems come from, and why. Homer was inspired by the divine muse; Horace saw himself as a kind of priest-poet: a vates. Literary talent, in other words, has both rights and obligations: the obligation to learn your craft and to push yourself, and the right to speak and to be heard. This old idea merged with the humanist ideal of a Republic of Letters—a sort of democracy of scholarship and intellectual activity. It was a natural development of this humanist ideal (after the barbarities and dislocations of war) that men (and occasionally women) should be free to speak, to create, and to criticize. This was an idea that took hold slowly and irregularly in the second half of the 17th century. Germany, for example, remained very divided into different principalities and cities. England, by contrast, and the Low Countries, were the countries that most rapidly embraced this connection between a progressive republic of literature and the ideal of freedom of political expression.

CROMWELL AND MILTON

Here Oliver Cromwell is dictating to the poet John Milton, Latin Secretary to the Council, who latinizes foreign dispatches.

England

Under James I, England was united with Scotland and the centralizing of authority continued apace. Conflicts between the increasingly high-handed actions of James I's son, Charles I, and the parliament soon became apparent. If the court attempted to be the center of cultural production, it faced a losing battle. Literacy increased; the clergy were better educated than ever before; Oxford and Cambridge were once again at the center of European culture; London's scientific revolution was as much dependent on humble apothecaries and mechanics as it was on the king or the nobility; the theaters were a new site of popular discussion

SIR THOMAS BROWNE

of ideas; even women were venturing into print. Although the parliament should not be seen as any protector of free speech or human rights in the modern sense, the conflicts succeeded in underlining how many different sources of authority existed in England. Moreover, the English language was entering a period of astonishing richness. A new complexity and density had been added to poetry in the late Elizabethan period, by writers such as Shakespeare, John Donne, and Samuel Daniel. Prose, perhaps, had lagged behind. By the middle of the century, however, England was to produce writers of subtlety, power, and grace, such as Sir Thomas Browne (1605–1682), whose *Hydrotaphia* is seen as the finest achievement of English prose in the 17th century. Most poets reacted against the complexities of Donne, for the poetry of the period emphasized song-like qualities, in imitation (successful at last) of the Italian lyric tradition. Edmund Waller

(1607–1687) is perhaps the best of these: "Go, Lovely Rose/Tell her that wastes my time, and me/That now she knows/When I resemble her to thee/How sweet and fair she seems to be."

To some writers, such poetry seemed politically irresponsible. The conflict between Charles I and parliament reached a crisis with a civil war in the 1640s, which ended with a temporary ending of the monarchy and the beheading of Charles. The literary figure who best represents this period of republican rule, and the inheritance of the notion of poetical authority and the republic of letters, is John Milton (1608–1674). The republican Protectorate, which emerged after Charles I, was led by Oliver Cromwell, and Milton spent time in Cromwell's service, closely involved with the production of documents directly related to the new political order. The transformation from early humanist poet to political civil servant is best understood through the idea that Milton had of his authority to speak, an authority both secular and poetic. Milton had set himself, more consciously than anyone before him in the history of England, to be a poet. His model, like Edmund Spenser before him, was Virgil. The first poetry he wrote during and after his studies at Cambridge University was notable (just like Virgil's early pastoral poetry) for its elaborate sound structures. He was a full participant in the European culture of learning and literature, and he traveled

JOHN MILTON (1608-1674)

Milton composed *Paradise Lost* in *c*. 1666. Having become blind, he was forced to dictate the poem to his two daughters. Milton first wanted to base his epic poem on the Arthurian legends, which were foundation myths of English nationalism, but later turned to the universal theme of genesis.

Right: Satan and Beelzebub, as illustrated in Milton's *Paradise Lost* 1868.

THE DESCENT OF TYPHON AND THE GODS INTO HELL
Milton's *Hymn on the Morning of Christ's Nativity*, illustrated by William Blake. (watercolor on paper, Whitworth Art Gallery, The University of Manchester, UK).

Paradise had also been lost. In 1660, monarchy was restored to England, and England's subjects were no longer "free." Milton passionately believed in the importance of independent political judgment—not all dissent was disobedience. While we must submit to the will of God he believed, God cannot be, as Charles I was, a tyrant. The figure of a rebellious Satan has, throughout the poem, the best and most memorable lines. Perhaps Milton's attitude to Satan is more admiring, and more political, than Biblical tradition allowed. It is, then, Milton's last adaptation of Renaissance humanism and the authority of the poet to the changing political circumstances of the day that make him a fitting end to this rich period of English literature.

Low Countries

England did not have a monopoly, however, on innovative forms of government and an emphasis on parrhesia. The Low Countries were the other beneficiary of the new ideas of freedom of expression in this period. Whereas in the 16th century, Italy had been seen as the center of all of the latest trends, be they literary or intellectual, by the middle of the 17th century, this had shifted to, above all, the Dutch Republic. From a literary perspective, however, certain disadvantages would need to be overcome. The most serious of these was the Dutch language, for it had neither a long, nor a distinguished history. To some, it might even seem to be an inferior version of German. Dutch was not a tongue that many men or women in Europe knew and the emphasis on international trade that formed the core of the power of the Dutch empire meant that the Dutch tended to be good linguists.

The reputation for intellectual and political freedom and their high quality universities (above all the University of

to Italy where he was warmly received by various poets and scholars. Of convinced Puritan sympathies, his respect for the ancient ideal of parrhesia (embodied in an impassioned defense of free speech and press in his *Areopagitica*) combined with a belief in the importance of constructing a new Jerusalem for the godly.

Milton eventually turned to writing a much bigger work, *Paradise Lost*. This epic retold the tale of how Adam and Eve were banished from the Garden of Eden. Their sin was that they had eaten the fruit from the tree of knowledge of good and evil, despite having been forbidden by God to do so. The words "Of man's first disobedience" begin the poem. But another

JOOST VAN DEN VONDEL, *c.* 1650, Engraving by De Visscher

Poet and playwright Joost van den Vondel produced some of the greatest works of Dutch literature. Besides his plays and lyrics, Vondel also became renowned for his biting political satire.

RIGHT: The Dutch poet Joost van den Vondel is honored with a literary and musical fete at Ruremonde, Netherlands.

Leiden) meant that the Low Countries were soon exposed to influences from all over Europe—and the wealth that flowed in from their trading enterprises was soon put to use in the creation of vast amounts of distinctively Dutch sculpture, painting, and architecture. Literature often played second fiddle to both these academic and visual forms of cultural identity, but it did slowly emerge. The most famous figure is Joost Van Den Vondel (1587–1679), who wrote a range of biblical and historical tragedies that fully commented on the problems of the day with a command of the Dutch language that, his fellow poets said, raised their tongue to new heights of grandeur and new depths of subtlety. To show how multi-polar the literary world had become, we should remember that the Silesian Andreas Gryphius visited Van

Den Vondel. Gryphius's own later development is attributed to this Dutchman's influence, who indeed, affected the future of German Baroque..

The Renaissance was a revolution, that looked to the past for answers to the woes of society and models for how to write in the works of the classical past. The new sense of the possibilities for literary expression, scientific development, and new tools for the exchange of ideas show how the 17th century was both the death knell of humanist culture, and yet wholly dependent on its achievements and methods. The stage was set for new revolutions.

Chapter 5
ENLIGHTENMENT TO CLASSICISM
REASON AND KNOWLEDGE

DENIS DIDEROT

Diderot was the chief editor of the *Encyclopédie*, along with the mathematician Jean Le Rond d'Alembert. He is responsible for enlarging the scope of *Encyclopédie*, making it a tool for radical and revolutionary opinion. Here, Diderot is seen discussing the encyclopedia with colleagues.

FACING PAGE: Goethe's Faust, *The Meeting of Faust and Marguerite*, 1860, James Jacques Joseph Tissot (1836-1902), Oil on canvas, Musée d'Orsay, Paris, France

FRANCE

The text that most accurately defines the Enlightenment movement within French culture is the *Encyclopédie, ou dictionnaire raisonné des sciences, des arts et des métiers* (in English, *Encyclopedia, or a systematic dictionary of the sciences, arts, and crafts*). Published between 1751 and 1772, with larger supplements and revisions added in 1772, 1777, and 1780, it included articles from many of the most prominent figures of the French Enlightenment, including Voltaire, Rousseau, and Montesquieu. It was Louis de Jaucourt, however, who contributed most significantly to the *Encyclopédie*, writing 17,266 articles between 1759 and 1756. But the completion of this ambitious project would probably never have happened without the efforts of the philosopher and writer Denis Diderot (1713–1784), who became co-editor with Jean d'Alembert in 1751, remaining in an editorial position for 25 years.

The aim of the *Encyclopédie* was the dissemination of knowledge, inspired by Francis Bacon's *Advancement of Knowledge*, which divided knowledge into the three branches of history, philosophy, and poetry. On a more clandestine level, the editors also hoped that it would act as a manifesto for Enlightenment thinking. In France, the *ancien régime*, upset particularly by the *Encyclopédie's* plea for religious tolerance, banned the whole work by royal decree, closing down the project in 1759. However, the work continued in secret, as the editors enjoyed the favor of high-profile supporters, such as Madame de Pompadour. Needless to say, the work had a huge influence on the kinds of political thinking that would spark the events of the French Revolution.

Aside from working on the *Encyclopédie*, Diderot was a writer and dramatist; he is particularly remembered for his work *Jacques le fataliste et son maître* (*Jacques the fatalist and his master*, 1796), in which a master tells stories of his love affairs to his valet, Jacques. The roundabout plot and narrative interruptions have encouraged comparisons with Laurence Sterne's *Tristram Shandy*; however, the novel's broader philosophy, that there is a "great scroll" on which all past and future events are written, has led some critics to regard the work as deterministic. Diderot is also known for sentimental

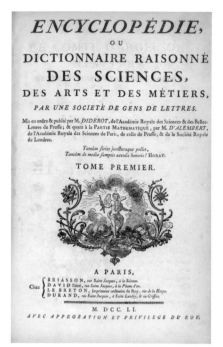

witty style that earned him comparisons with Jonathan Swift. He is remembered for his plays, of which he wrote over 50, and left some unfinished, including *Œdipe* (1718), *Zaïre* (1732), and *Eriphile* (1732). But his most important works are arguably his philosophical writings, which he started composing on his return from a two-year exile in England, publishing his *Lettres philosophiques*, translated as *Philosophical Letters on the English Nation*, in 1734. However, their celebration of the liberal spirit of England was not well received in Paris; Voltaire had to move to the countryside in fear of being arrested. After living for 15 years in Lorraine, and then for a short period in Prussia, he settled near Geneva in 1755, publishing his *Essai sur les mœurs et l'espirit des nations* (1756), translated as *Candide, or All for the Best*, in 1759. Although he did move back to France, he only returned to Paris shortly before his death; here he was upheld as the most daring spokesperson for Enlightenment principles of liberation and understanding. His ideas, which are perhaps best illustrated in his compendium *Dictionnaire Philosophique* (1764), can be compared to those of Newton and Locke, who similarly combined science and empiricism with a religious belief that eschewed formal religion, while clinging to the mysteries of faith. In this way he is often described as a deist in his philosophy, and a humanist in his politics.

Another figure of the Enlightenment, whose controversial writings helped shape French revolutionary thinking, was the philosopher and novelist Jean-Jacques Rousseau (1712–1778). Rousseau first came into contact with the philosophers of the Enlightenment when working as a tutor to the family of the Abbé de Mably in Savoy; he would also make the acquaintance of Diderot in Paris. Later, after being dismissed from the service of the Ambassador in Venice, and becoming secretary to a rich tax-farmer, Rousseau began to write articles for the *Encyclopédie*. In 1749 he wrote a prize-winning essay for the Dijon Academy, the *Discours sur les sciences et les arts* (1751, now referred to as *The First Discourse*), which began to develop

dramas, and for a dialogue, *"Le Rêve d'Alembert"* (*"D'Alembert's Dream,"* 1769), the title traditionally given to three related dialogues, published posthumously, in which he imagines dialogues with D'Alembert, his co-editor on *Encyclopédie*. Jean le Rond d'Alembert (1717–1783), a mathematician, mechanician, physicist, and philosopher (who is also remembered for his method for a wave equation), edited the mathematics and science articles in the *Encyclopédie* from the late 1740s until 1757. He wrote over 1,000 articles for the project, including the famous *Preliminary Discourse*, which laid out the principles of the *Encyclopédie*, outlined its structure, and described the history and thinking behind it.

One of the most important figures of the French Enlightenment, and a contributor to the *Encyclopédie*, was the writer, dramatist, and poet François-Marie Arouet (1694–1778), who wrote under the pseudonym of "Voltaire." Voltaire's early passion for writing poetry gave way to prose, and he soon adopted an ironical, his philosophy, through suggesting that neither the arts nor science could bring happiness to the individual. Then, in 1753, he entered the competition again with his *Discours sur l'origine et les fondements de l'inegalité parmi les homes* (1755, *A Discourse on the origin and the foundations of inequality among men*, translated in 1762 and known as the *Second Discourse*). This second essay expanded upon the arguments of the first to contend, as some of his Romantic counterparts in Britain would later hypothesize, that society could only damage the human condition, whereas by living in a state of communion

MR HARLEY as DOCTOR PANGLOSS

FAR LEFT: VOLTAIRE

This French writer, especially of satire, is remembered as a crusader against tyranny and bigotry. Along with Montesquieu, John Locke, Thomas Hobbes, and Jean-Jacques Rousseau, Voltaire is one of the key figures of Enlightenment.

LEFT: VOLTAIRE'S *CANDIDE*, Dr Pangloss played by Harley in the stage version, 1759

Candide is Voltaire's most famous work, in which he parodies the optimism philosophy of Gottfried Wilhelm Leibniz. According to Leibniz, everything in the world is perfect. Voltaire's world in contrast, where his hero Candide goes through a series of misfortunes, is far from perfect.

LEFT: JEAN-JACQUES ROUSSEAU, Oil on canvas, Musée Historique de la Ville de Paris, Musée Carnavalet, Paris, France

Rousseau was a French philosopher and political theorist, whose various treatises greatly influenced the leaders of the French Revolution.

RIGHT: THE RACE, Illustration from *Émile* by Rousseau

Émile is a seminal treatise on education.

with nature, man would be free, independent, and innocent. In contrast to his British contemporary Hobbes, Rousseau viewed the legal system as unjust and subjective, and as a way for the rich to control and deceive the poor. He also juxtaposed the simplicity and naturalness of sex against the artificiality of love, which he viewed as means of manipulation through which women could assert power over men.

Later works included *Le Contrat Social* (1762, translated as *The Social Contract* in 1764), in which Rousseau advocated upholding democratic, republican ideals influenced by ancient Sparta, and described how freedom could be used as a means of engaging with law and politics. If everyone acted according to his or her personal freedoms, he argued, society would be governed by the "volonté" or general will. This reaction against the kind of uniformity upheld by Enlightenment thinkers led to new ways of thinking about society; Rousseau showed how it could be viewed as a single, evolving entity. Linked to this was Rousseau's view of religious faith as a natural instinct generated by the heart rather than the head. These ideas reached their full expression in *Émile, ou de l'éducation* (1762, translated in 1764), which

dismissed existing systems of education, advocating instead a more instinctive, natural approach to learning. The work was banned (*The Social Contract* had already been banned), leading Rousseau to flee to Switzerland, where the local pastor did his best to turn the community against him. As a result Rousseau's later years were spent traveling in weakening mental health; however they did produce *Les Confessions* (1782–9, translated in 1783–90), a ground-breaking autobiography. Rousseau's work had a lasting legacy, influencing the ideals of the French Revolution, and paving the way for the European philosophers of the late Romantic period.

GERMANY

Although the era of confessional conflict and war had ended in 1648, culture had continued to decline in the Holy Roman Empire and the German states throughout the remainder of the 17th century. By the middle of the 18th century, however, after decades of cultural stagnation, a significant literary and cultural revival took place that would culminate in the Weimar Classicism of the 1790s, a period also referred to as the Age of Goethe. The recovery was aided by a new understanding of human ability to assert control over nature and instead set personal rules of morality. Enlightenment thinking saw that progress might be made through harnessing the powers of education and science. The roots of this rationalist argument might be traced to the English scientist Sir Isaac Newton and the German philosopher Gottfried Wilhelm Leibniz. Leibniz's essays, published in the early years of the 18th century, viewed the universe as an absolutist state with God as the monarch, or central monad, upon whom all other monads, humans included, strove to model themselves. This metaphysical model influenced German writers, including Goethe, who depicted the protagonist of Faust as a monad seeking salvation.

During the economic downturn of the late 17th century, the German Counts and educated classes had attempted to model themselves on their French counterparts in order to benefit from the changes that had been taking place in the French culture. Leibniz wrote most of his essays in French and Latin, while the aristocracy, viewing German culture as vulgar, turned to France and Italy for cultural inspiration. By the 1750s the effort to demonstrate that Germany was capable of literary expression had led to a search for indigenous qualities in the German culture that might be revived in order to discover a unifying cultural identity.

Nevertheless, the first literary reforms in Germany, which took place between 1724 and 1740, were inspired by 17th-century French classicism. Their primary proponent was the conservative Leipzig professor Johann Christoph Gottsched (1700–1766), who wrote his *Versuch einer Critischen Dichtkunst vor die Deutschen* (*Essay on a German Critical Poetry Theory*) in 1730 as a model for Germans to follow. Gottsched saw reason as the primary criterion for the production and dissemination of literature; basing his theories on a literal interpretation of Aristotle's *Poetics*, he contended that as nature was governed by reason, poets should convey the manifestation of that reason in nature. Another of Gottsched's projects was a reform of German theater, for which he wrote tragedies and comedies based on the French classical model, and particularly on the works of Molière, to banish what he saw as the extravagance and vulgarity of the existing theatrical modes. This included expelling from the stage the enduring figure of the clown. Gottsched also edited some of the first German moral weeklies, which aimed to improve the moral standards of the German middle class. These weeklies, which enjoyed more popularity than Gottsched's plays, voiced middle-class public opinion in Germany.

JOHANN CHRISTOPH GOTTSCHED

German critic and author, a product of the Enlightenment, who advocated the use of a rationalist philosophy of esthetics for German literature.

Naturally, opposition arose to Gottsched's moralistic, derivative, and restrained literary style. Two Swiss critics, Johann Jakob Bodmer and Johan Jakob Breitinger, used John Milton's epic *Paradise Lost* (1667) as a model for their argument that literary production should place stronger emphasis on the imagination, a factor that had been virtually ignored by Gottsched's scheme for writing poetry. Poets in Germany soon joined this progressive group. Friedrich Gottlieb Klopstock (1724–1803) was also inspired by *Paradise Lost*; his patriotic odes, and his religious epic *Der Messiah* (1748–1773, *The Messiah*), celebrated a Miltonic delight in pietistic sentiment and displayed a disinclination toward action. Klopstock, who began writing *The Messiah* as a student, lived for many years in Denmark under the patronage of King Frederick V. His work influenced other poets including Goethe, Rilke, and Hölderlin, and anticipated the *Sturm und Drang* movement of the mid- to late-18th century.

A more general reaction to Gottsched's conservative philosophy can be seen in the development of *Empfindsamkeit*, an esthetic movement that flourished in Europe, and in northern Germany in particular, in the middle of the century. Its origins lay partly in the cult of "sensibility" propounded by writers such as Samuel Richardson and Laurence Sterne in Britain. The musician and publisher Johann Christoph Bode translated Sterne's *A Sentimental Journey through France and Italy* in 1768 under the title *Yoriks empfindsame Reise* to great commercial success. Bode's coinage "empfindsame," or "sensitive," became a buzzword for the period. German poets who employed sentimentalism in their work included Klopstock himself, Christian Fürchtegott Gellert (1715–1769), and Sophie de la Roche (1730–1807), the author of the first epistolary novel in German. The

JOHANN JACOB BODMER (LEFT) AND JOHANN JACOB BREITINGER

Swiss scholars Bodmer and Breitinger advocated the freedom of imagination from the restriction imposed upon it by French pseudo-classicism.

influence of *Empfindsamkeit* can also be traced to the early works of Goethe.

Meanwhile, other Enlightenment figures were making their presence known. The first was Gotthold Ephraim Lessing (1729–1781), a vocal opponent of Gottsched's reforms. While working as a librarian in Wolfenbüttel, northern Germany, in 1774, Lessing discovered the 12th-century treatise on painting, *De diversis artibus*. Inspired by this text, he wrote *Laokoon oder über die Grenzen der Malerei und Poesie* (1766), in which he attacked the neoclassical ideal of antique beauty, instead deriving inspiration from the Laocoon group, an ancient marble sculptural group depicting the Trojan priest Laocoon with his sons. For Lessing this group displayed a profound ability to select the "fruitful" moment that not only summed up its age but also stimulated the imagination. The impact of *Laokoon*

FRIEDRICH G. KLOPSTOCK

German poet who influenced Goethe, the Göttingen poets, and the *Sturm und Drang* movement.

stemmed from its emphasis upon art as an expression of estheticism rather than of religion and philosophy; art could be beautiful rather than dutiful. Lessing's broader suggestion was that German writers should look to English literature, and particularly to the works of Shakespeare, rather than to the French classical school. Essays including the *Briefe die neueste Litteratur betreffend* (*Letters relating to recent literature*, 1759–1765), and the *Hamburgische Dramaturgie* (1767–1769), led the republican historian Catherine Macaulay to term Lessing "the first critic in Europe." Lessing also played a leading role in the development of German theater. His tragedies included *Emilia Galotti* (1772) and *Miss Sara Sampson* (1755), the first significant domestic tragedy in German, while his comedies included *Minna von Barnhelm* (1767) and the dramatic poem *Nathan der Weise* (1779), which advocated religious tolerance. Several English authors and poets, including Samuel Taylor Coleridge and George Eliot, commended Lessing's ability to convey his humanist and liberal beliefs in clear, precise prose.

The intense literary activities of the German Enlightenment writers culminated in the *Sturm und Drang* ("Storm and Stress") movement of the mid- to late-18th century. The name of the movement was derived from the title of a 1766 play on the American Revolution by Maximilian Klinger. The movement, influenced by the thinking of Rousseau and the dramatic style of Shakespeare, was characterized by the expression of emotional turbulence and the rejection of neoclassical literary models. The movement's adherents aimed to portray violent emotions as dramatically as possible. Seen now as the first Romantic reaction in Germany against the classical calm of the Enlightenment, *Sturm und Drang* arguably reached its high point in the literature of the 1760s and 1770s in the works of Jakob Michael Reinhold Lenz (1751–1792), and in the early works of Schiller and Goethe.

Although Goethe's early work *Götz von Berlichingen* (1773) and Schiller's *Die Räuber* (1780–1781) are seen as providing the ultimate expression of *Sturm und Drang*, the writings of

FAR LEFT: LAOCOON AND HIS SONS STRANGLED BY SERPENTS, Sculpture, 2nd century BC, Discovered at Rome in 1506

Lessing's ethetic's during *Laocoon: An Essay on the Limits of Painting and Poetry* is the first systematized treatment of the Enlightenment, which establishes poetry and painting as two independent arts.

NATHAN THE WISE A 2002 production of Lessing's *Nathan der Weise* at the Wiener Volkstheater in Vienna, Austria.

Lenz are also highly significant. The Latvian-born dramatist and poet, now considered a forerunner of 19th-century Naturalism and 20th-century German expressionist theater, met young Goethe in a literary group in Strasbourg in 1771. His works include the verse epic *Die Landplagen* (*The Torments of the Land*, 1769); the dramas *Der Hofmeister, oder Vorteile der Privaterziehung* (*The Tutor*, or the *Advantages of Private Education*, 1774), *Der Neue Menoza* (1774) and *Die Freunde machen den Philosophen* (*Friends Make the Philosopher*, 1776); and the essay *Anmerkungen übers Theater* (*Observations on Theater*, 1774). Another well-known adherent of the *Sturm und Drang* movement was Johann Gottfried Herder (1744–1803), a philosopher, critic, and collector of folk-songs.

The early works of the dramatist, historian, poet, and critic Johann Christoph Friedrich von Schiller (1759–1805) bear the hallmark of the movement. With his early play *Die Räuber* (*The Robbers*, 1781), written at the young age of 22, Schiller established himself as a major figure of *Sturm und Drang*. The play displayed the influence of Shakespeare's works *Richard III* and *King Lear*. In his next important play, *Kabale und Liebe* (*Intrigue and Love*, 1784), Schiller attacked contemporary society by conveying the damaging interference of a despotic state in a fated love affair. He achieved commercial success with his play *Wallenstein* (1799), some of which was translated into English verse by Coleridge in 1800. His last finished play was *Wilhelm Tell* (1804).

Schiller was also known as a poet and lyricist. In 1797–1798, he and Goethe collaborated on a series of ballads at the same time that Coleridge and Wordsworth were compiling their *Lyrical Ballads* in England. Additionally, in his position as professor of history at Jena from 1789, Schiller wrote historical works on the *Revolt of the Netherlands* (1788) and the Thirty Years' War. He was a voracious student of Kant and wrote the *Philosophische Briefe* (*Philosophical Letters*, 1786) based on his philosophy, while his many essays on esthetics would have a significant influence on the work of the German philosopher Schlegel. Notably, in 1795 he produced an essay that suggested that his ideas were moving away

WOLFGANG VON GOETHE

The career of the poet, dramatist, scholar, scientist, and statesman Johann Wolfgang von Goethe (1749–1832) encompasses most of the movements that defined the period: rationalism of the Enlightenment, *Sturm und Drang*, and Weimar Classicism to name a few. Initially influenced by the *Sturm und Drang* movement, Goethe's style became progressively measured and classical, as illustrated in his "Wilhelm Meister" novels. However Goethe is best known for his dramas, such as *Götz von Berlichingen* (1773) and *Tasso* (1790), while internationally he is probably best remembered for his masterpiece *Faust* (1808–1832).

Goethe had already written a couple of dramatic comedies when, in the late 1760s, he was introduced to the plays of William Shakespeare. He wrote his first play in the Shakespearian style, *Götz von Berlichingen*, in 1773, which was produced in Berlin in the same year. Its idealistic depiction of a robber baron became the spearhead of the *Sturm und Drang* movement, while its offshoot Ritterdrama, a style of drama that employed medieval settings to indulge a growing taste for the romantic, became popular throughout Germany. Further plays included *Stella* (1776), the Spanish-set domestic tragedy *Clavigo* (1779), and *Egmont*, a play about the revolt of the Netherlands in 1567, which was not completed until 1787. Schiller made extensive revisions to this latter play for its first performance in 1791, while the original version was not performed until 1810.

In 1775 Goethe moved to the Duchy of Weimar, having been invited by the Duke to serve as Privy Councillor. As part of his duties Goethe was expected to put on plays for ducal entertainment; the first of these was an early prose version of his own play *Iphigenie auf Tauris* (*Iphigenia in Tauris*, 1779). During a stay in Italy between 1786 and 1788, he put the play into verse, using the situation of Euripides's *Iphigenia* as a prism through which to refract 18th-century moral thinking. The play was produced in the new version in 1802. While in Italy, Goethe also wrote *Torquato Tasso* (1807), which was comparable with *Iphigenie* in terms of its iambic meter and its emphasis on the personal world of poetry rather than on the objective sphere of action. In 1791, following his return from Italy, he was appointed director of a professional company established in the Court theater, which became famous throughout Europe.

The play that most accurately portrays Goethe's skills as a dramatist, poet, and philosopher is his labor of love, *Faust*. Inspired by a puppet play he had seen

GOETHE'S FAUST, MEPHISTOPHELES PRESENTS FAUST WITH A VISION OF GRETCHEN

JOHANN WOLFGANG VON GOETHE, At the age of 23 in Wetzlar

In Wetzlar, Goethe practiced law. He contributed to the periodical *Frankfurter Gelehrte Anzeigen* in 1772, and two years later published his first novel *The Sorrows of Young Werther*, in which he created the prototype of the Romantic hero.

in his youth, Goethe began working on the play in the 1770s; but its subject and scope were to obsess him throughout his life. He abandoned the original draft, but it was later discovered and published as the *Ur-Faust* in 1887. A second version, which had not been performed, was included in an edition of Goethe's works that he published in 1790. It was actually Goethe's colleague Schiller who persuaded him to return to the play; he did so in 1799, eventually finishing Part I. This part, which tells the story of the seduction and downfall of Gretchen, was published in 1808; while Part II, which includes the story of Helen of Troy as told by Marlowe in *Dr Faustus* in 1604, was finished in 1832 and published after Goethe's death. The two parts when read together convey Goethe's reflective wisdom at the end of

his life, while reflecting an increasingly nostalgic classicism that would separate him from the early voices of the German Romantic movement.

Given to its complexity, *Faust* has always been notoriously difficult to stage; hence many companies perform the simpler *Ur-Faust* instead. Part I was not staged in Germany until 1829, while Part II was not seen until 1854. The first production of both parts took place in Weimar in 1876, while significant later productions include those by Max Reinhardt (in 1909) and Gustaf Gründgens (in 1932). Although most of Goethe's works have been translated into English, there have been relatively few performances of the longer version in Britain, except for notable productions at the Bristol Old Vic in 1963 and in London

from those of his contemporary Goethe. In *Über naïve und sentimentalische Dichtung* (*On Naïve and Reflective Poetry*, 1795–96), Schiller contrasted his apparently modern and self-reflexive style against Goethe's older and less self-concious genius.

Schiller and Goethe were the primary figures in the period of German literature now referred to as Weimar Classicism. This is so called because the two writers, as inhabitants of the Duchy of Saxe-Weimar, became part of a group of cultural figures and intellectuals who enjoyed the patronage of Anna Amalia, Duchess of Saxe-Weimar (1739–1807). While the ideas of Weimar Classicism were traditionally seen as being developed between the return of Goethe from Italy

GOETHE AND SCHILLER, Monument in Weimar

It was in 1794, six years after becoming acquainted with each other, that Goethe and Schiller became close friends. Their friendship, which came to end with Schiller's death in 1805, profoundly influenced the lives of the two poets. It was at Schiller's insistence that Goethe resumed his major work, *Faust*, Part I, which he completed three years after Schiller's death.

in 1788 and the death of Schiller in 1805, they are now seen as ending with the death of Goethe himself in 1832. Responding to the works of Johann Joachim Winckelmann (1717–1768), Goethe and Schiller developed a literary pursuit and praxis of the imitation of ancient Greek and classical models, and an understanding of social and cultural reforms through the prism of esthetics, where organic unity and harmony were of primary inspiration and importance. Weimar Classicism might be viewed as Schiller and Goethe's attempts to reconcile the *Sturm und Drang* movement with the Enlightenment, thus fusing the vividness and energy of the former with the harmony and rationalism of the latter. The attempt at reconciliation meant ultimately that although some of Schiller's work anticipated German Romanticism, the broader principles of Weimar Classicism were at odds with this subjective and modernizing movement.

BRITAIN

The year 1702 saw the succession of Queen Anne, sister of Mary, to the English throne following the death of William III. On May 1, 1707, under the Acts of Union, England and Scotland were united as a single state, the "Kingdom of Great Britain," with Anne becoming its first sovereign. Anne reigned for 12 years until her death in 1714, marking the end of the House of Stuart, when she was succeeded by her second cousin, George I, the first of the House of Hanover. Their reign began the period known as the "Augustan Age" (lasting until around 1745), which, in echoing the period of Virgil, Horace, and Ovid under the Roman emperor Augustus in 27 BC–AD 14, reflected Europe's new dedication to rationalism.

ALEXANDER POPE (1688-1744)
Alexander Pope, English poet and satirist. Color illustration.

As part of this nostalgia for classical values, the late 17th and early 18th centuries witnessed the resurgence of satire, a literary form firmly rooted in ancient Greek poetry. However, it was the Roman satirical poets, and particularly Horace, who had the strongest influence on English satire in this period; and Alexander Pope (1688–1744) was its most notable and successful exponent. Pope's "mock-heroic" narrative poems, such as *Essay on Criticism* (1711) and *The Rape of the Lock* (1712, expanded 1714), began a new tradition for poetry that contrasted a complex formal structure with a relatively superficial subject matter, in parody of the heroic poems that had come before. *The Rape of the Lock*, which describes the inconsequential events of stealing a lock of hair, questions the suitability of "high" style in a society that is morally corrupt, but self-important. At the same time, however, Pope was careful to confirm allegiance to Queen Anne: this is indicated in his pastoral poem *Windsor Forest* (1913). Pope, the son of a Catholic linen-draper, was one of the first generations of professional writers, securing his financial independence by translating Homer's *Iliad* into heroic couplets in 1720 and the *Odyssey* in 1726 (final version 1743), and by bringing out a new edition of Shakespeare's *Works* in 1725.

Pope, as a staunch supporter of the Tories, symbolized the new confrontational politics of the age, during which one Whig minister, Robert Walpole, rose to prominence, becoming First Lord of the Treasury, and the first unofficial Prime Minister, in 1721 (the term had no recognition in law at the time). Walpole became the undisputed leader of the Cabinet in 1730, governing until his resignation in 1741, making his administration the longest in Britain. His growing influence was reflected in the

JONATHAN SWIFT, c. 1718, Charles Jervas, Oil on canvas, National Portrait Gallery, London, UK

Famous Anglo-Irish poet, pamphleteer, and satirist, Swift is popular for his masterpiece *Gulliver's Travels*. Although largely known as a children's adventure story, *Gulliver's Travels* is a socio-political satire, ridiculing political events as well as English values and institutions.

The giddying changes of the new age led writers to seek explanations and definitions that could give them a handle on events. Samuel Johnson's *Dictionary*, published in 1755 after eight years' work, reflects an attempt to define a shifting linguistic and cultural world. Meanwhile, writers including John Dryden, Daniel Defoe, and Swift called for the introduction of an Academy that could regulate the language. In this context, it is not surprising that the 18th century saw the emergence of the novel, as its ability to give voice to the individual in an unstable and evolving society, and its potential to convey that society in all its manifestations, provided inspiration for writers, and middle-class writers in particular, who wanted to make their voices heard.

competitiveness of English society, and in the increased emphasis on trade and individual interest groups.

One writer who felt alienated by the political changes in society was Jonathan Swift (1667–1745), who, like Pope, had enjoyed political favor under the reign of Queen Anne and had been a pamphleteer for the Tories. As a result, his writings, like Pope's, portray a society that he neither understands nor condones. Following the return to power of the Whigs in 1714, Swift left England and took up his Deanery at St Patrick's Cathedral, Dublin, Ireland. In the 1720s he wrote the majority of his most significant works, including a series of satiric pamphlets—such as *The Drapier's Letters* (1724) and *A Modest Proposal* (1729), a savage satire advocating the breeding of children by the poor to be fed to the rich—and his extended satirical work *Gulliver's Travels* (1726). *Gulliver's Travels* tells the story of Lemuel Gulliver's journeys to fantastical and allegorical lands, each symbolizing aspects of the new society. Ironically the work of Swift and Poe was somewhat regressive in its satirical emphasis, as its criticism of the increasingly political, divided society reflected an entrenched distrust of progress and change.

The novel as we have come to regard it today first emerged in 1719 with the publication of *Robinson Crusoe*. The novel's middle-class focus, which centers on the individual's need to work for his living within a commercial society, coupled with its direct, business-like style, and its allusions to questions of race and class, embodies the preoccupations of the new age. The emphasis on individuality, as Crusoe makes his way

GULLIVERS TRAVELS c. 1850: An illustration from Jonathan Swift's book *Gullivers Travels* with Gulliver looking at one of the Lilliputians on a table. (Photo by Hulton Archive/Getty Images)

the first novelist—the restoration dramatist William Congreve had published *Incognita* in 1713, which he described as a novel, while the female Restoration dramatist Aphra Behn had written an early novel, *Oroonoko*, in *c.* 1688—Defoe's novels were so contemporaneous with his live and times that they came to define the genre itself. The next important novelists, Samuel Richardson and Henry Fielding, acknowledged the same preoccupations as Defoe, while adapting them to suit their own intentions. However, while Defoe was keen to use exotic locations to reflect the wider concerns of a changing society, Richardson and Fielding turned the focus inward, depicting more private, domestic concerns.

Samuel Richardson's epistolary novels *Pamela* (1740), *Clarissa* (1747–1748), and *Sir Charles Grandison* (1753–1754) reflected this return to the domestic sphere in their depictions of individuals facing personal challenges against the background of contemporary British society. Richardson's characters were constantly preoccupied with love and romance, so much so that *Pamela* came to be seen as the quintessential sentimentalist novel. Some of Richardson's

through the world, also draws the reader's attention to the nature of man's relationship with God, a subject of growing debate during this period. In Defoe's second novel *Moll Flanders* (1722), his depictions of characters as commodities to be traded place the market system, rather than the church, at the center of everyday life. The fact that Defoe is one of the most prolific writers in the history of English literature—he wrote several novels, poetry, political pamphlets, and even a guidebook to Britain—reflects his attempt to write himself, and by extension the middle class itself, into the very fabric of society. Defoe's influence on the history of the novel is hugely significant, as by discussing the concerns of his society, he also established the themes that would become the mainstays of the novel genre. Although he cannot strictly be regarded as contemporaries disapproved of his sentimentalism. Henry Fielding, for example, published a parodic novel, *Shamela* (1741), as a critique of *Pamela*; he objected to the fact that in Richardson's novel, the heroine rejects her master's advances only to marry him at the end of the story. However, in contemporary terms, we would probably see Richardson as the more modern writer, thanks to his focus on psychological complexity—Pamela, for example, undergoes hundreds of pages of self-scrutiny before her "virtue" is "rewarded," as the subtitle of the novel tells us. Moreover, Richardson's continued explorations of the novel form are evidenced by the transition from the broadly comic *Pamela* to the complex tragedy of *Clarissa*.

Fielding's characters, however, are far less complex, their actions and responses to situations informed by a combination of instinct and social conditioning. Fielding's distrust of psychological introspection reflected his social standing as a gentleman and a magistrate—in contrast to Richardson's more worldly businessman—who had a traditional view of the world order and, by extension, of the novel form itself. For Fielding, it would have been shocking, and disquieting, that Pamela, a maid, would have been allowed such a degree of internal reasoning within a novel of which she was the heroine. As a result, Fielding's novels, such as *Shamela* and *The History of Tom Jones, a Foundling* (1749), advocate a return to traditional views of class and relationships: even sexual encounters are portrayed as inconsequential incidents with only momentary importance. The moralistic simplicity of Fielding's work is, nevertheless, a reaction against an increasingly complex, changing world, while his parodic representations problematize and ultimately reject these changes.

The novelist who dared to parody the genre itself, while questioning its new turn towards interiority, was Laurence Sterne. It is difficult to overstate the impact of Sterne's

THE HISTORY OF TOM JONES, A FOUNDLING

First published in England in 1749, *Tom Jones* is Henry Fielding's third novel. It is a comedy, which traces the development of the central character. The above illustration from one of the editions shows a man forcing himself into a room being occupied by a lady and a gentleman.

writings, and particularly of his most famous work, *The Life and Opinions of Tristram Shandy, Gentleman* (1759–1767), upon the development of the modern novel. In *Tristram Shandy*, Sterne upturns the already familiar story of an individual making his way through life by employing an anti-chronological structure and frustrating the reader's narrative expectations. The narrator is so self-indulgent and introspective that the plot somehow never quite gets underway. To a reader used to epistolary novels, in which the letters telling the story were arranged (and read) in chronological order, the thematic and structural idiosyncrasies of Sterne's so-called novel would have seemed baffling, and even shocking.

Indeed *Tristram Shandy's* idiosyncrasies, of which there are many, might baffle even a contemporary reader: the narrator adopts the dubious position of spectator at his moment of conception and at his own birth, while three volumes of the book detail the period before his birth, leaving very little space to tell the story of his own life. Meanwhile, the chapters are not numbered sequentially, leading readers to question whether they should adopt the conventional approach to reading and go from first page to last, or if they should follow Sterne's alternative numbering system; of course, this allows for two different readings of the book. Moreover, Sterne uses textual apparatus to underline events or convey emotion—for example, a black page is inserted wherever a death occurs— —which ironically render the event or emotion all the more artificial. *A Sentimental Journey through France and Italy* (1768), Sterne's other famous work, blurs the boundaries between travelog, novel, and memoir, and mocks gently the prevailing sentimental strain in contemporary novels. Although this later book was received more favorably than *Tristram Shandy*, the clergyman and novelist died in poverty just one month after its publication. Readers clearly were not yet ready for Sterne's alarmingly modern style.

Sterne's writings, and particularly *Tristram Shandy*, have received more critical appreciation in recent years, as they appear to anticipate many of the questions that concerned modernist writers at the beginning of the 20th century. Writers such as Joseph Conrad, Virginia Woolf, James Joyce, and D. H. Lawrence used their work not only to question the artifice of human relationships, but also to question the value of the novel form itself. Since the early days of Defoe and Richardson, through to the novel's heyday in the 19th century, when writers

LAURENCE STERNE, Oil on canvas, National Portrait Gallery, London, UK

Sterne is best known for his two works: the novel *Tristram Shandy, Gentleman* and the travel essay *A Sentimental Journey through France and Italy*. He introduced a novel form in which the story is secondary to the narrator's associations and digressions.

SENTIMENTAL JOURNEY

LAURENCE STERNE Sterne's alter ego Yorick in his novel, *Sentimental Journey*, in his encounter with the grisette.

such as George Eliot and Charles Dickens used the genre to comment on wider social and cultural issues, the novel was generally seen as the most suitable, if suitably flawed, form to present everyday life. Yet in the late 18th century Sterne had been a lone voice questioning these assumptions; like his modernist heirs, he had dared to interrogate the resilience of the novel form. It is perhaps of no surprise, then, that Joyce's epic masterpiece *Ulysses* (1922), and even Salman Rushdie's

Anglo-Indian novel *Midnight's Children* (1981), owe something of their narrative defiance to Sterne's progressive model.

ITALY

Two dramatists emerged in Italy in the mid-18th century who were determined to revive the moribund tradition of the *commedia dell'arte*, the style of Italian improvisational comedy, first recorded in 1545, which had flourished between the 16th and early 18th centuries. The Venetian playwright Carlo Goldoni (1707–1793) had originally intended to work in the law, but was drawn to the theater by a desire to reform the *commedia*. He implemented these reforms by replacing improvisational narratives with an outline plot with fully written, character-based comedies. Goldoni was influenced by French dramatist Molière, earning him the title of "the Italian Molière." In his efforts Goldoni was bitterly opposed by some of his actors and most notably by his fellow dramatist Carlo Gozzi (1720–1806), who had his own plans for reform. Goldoni's first attempt was *Momoló cortesan* (*Momolo the Court Man*, 1738), in which he wrote just one part out in full. He followed this play with *Il servitore di due padrone* (*The Servant of Two Masters*, 1743), which became one of his most popular works. For the first production he left out some of the scenes to be improvised by Truffaldino, the "servant" of the title, but wrote them out when the plays was published in 1755. In 1750 he produced his manifesto for the reform of the stage, *Il teatro comico*, and in the same year reached the height of his success with the comedies *Il bugiardo* (*The Liar*) and *La bottega del caffè* (*The Coffee House*). He followed this up with a play that is largely regarded as his masterpiece, *La Locandiera* (*The Landlady*, 1751). This delighted audiences in Europe and eventually reached America, inspiring adaptations into the 20th century; for example, in 1910 Lady Gregory translated the play as *Mirandolina*, named after Goldoni's heroine, for a production at the Abbey Theatre in Dublin, Ireland.

In 1751, Goldoni left the Teatro Sant'Angelo in Venice, where he had staged his popular comedies, and moved to the Teatro San Luca. However the size of the new space, which was too big for intimate comedies, coupled with the hostility of his fellow playwrights Gozzi and Pietro Chiari, compelled Goldoni to move to Paris. In Paris he wrote plays in Italian and French for the Comèdie-Italienne, but did not enjoy the success he had been hoping for. He died in poverty, having become embroiled in the turmoil of the French Revolution. However, his ability to

CARLO GOLDONI (1707-1793)

Italian playwright, who created modern Italian comedy in the style of Molière. Louvre, Paris, France.

GOLDONI'S *IL SERVITORE DI DUE PADRONE (THE SERVANT OF TWO MASTERS),* Tommy Steele as the servant Truffaldino

Truffaldino, the servant of the main character Beatrice, is the central figure of this play. He is always complaining of an empty stomach, and always trying to appease his hunger. One of the main themes of this play is found in the character development of Truffaldino, who, it is implied, is hungry for love. The characters of the play are in the tradition of the Italian Renaissance theater style *commedia dell'arte*. In classic *commedia* tradition, an actor learns a stock character (usually accentuated by a mask) that has characteristics of an archetype, and plays it to perfection throughout his career. The actors worked with a basic plot; they would improvise their roles and perform physical-comedy acts known as *lazzis* as they went along.

apply the hallmarks of the *commedia* to realistic comedy left a lasting legacy, influencing the *drame bourgeois* of Diderot in France; while much of his work, of which there are some 150 comedies in total, survives both on the Italian stage and in the international repertory.

Goldoni's rival Gozzi had attempted likewise to reform the *commedia*, but while he aimed to alter its character and methods, he did not approve of changing its subject matter. The result was a new type of play that he called *fiabe:* a combination of fantastical settings and light-hearted farce. In contrast to the realistic, bourgeois comedies of Goldoni, Gozzi preferred to tell stories of magicians, animals, and extraordinary characters, while

CARLO GOZZI

Italian playwright, a traditionalist who opposed the innovations of Goldoni.

the language he employed was "pure Tuscan," in opposition to his contemporary's use of local Italian dialects. His most successful plays were *L'amore delle tre melarance* (*The Love of Three Oranges*) and *Il corro* (*The Raven*) in 1761; *Il re cervo* (*King Stag*) in 1762; *Turandot*, based on a Chinese fairy-tale, in 1765; and *L'augellino belverde* (*The Beautiful Green Bird*), written in the same year. Gozzi's plays continued to be adapted and performed into the 20th century, while two were adapted as opera libretti: Prokofiev's *The Love of Three Oranges* (1921) and, famously, Puccini's *Turandot* (1926). His work might be seen as a forerunner to the drama of Luigi Pirandello, as his fantastical subjects arguably paved the way for Pirandello's use of mythology.

Chapter 6
ROMANTICISM TO REALISM
ESTHETICS AND EMOTIONS

GERMANY

The literary figure who bridged the gap between late Enlightenment and early Romantic thinking was Johann Christian Friedrich Hölderlin (1770–1843). Although he gained little recognition during his lifetime, and was almost completely forgotten until the mid-20th century, he is now recognized as one of the great German lyric poets. Hölderlin originally intended to make his living in the church; however, torn between his devotion to Protestant theology and his passion for Greek mythology, he decided instead to become a poet. Like his Romantic counterparts in Britain, Hölderlin thought that poets could act as mediators between men and god(s).

Schiller published some of Hölderlin's poetry, together with a fragment of his unfinished novel *Hyperion*, a tale of the liberation of Greece, in his periodical *Neue Thalia* in 1793. The older writer, whose influence can be detected in some of Hölderlin's early poetry, suggested that Hölderlin become a tutor to support his burgeoning literary career. In 1795, living in Frankfurt, Hölderlin fell in love with his employer's wife; she appears under the Greek name "Diotima" in his poems and in the second volume

of *Hyperion* (1799). Upon the discovery of the affair, and his dismissal from employment, Hölderlin began writing a tragedy, *Der Tod des Empedokles* (*The Death of Empedocles*), the first version of which he nearly completed (fragments of a second and third version also exist). Despite ongoing mental illness, the years 1798–1801 were extraordinarily productive, with Hölderlin writing, in addition to several odes, the great elegies *Menons Klagen um Diotima* (*Menon's Lament for Diotima*) and *Brod und Wein* (*Bread and Wine*).

After spending time in Bordeaux, France, Hölderlin returned to his home town of Nürtingen, making the journey on foot. On arrival it became evident to family and friends that he was suffering from acute schizophrenia. Nevertheless Hölderlin continued to write, although the compositions from this period (1802–1806) bear the hallmarks of a struggle with insanity: these include *Friedensfeier* (*Celebration of Peace*), *Der Einzige* (*The Only One*), and *Patmos*. During this time Hölderlin also completed verse translations of Sophocles's *Antigone* and *Oedipus Tyrannus* (1804). After the false imprisonment of his friend and patron Isaak von Sinclair in 1805, Hölderlin's mental state declined considerably. Following a spell in a clinic at Tübingen, he was removed to a carpenter's house, where he lived for the next 30 years. Hölderlin's talent was also his undoing: by attempting to fuse Christian and classical modes harmoniously within the German lyric, he created a unique form of expression, but was unable to find a satisfactory resolution.

Hölderlin's troubled idealism influenced two groups that emerged at the turn of the 19th century. The Jena Romantics (in German, *Jenaer Romantik*) marked the first phase of German Romanticism. The group, centered on Jena, Germany, between 1798 and 1804, was led by the writer Ludwig Tieck. Two other important members were the brothers August Wilhelm and Friedrich von Schlegel. In the group's periodical, the *Athenäum*, the brothers laid down the theoretical basis for Romanticism, arguing that the first duty of criticism was to understand and appreciate the right of genius to follow its own inclination. Other members of the group included Johann Gottlieb Fichte and Friedrich von Schelling, whose works emphasized the philosophical bent of Romanticism; meanwhile the theologian Friedrich Schleiermacher expounded the notion of individualism in religious thought.

The most lasting achievements of the Jena Romantics are to be found in the lyrics and fragments of Friedrich Leopold von Hardenberg (1772–1801), who wrote under the pseudonym of "Novalis." Novalis studied law at the University of Jena, where he became acquainted with Schlegel. He completed his studies at Wittenberg in 1793, and in 1796 was appointed auditor to the Saxon government saltworks at Weissenfels. During this time he became engaged to 12-year-old Sophie von Kühn; her death from tuberculosis in 1797 led to his outpourings of grief in *Hymnen an die Nacht* (*Hymns to the Night*, 1800), six prose poems interspersed with verse. In this work Novalis celebrates night, a symbol of death, as a means of communing with God; in his verse he envisages seeing Sophie again after his own death.

JOHANN LUDWIG TIECK (1773 - 1853)

Tieck, a prolific writer of the early Romantic movement in Germany, is seen being sculpted by David d'Angers, while Dorothea Tieck (on the right) watches the proceedings.

Novalis's last years, during which he worked on a draft of a philosophical system based on idealism and on several poetic pieces, were very creative. Two collections of fragments were published in his lifetime—*Blütenstaub* (*Pollen*, 1798) and *Glauben und Liebe* (*Faith and Love*, 1798)—each underscoring his attempts to bridge the gap between poetry, philosophy, and science. His mythical romance *Heinrich von Ofterdingen* (published posthumously in 1802) describes the romantic endeavors of a young poet, while its recurring motif of the blue flower became an enduring symbol of Romantic longing. In the essay *Die Christenheit oder Europa* (*Christendom or Europe*, 1799), Novalis argued that the Christian church should be united as it had been before the Reformation and the Enlightenment, in order to embrace medieval ideals of cultural, social, and intellectual accord. He died of tuberculosis in 1801.

Although the Jena group had dispersed by 1804, a second phase of Romanticism was initiated two years later in Heidelberg. The leaders of the Heidelberg group were Clemens Brentano, Achim von Arnim and Joseph von Görres; their periodical was entitled the *Zeitung für Einsiedler* (*Journal for Hermits*, 1808). The group is best remembered for its production of a collection of folk songs entitled *Des Knaben Wunderhorn* (*The Boy's Magic*

1781-1790 Immanuel Kant publishes *Critique of Pure Reason*.

1782-1789 Jean-Jacques Rousseau publishes *Les Confessions*.

1789-1799 The French Revolution.

1792 Johann Gottlieb Fichte writes *An Attempt at a Critique of All Revelation*.

1794 William Blake publishes *Songs of Innocence* and *Songs of Experience*.

1795 Friedrich Wilhelm Joseph (von) Schelling publishes his first philosophical work *On the Possibility and Form of Philosophy in General*. His emphasis on nature, and philosophy of the absolute, earn him recognition in Romantic circles.

1798 William Wordsworth and Samuel Taylor Coleridge write the *Lyrical Ballads*.

1801 United Kingdom of Great Britain (England and Scotland) and Ireland established

1804-1815 The reign of Napoleon Bonaparte.

1812-1818 George Gordon, Lord Byron, writes *Childe Harold's Pilgrimage*.

1818-1820 Lyrics by Percy Bysshe Shelley and John Keats.

1820 Alphonse de Lamartine publishes *Poetic Meditations*, his first collection of poems.

1824 Giacomo Leopardi writes *Canzoni*, his first collection of poems.

1834 Alexandr Sergeyevich Pushkin publishes *The Queen of Spades*.

1837 Victoria takes the throne and becomes Queen of the United Kingdom.

1840 Percy Bysshe Shelley's *A Defence of Poetry* is published posthumously.

1847 Charlotte Brontë publishes *Jane Eyre*; Emily Brontë publishes *Wuthering Heights*.

Horn, 1805–1808). The title is taken from the opening poem, in which a boy brings an empress a magic horn. The first volume, published in 1805 (dated 1806), was dedicated to Goethe; he reviewed it well, but other reviewers criticized its philosophical inaccuracies.

The poet, novelist, and dramatist Clemens Brentano (1778–1842) was acquainted, through his family, with Goethe and the Jena Romantics. On abandoning his studies at the University of Jena, Brentano met Arnim, co-publishing *Des Knaben*

NOVALIS

Novalis, pseudonym of Friedrich Leopold von Hardenberg, greatly influenced later Romantic thought. When he died in 1801, his two philosophical romances, *Heinrich von Ofterdingen* and *Die Lehrlinge zu Sais*, were left incomplete. In the former, Henry, a young medieval poet, seeks the mysterious blue flower. The blue flower was the central image of Novalis' visions, which later became a symbol of longing among Romantics.

E.T.A. Hoffmann is known for his stories in which supernatural characters reveal people's hidden secrets. Having an inclination toward music and painting in his early career, Hoffmann became interested in writing in his middle life, producing his best works in the last 10 years of his short life. Hoffmann's fiction comprises the first examples of horror and fantasy short story.

Wunderhorn with him. As a writer he had most success with his fairy tales, and particularly with *Gockel, Hinkel und Gackelia* (1838). Brentano's attempts to fuse folklore and fantasy are underlined in his novella *Geschichte vom braven Kasperl und dem schönen Annerl* (*The Story of the Just Casper and Fair Annie*, 1817), while his novel *Godwi* (1801) transverses the two phases of German Romanticism. Other notable works include the dramas *Ponce de Leon* (1801) and *Die Gründung Prags* (*The Foundation of Prague*, 1815). The contributions of Achim von Arnim (Karl Joachim Friedrich Ludwig von Arnim, 1781–1831) are perhaps less notable than those of his co-publisher Brentano, but his attempts to combine realism and fantasy within his short stories were influential. As a group, the Heidelberg Romantics were more practical and focused than their Jena predecessors, stimulating their fellow citizens' interest in Germany and founding the study of German philosophy and medieval literature.

A significant figure of late German Romanticism was the writer, composer, and painter Ernst Theodor Amadeus Hoffmann (1776–1822). Throughout his career, Hoffmann supported himself by working as a legal official in Berlin. However his first love was music; in 1813 he changed his third name from Wilhelm to Amadeus in honor of Mozart. His early compositions were musical—the ballet *Arlequin* (1811) and the opera *Undine* (first performed in 1816)—but he followed these with the four-volume short story collection *Phantasiestücke in Callots Manier* (*Fantasy Pieces in the Manner of Callot*, 1814–1815). In these stories, supernatural, sinister characters insinuate themselves into men's lives, with the aim of revealing the seamier side of human nature. Hoffmann also wrote two novels, *Die Elixire des Teufels* (*The Devil's Elixir*, 1815–1816) and *Lebens-Ansichten des Katers Murr nebst Fragmentarischer Biographie des Kapellmeisters Johannes Kreisler* (*The Life and Opinions of Kater Murr, with a fragmentary biography of Conductor Johannes Kreisler*, 1820–1822). Before his death from progressive paralysis in 1822, Hoffmann wrote more than 50 short stories, some of which were published in the later collections *Nachtstücke* (translated as *Hoffman's Strange Stories*, 1817), and *Die Serapionsbrüder* (*The Serapion Brethren*, 1819–1821). These later works proved popular in England, France, and even the United States, and publication continued into the 1950s. Hoffmann's bureaucratic lifestyle lent his stories an air of accuracy in their enactment of the struggle between everyday life and the world of the imagination. His flights of fancy have inspired operas by Richard Wagner, Paul Hindemith, and Jacques Offenbach, and ballets by Léo Delibes and Pyotr Ilyich Tchaikovsky.

The painstaking collection of fairy tales might be seen as an inevitable consequence of the efforts of the German Romantics to reawaken a love of folklore and myth. *Kinder-und Hausmärchen* (known in English as *Grimm's Fairy Tales*, 1812-1822), collected by Jacob Ludwig Carl Grimm (1785–1863) and Wilhelm Carl Grimm (1786–1859), marked the birth of the science of folklore. The brothers were introduced to folklore by

Brentano and Herder, whom they met while studying law at the University of Marburg; by 1816, had given up the law to pursue literary research full-time. First they collected folksongs and tales for Arnim and Brentano, and then they worked on their own projects, adopting an empirical and methodical approach. They collected material from the literary traditions of England, Ireland, Scotland, Spain, the Netherlands, Scandinavia, Serbia, and Finland. *Kinder-und Hausmärchen* implied through its title —translated literally as "Children's and Household Tales"—that it might be read by adults and children alike. It consisted of 200 stories, most derived from oral traditions. The collection, which was published widely in Germany and was soon distributed throughout the world, is still available in 70 languages. Other significant works by the Brothers Grimm include a collection of historical and local legends of Germany, *Deutsche Sagen* (1816–1818), and Jacob's intensive works *Deutsche Grammatik*, a study of German grammar, and *Deutsche Rechtsaltertümer* (1828), an overview of German law practices and beliefs.

RED RIDING HOOD FROM *GRIMM'S FAIRY TALES*

Little Red Riding Hood hides from the wolf in the forest in this postcard taken from *Grimms' Fairy Tales*, a collection of fairy tales, first published in 1812 by Jacob and Wilhelm Grimm, also known as the Brothers Grimm.

DENMARK

In Denmark, a writer emerged whose fascination for folklore would earn him the title of 'Master' of the fairy tale. Hans Christian Andersen (1805–1875) wrote his first significant work, in the style of E. T. A. Hoffman, while studying at the University of Copenhagen; a fantastical story, it was entitled *Fodrejse fra Holmens Kanal til Østpynten af Amager i aarene 1828 og 1829* (*A Walk from Holmen's Canal to the East Point of the Island of Amager in the Years 1828 and 1829*). Although the story was an immediate success, Andersen abandoned writing storys for several years, so that when his first book of tales appeared in 1835, he was regarded as a novelist. Yet the three installments of *Eventyr, fortalte for børn* (*Tales, Told for Children*, 1835 and 1837) earned him instant recognition, thanks to an idiomatic style that dismissed elevated rhetorical modes. *Billedbog uden billender* (*A Picturebook Without Pictures*) appeared in 1840, while a second volume of *Eventyr* was completed in 1842; new collections were published in 1843, 1847, and 1852. Andersen expanded his body of work with *Nye eventyr og historier* (*New Fairy Tales and Stories*, 1858–1872). His legacy is enduring: included among his many stories are *The little Mermaid*, *The Tinderbox*, *The Princess and the Pea*, and *The Snow Queen*. Like the Brothers Grimm, Andersen's tales combine the perspective of a child with the perspicacity of an adult to comment on the nature of suffering and the conflict

Although he wrote in many genres—novels, poems, plays, and travelogs–—Hans Christian Andersen is primarily remembered as the author of fairy tales, of which many, such as *The Ugly Duckling* (1843), *The Emperor's New Clothes* (1837), and *The Little Mermaid* (1837), have become world famous. Andersen wrote more than 150 tales, mostly between 1835 and 1874. He established the literary genre of folk tales, which had so far only been part of the oral tradition of literature. He used easy language and combined an adult sensibility with a child-like simplicity in his tales.

---

la Bretonne. Although these works varied widely in subject matter, they marked a shift in emphasis from the community to the individual.

A very different reaction to this period of change came from Donatien-Alphonese-François, comte de Sade, more commonly known as the Marquis de Sade, whose interest in the connections between power, pain, and pleasure gave rise to the term "sadism." In a deliberate corruption of Enlightenment thinking, de Sade argued that to pursue total freedom meant pursuing individual desires; hence the pleasure derived from cruelty in his works *Justine: ou, les malheurs de la vertu* (*Justine, or the misfortunes of virtue*, 1791), and the tale of her sister, *Juliette* (1797). The text he composed while imprisoned in the Bastille, *Les 120 Journées de Sodome* (*120 Days of Sodom*, 1784–1785, published in 1804), is now viewed as an influential study of the imaginative forms of the modern unconscious.

between good and evil. Despite widespread acclaim for his work, Andersen always viewed himself as an outsider. This sadness permeates the most memorable stories, many of which continue to be reinterpreted today.

FRANCE

The French novel in the later years of the 18th century was concerned with preparations for, and the consequences of, the French Revolution. Several novelists, influenced by the ideals of Rousseau, produced work of foment and possibility; these included *Les Liaisons dangereuses* (1782) by Pierre Choderlos de Laclos, the utopian, Mauritius-set novel *Paul et Virginie* (1788) by Jacques-Henri-Bernardin de Saint-Pierre, and the Parisian writings of Nicolas-Edme Restif de

THE MARQUIS DE SADE IN PRISON, Engraving

However, because of the centralizing Napoleonic regime, which encouraged a return to the Classical mode, there was little evidence of change in literary form between 1789 and 1815. Nevertheless, bubbling under the surface was the sense that Rousseau's emphasis on subjectivity and expression still found its adherents. André Chenier (1762–1794), although executed during the last days of the

CHATEAUBRIAND
(1768 - 1848)

Francois-Auguste-René, vicomte de CHATEAUBRIAND French writer and statesman, Mary Evans Picture Library

Staël-Holstein, 1766–1817).Initially a liberal-thinking supporter of Revolutionary ideals, she later became fiercely anti-Napoleonic when her offer of support was rejected. Her two novels *Delphine* (1802) and *Corinne* (1807) focus on the limits society tries to impose on independent women. Her most influential works were *De la littérature* (translated as *The Influence of Literature upon Society*, 1800) and *De l'Allemagne* (*Germany*, 1810), which claimed that post-revolutionary societies required new literary forms of expression. She even suggested, to the disgust of her neoclassical counterparts, that the French might draw upon writers as diverse as Shakespeare, Ossian, and the German Romantics for inspiration.

Thanks to the ravages of the French Revolution, and the impact of the Napoleonic regime, full-blown Romanticism developed much later in France than in Britain or Germany. French writers coined the terms *mal du siècle* and *enfant du siècle* to illustrate their distress; the poet and playwright Alfred de Musset (1810–1857) entitled his autobiography *La confession d'un enfant du siècle* (*The Confession of a Child of the Century*, 1836). Although most French Romantics commented on the ills of their country,

Terror, is associated with the first generation of French Romantics as his work was first published in 1819. His writings used classical myths to understand the modern condition; this is particularly evident in his unfinished epic *Hermes*, and in his more political lyrical satires, the *Ïambes*, which he wrote in prison. Meanwhile, the writer whose work during the French Revolution had the most profound impact was actually an émigré. François-Auguste-René, vicomte de Chateaubriand (1768–1848), published *Essai sur les revolutions* (translated as *An Historical, Political and Moral Essay on Revolutions, Ancient and Modern*) in 1797, a complex and often rambling attempt to make sense of revolutions, and of the French Revolution in particular. Like his contemporaries in Britain, Chateaubriand viewed nature as a source of spiritual repose and renewal. Common to all of Chateaubriand's work is a sense that the French Revolution has damaged society; this is most evident in his autobiography *Mémoires d'outre-tombe* (translated as *The Memoirs of Chateaubriand*, 1848–1850), which uses the non-fictional frame to meditate on the history of France.

Another influential figure was the eclectic writer and thinker Mme de Staël (Anne-Louise-Germaine Necker, Baronne de

ALFRED DE MUSSET WITH GEORGE SAND

Musset's love affair with the novelist George Sand (1804–1876) between the years 1833 and 1835 inspired some of his finest lyrics. *La Confession D'un Enfant Du Siècle* (1835), a fictionalized account of the love affair, reflects the *mal du siècle*, the disillusioned moral atmosphere in the period of strife between liberals and monarchists. Musset wrote the first modern dramas in French.

DEATH OF CHATTERTON,
1856, By Henry Wallis,
Oil on canvas, The Tate
Gallery, London, UK

Thomas Chatterton (1752–1770) died at the age of 17 from arsenic poisoning. The English writer is famous for fabricating the existence and poetry of a 15th-century Bristol monk called Thomas Rowley. Chatterton's genius and his tragic death are commemorated by the Romantic poets—by Shelley in *Adonais*, by Wordsworth in *Resolution and Independence*, by Coleridge in *A Monody on the Death of Chatterton*, by Dante Gabriel Rossetti in *Five English Poets*, and by John Keats in *To Chatterton*. Keats also dedicated his *Endymion* to him. Alfred de Vigny's *Chatterton* gives a fictitious account of the poet.

a distinction emerged between the pessimism of the aristocratic generation of 1820 and the dynamic frustrations of the more bourgeois generation of 1830. The works of an 1820 poet, Alphonse de Lamartine (1790–1869), including his *Méditations poétiques* (*Poetic Meditations*, 1820) and *Harmonies poétiques et religieuses* (translated as A *Biographical Sketch*, 1830), generated a sense of unfulfilled longing tempered only by bouts of revolt and despair.

In comparison, the generation of 1830 marked a turning point in French Romanticism by giving way to the sufferings and indulgences of the Romantic mode, and envisaging the poet as a prophet or visionary. The poetic works of Alfred-Victor, comte de Vigny (1797–1863), such as *Les Destinées* (1838–1863, translated as *The Fates* in 1864), view the poet as a moral philosopher, elegant in his despair. Meanwhile the young Alfred de Musset was writing works of great exuberance, such as the hugely successful *Contes d'Espagne et d'Italie* (*Tales of Spain and Italy*, 1830), which soon gave way to poetry on the solace of suffering, such as his famous collection *Nuits* (*Nights*, 1835–1837). De Vigny and de Musset are also remembered for their dramatic works; de Vigny composed the bourgeois drama *Chatterton* (1835), focusing on the suicide of the 18th-century English writer Thomas Chatterton, while de Musset had significant success with his historical tragedies and comedies. French Romantic poetry arguably reached its peak of expression in the writings of Gérard de Nerval (1805–1855), including the 12 sonnets of *Les Chimières* (*The Chimeras*, 1844–1854) and the spiritual odyssey *Aurélia* (1853–1854); his use of mysticism and symbols anticipated the French symbolist movement of the 1850s.

However the most rapidly developing literary form during this period was the novel. Presented as fictional autobiography, *Adolphe* (1816), by the novelist Benjamin Constant (1767–1830), continued and extended the tradition of the French psychological novel in its focus upon an individual character.

The novel is remarkable for its modern take on morality, which contrasts with its narrative simplicity and neoclassical intensity. A prolific writer of the period was George Sand (1804–1876). Her early novels *Indiana* (1832), *Valentine* (1832), and *Lélia* (1833) discuss the position of women within marriage and society; while her "rustic" novels, such as *La Mare au diable* (1846), *François le Champi* (1848), and *La Petite Fadette* (1849), combine a love of the pastoral with sympathy for the poor. Just as prolific was the dramatist and historical novelist Alexandre Dumas père (1802–1870), author of such memorable works as *Les Trois Mousquetaires* (*The Three Musketeers*, 1844) and *Le Comte de Monte Cristo* (*The Count of Monte Christo*, 1844–1845). Another influential figure of the period was the novelist, poet, critic, and journalist Théophile Gautier (1811–1872), who coined the expression "l'art pour l'art" ("art for art's sake") to refer to literature whose purpose was purely esthetic. In many ways his writings demarcated the transitions that occurred in French literary circles during the 19th century, as literature adopted Romantic, esthetic, and lastly naturalist models.

ITALY

The two notable Romantic writers in Italy were the poet and novelist Alessandro Manzoni (1785–1873), and the poet, scholar, and philosopher Giacomo Leopardi (1798–1837). Manzoni began his career as a poet. Although his first notable poem was the anti-clerical work "Il trionfo della libertà" ("The Triumph of Liberty", 1805), he returned to Catholicism in 1810, composing a series of religious poems entitled *Inni sacri* (*Sacred Hymns*, 1815–1822). Other works included odes on the Piedmontese revolution of 1821 and on the death of Napoleon (1822); a treatise on Catholic ethics (1819); and two historical tragedies influenced by Shakespeare, *Il conte di Carmagnola* (1820) and *Adelchi* (performed in 1822).

Manzoni's masterpiece, *I promessi sposi* (translated as *The Betrothed*), was published to critical acclaim between 1825 and 1827. The novel, set in early 16th-century Lombardy during the Thirty Years' War, is notable for its sympathetic portrayal of a love affair between two peasant workers. Its language recreates contemporary educated Florentine speech, symbolizing a loyalty toward Italian middle-class culture. Manzoni's opposition to elitism in literature, and his deep religious faith, made him a national icon: he was made a senator in 1860 and was buried with a state funeral in 1873. His prose, meanwhile, became the model for many Italian writers.

ALESSANDRO MANZONI,
Italian novelist and poet

Manzoni's near-contemporary Leopardi is noted for his superb lyrical poetry and his outstanding scholarly and philosophical works. A child prodigy troubled by weakening eyesight and his difficult relations with his parents, he poured his hopes and bitterness into poems such as *Appressamento della morte* (*Approach of Death*, 1835), a visionary work written in imitation of Petrarch and Dante. His unrequited love for his cousin, coupled with the death of a close family friend, led to his elegies *Il primo amore* and *A Silvia* in 1817–1818. Leopardi's poetry collections include *Canzoni* (1824), *Versi* (1826) and *Il Canti* (1831). He also completed *Operette Morali* (*Minor Moral Works*, 1827), a philosophical piece on despair and longing. His final work, and his longest canto, was *La Ginestra*, also known as *Il Fiore del Deserto* (*The Flower of the Desert*, 1836). It is seen as his moral testament as a poet, thanks to its attempt to enhance the power of pessimism as a means of instigating change. His poetry is celebrated for its apparently artless lyricism.

BRITAIN

The message of the French Revolution sent ripples through British culture, influencing the thinking of virtually every British writer at this time. The Anglo-Irish historian Edmund Burke worried in *Reflections on the Revolution in France* (1790) that the Revolution marked a dangerous severance with the old order; his thesis was soon rebuffed by Thomas Paine's *Rights of Man* (1791) and Mary Wollstonecraft's *A Vindication of the Rights of Men* (1791) and *A Vindication of the Rights of Women* (1792). Britain was drawn further into the debate when it entered into a war with France in 1793, which ended with the defeat of Napoleon's army at Waterloo in 1815. Amidst this

political and social turbulence, writers had to assess the impact of the new order in France, and to address their own sense of national pride and responsibility.

The poet, painter, and engraver William Blake (1757–1827) saw the French Revolution as a chance to shake things up and start afresh. Questioning the rationality and materiality of the 18th century, he saw in the aftermath of the Revolution the possibility of introducing more radical and spiritual ways of thinking. In Blake's collections *Songs of Innocence* (1789) and *Songs of Experience* (1794), poems in one collection provided counterpoints to poems in the other. Yet the very artifice of this structure encourages the reader to question the validity of binaries such as "innocence" and "experience." The poems become, then, a reflection of British society as a whole, where old values, and old ways of seeing the world, are questioned: and where new ideas provide inspiration as they generate fear. Blake hypothesized that an unquestioning faith in God was harmful to one's spiritual development. This argument is developed in his longer works *The Book of Thel* (1789), *The Marriage of Heaven and Hell* (1790–1793), *Visions of the Daughters of Albion* (1793), *The Book of Urizen* (1794), *The Four Zoas* (1794–1804), *Jerusalem* (1804–1820), and *Milton* (1804–1808), all of which celebrate the freedom of the individual as they condemn the constraints of institutions. Blake's radical vision for society was conveyed through a symbolic lexicon that led his later work to be largely neglected. It only began to be appreciated fully when the Irish poet W. B. Yeats (1865–1939), himself an advocate of symbolism, rediscovered Blake in the late 19th century.

William Wordsworth (1770–1850), in contrast to Blake, enjoyed more immediate popularity. Having been in favor of the French Revolution, Wordsworth changed his mind following the Reign of Terror in 1793, and soon retreated from public life completely. Wordsworth's focus on the natural world as a conduit for emotions is evident in the *Lyrical Ballads* (1798), a joint project with Samuel Taylor Coleridge. This work, considered a defining Romantic text, turned the focus upon the individual, in a language that attempted to mirror the speech of everyday life. This emphasis on individual insight implied a renunciation of church and state that was in fact profoundly revolutionary. However Wordsworth's theses are complicated by self-doubt that is evident in both the *Lyrical Ballads* and in his semi-autobiographical epic poem *The Prelude* (1799; revised 1805, and published in a new version in 1850).

Where Blake was an idealistic visionary, and Wordsworth an imaginative introvert, Samuel Taylor Coleridge (1772–1834)

was a pessimistic visionary with an extroverted imagination. On the one hand, his ability to convey the full powers of his imagination is extraordinary: this is most evident in his famous poem *Kubla Khan; or, A Vision in a Dream: A Fragment* (1797; published in 1816). On the other, Coleridge's view that human nature is incompatible with religion, as seen in *The Rime of the Ancient Mariner* (1797–1798), and his tendency to revise works or leave them unfinished, highlight his sense of failure at being unable to fuse his radical, philosophical, and religious selves into a single poetic vision. Nevertheless, his philosophy of poetry, and particularly his critical writings on Shakespeare, had a huge impact on the development of literary criticism in the early 20th century.

George Gordon, Lord Byron (1788–1824), one of the "second generation" of Romantics, enjoyed more immediate popularity—and notoriety—than any of his predecessors. Following a series of indiscretions, including an affair with a married aristocrat and an alleged liaison with his half-sister, Byron spent most of his life in exile, dying eventually in Greece where he was organizing forces fighting for independence from the Turks. He wrote politically engaged, energetic, often humorous poetry that featured a hero at the fringes of society whose *laissez-faire* approach to life revealed the hypocrisy of others. Byron developed this character in his poetic dramas *Manfred* (1817) and *Cain* (1821), and ultimately in the charming libertine of Don Juan, the eponymous hero of Byron's most famous work (1819–1824). In *Don Juan*, however, the synthesis between the hero's personal and sexual freedoms complicates Byron's political stance, so that Don Juan might be viewed either as a character of a bygone age, content to sport and squire as if he were in a Henry Fielding novel, or as a forward-thinking revolutionary.

The poetry of Percy Bysshe Shelley (1792–1822) was, superficially at least, more sincere in its revolutionary aims than the work of Byron. On the one hand, Shelley was the most radical of the Romantic poets: he was expelled from University College Oxford for publishing the pamphlet *The Necessity of Atheism* (1811), and read texts by political radicals such as William Godwin. One the other hand, however, Shelley's privileged middle-class upbringing was coupled with an egotism that is evident in his essay *A Defence of Poetry* (first published 1840), which describes poets as the "unacknowledged legislators of the world." Some critics view Shelley's political stance as little more than a poetic posture, while others see it as an attempt to gain popularity within the working classes, and notoriety within his own intellectual circle. Nevertheless, Shelley's belief in the power of the individual to change society has lent his work lasting resonance. For example, his epic poem *The Mask of Anarchy* (1819), written in response to the Peterloo massacre of 1819, seems fitting in its use of trochaic marching meter to appeal to everyday workers. Meanwhile, his idealistic vision, outlined in his epic poem *Queen Mab* (1813), would influence later poets including Swinburne, Rossetti, Tennyson, and Yeats. Despite his apparent revolutionary aims, then, the poets, rather than the proletariat, thus claimed Shelley as one of their own.

Shelley's *Mask of Anarchy*, with its emphasis on the working-class British man, reflects a change in society that occurred with the end of hostilities with France in 1815, which left 300,000 members of the British Army and the Royal Navy unemployed, and with the beginnings of the Industrial Revolution. It is initially surprising, then, that this period also saw the emergence of a sensual poetic voice in John Keats (1795–1821). However, Keats's focus on the

ABOVE: JOHN KEATS, 1818, Joseph Severn

The "second generation" of English Romantic poets consists of Lord Byron, John Keats, and P. B. Shelley. Shelley knew both Keats and Byron; he wrote *Adonais* elegy on Keats's death.

LEFT: PERCY BYSSHE SHELLEY, 1845, Joseph Severn, Oil on canvas, Keats–Shelley Memorial House, Rome, Italy

THE GOTHIC NOVEL AND MARY SHELLEY

Gothic fiction, a hugely popular genre from the 1760s until the 1820s, is an enduringly influential narrative form. Just as the sentimentalist refuses to see life as it is really lived, a similar comment might be made about writers of Gothic fiction. The genre, sometimes referred to as "Gothic horror," is widely believed to have been invented by the English author Horace Walpole (1717–1797), with his 1764 novel *The Castle of Otranto*. The gothic mode extended Romantic notions to their extremes, incorporating melodrama, parody, and even self-parody. Gothic literature is linked closely to the Gothic Revival architecture of the same period, which rejected the rationalism of the neoclassical style; Gothic fiction similarly rejects civilized or tempered modes in order to relish in the extremes of emotion and experience.

Whereas Walpole's Gothic writings aimed to combine medieval romances with the narrow focus of the British realist novel, the Gothic novelist Anne Radcliffe (1764–1823) earned greater popularity for her work by employing sensible heroines to whom extraordinary phenomena would ultimately be explained by natural causes. This is particularly prevalent in *The Mysteries of Udolpho* (1794). However Walpole's and Radcliffe's Gothic writings

FRANKENSTEIN BY MARY SHELLEY,
Frontispiece engraving, First published 1818

The Gothic novel resonates with philosophical and moral ramifications, themes of nature versus man-made, good versus evil.

are united in their attempts to explore the possibilities of the unconscious mind. This new style of expressive literature influenced similar movements in Europe. In France, Gothic novels were termed "black novels" and in Germany, they were known as "shudder novels." Often these works were much darker and more violent than their British counterparts.

The most remarkable work of Gothic fiction, however, is one by Mary Shelley (1797–1851), the wife of Percy Shelley, *Frankenstein* (1818) which uses the Gothic model to explore the possibilities and the uncertainties of the period. *Frankenstein* challenges narrative perspectives, and

overturns societal assumptions, by making the world of *Frankenstein* and his monster the "real" world, and the everyday world a place of secrets and misunderstandings. This enables the reader to assess the individual's relationship with the outside world, and to question how "real" that world actually is. There is also a feminist dimension to this argument; by placing an outsider at the center of her novel, and challenging the assumptions that surround this character, Mary Shelley is asking what it means to be a woman author in the center of a literary world dominated by men. Moreover, by pushing the genre to its extremes, Shelley anticipates the advent of the science fiction novel in the 20th century; indeed some critics have called her, retrospectively, the author of the first science fiction novel.

Gothic fiction impacted upon other genres of writing in the Romantic period and beyond, making its presence felt in a wide variety of literature. In France, its influence can be noted in the works of the Marquis de Sade and in Victor Hugo's drama *Notre Dame de Paris* (translated as *The Hunchback of Notre Dame*, 1831). The Cathedral of Notre Dame is one of the finest examples of Gothic architecture in the world. In America, Gothic fiction inspired the dark and savage stories of Edgar Allen Poe; it can even be linked to the black humor of the "Southern Gothic" writers Harper Lee, Flannery O'Connor, and William Faulkner. Gothic language also resounds in 20th-century dystopian fictions, such as *Nineteen Eighty-Four* by George Orwell (1949) and *The Handmaid's Tale* by the Canadian author Margaret Atwood (1985), and in the horror fiction of Stephen King.

In Britain, Gothic fiction has had an enormous and lasting impact. Jane Austen's novel *Northanger Abbey* can be read as a parody of the Gothic: its heroine imagines her life as a series of exciting calamities when in fact it is far more prosaic. Meanwhile the character of Bertha Rochester in Charlotte Brontë's 1847 novel *Jane Eyre* derives its inspiration from Gothic sources. Many Victorian writers explored Gothic themes in their literature as a means of addressing the scientific and industrial changes that were taking place in society; Bram Stoker's *Dracula* (1897) is a natural successor to *Frankenstein*, while Wilde's *The Picture of Dorian Gray* (1891), Robert Louis Stevenson's *The Strange Case of Dr. Jekyll and Mr. Hyde* (1886) and Henry James's novella *The Turn of the Screw* (1898) are all beholden to the Gothic genre. Moving into the 20th century, Daphne Du Maurier's novel *Rebecca* (1938), and Jean Rhys's *The Wide Sargasso Sea* (1966), a "prequel" to *Jane Eyre*, are heavily influenced by the Gothic. In contemporary times, media as varied as cartoons, movies, and rock songs—there is even a type of music termed "Gothic metal"—incorporate elements of the Gothic. It is a testament to the enduring legacy of Gothic fiction that humanity is still fascinated by the extremes of experience it conveys.

JANE EYRE AND GYPSY, From Charlotte Brontë's 1847 novel *Jane Eyre*.

individual's fractured relationship with society can be viewed as a counterpoint to the growing divisions in British society. Keats's *Odes* (1819), with their idealization of youth, and their emphasis on the connection between beauty and truth, influenced the thinking of the Esthetic movement of the 1860s. Meanwhile, his longer dramatic poems such as *Lamia* (1819) and *Endymion* (1817), which use myth to problematize (and sexualize) human experience, had a huge impact upon the painting and poetry of the Pre-Raphaelite Brotherhood of the 1850s. Keats's legacy lies not just in this enduring literary influence, but also in his bold suggestion that a capacity for hidden depths, some of them dark and unpleasant, lies in everyone.

There was, however, a counter-current to the psychological intensity and self-questioning despair of the Romantic poets. The novels of Jane Austen (1775–1817) use wit and irony, rather than allegory and allusion, to comment on the shifting nature of society, and focus on the realignments apparent in the middle classes at the beginning of the 19th century. Austen's novels reveal the influence of the sentimental novelist Samuel Johnson, through their nods to the epistolary style, the emphasis on female heroines, and focus on relationships within small societal groups. However, her social commentary, which includes a concern for the freedoms and opportunities of women, lends her writings a sensibility that is entirely suited to

19th-century Britain. Moreover, her masterful narrative control, and her deep insight into human relationships, have lent her six novels—*Sense and Sensibility* (1811), *Pride and Prejudice* (1813), *Mansfield Park* (1814), *Emma* (1816), *Northanger Abbey* (1818) and *Persuasion* (1818)—an enduring quality that means they continue to be read, taught, and adapted today.

Austen's work did not earn her immediate critical success or acclaim; the same, however, cannot be said of Sir Walter Scott (1771–1832), the most popular novelist of the period. Scott, who began his career as a poet, has been termed the

first international English-language author, as his novels were published in Europe, Australia, and North America. Scott's ability to tell a good story is apparent in his first series of novels, to which he did not give his name, all set in Scotland around the period of the Jacobite Risings (1688–1746); these included *Waverley* (1814) and *The Heart of Midlothian* (1818). Scott soon began work on another series of historical novels, this time set in 12th-century England, which included *Ivanhoe* (1819), noteworthy for including a sympathetic Jewish heroine, Rebecca. In each series Scott describes a period of transition in order to comment on the changes occurring within his own society. Viewed as a whole, they kick-started a fashion for historical fiction. However, Scott's popularity waned in the 20th century when E. M. Forster savaged his plots and awkward style in his essay *Aspects of the Novel* (1927). It was around this time that Scott's popularity dwindled, and Austen's star ascended —through favorable comparison with her contemporary.

EASTERN EUROPE

The Polish-born writer and philosopher Johann Gottfried (von) Herder (1744–1803), a leading figure of the *Sturm und Drang* movement in Germany, was apparently the first person to use the work "folk" (*Volk* in German) in print. He recorded and analyzed folk languages, his particular interest in traditional song texts leading him to collect old songs from many parts of the world. His rediscovery

PERSUASION

Persuasion was Jane Austen's last novel, written in 1816 and published posthumously in 1818. Like in her other novels, Austen presents the day-to-day lives of her characters in great detail—upper-middle-class men and women in 19th-century England. Anne Elliot, the story's heroine, is "persuaded" not to marry the man she loves because of their class distinction. Through this love story, Austen offers a penetrating critique of the standards of the British class system.

**JOHANN
GOTTFRIED VON HERDER**

Herder advocated the emancipation of German literature from foreign influences. His subsequent essays promoted folk literature and developed the idea of *Volksgeist* ("national character"), as expressed in the language and literature of a nation. He collected folk songs of all nations in *Stimmen der Völker in Liedern* (1778-1779).

of folk traditions, an act of preservation and a means of encouraging national pride, left a legacy for the *Volk* of Europe. As towns and cities continued to grow, those who still pursued an agrarian lifestyle were viewed with nostalgia by Romantics throughout Europe. Collecting the traditions of the *Volk* became a popular and respected pastime, with the consequence of forming the image of the "happy peasant."

Painters, choreographers, and musicians portrayed this character in their works.

Herder's influence can be seen more particularly in the growth of indigenous folk literature in Eastern Europe. In Serbia, the language scholar Vuk Stefanovic Karadzic (1787–1864), a reformer of the Cyrillic alphabet for Serbian usage, was busy earning himself the title of "father" of Serbian folk literature. Karadzic traveled throughout Serbia, Bosnia, and Croatia collecting stories, which appeared mostly in his four-volume work *Srpske narodne pjesme* (*Serbian Folk Poems*, 1822–1833). Slovenian literature also blossomed in the first half of the 19th century, when France Prešeren (1800–1849), and his friend and collaborator Matija Cop, introduced new poetic genres. Prešeren, Slovenia's national poet, composed complex Romantic sonnets, such as the *Sonetni venec* (*Wreath of Sonnets*, 1834). Meanwhile, the national consciousness of Bulgaria was being awakened through the formation of *novobulgarski*, the new (or modern) literary Bulgarian language based on the vernacular of its eastern dialects, as opposed to Church Slavonic. Its pioneers were Bishop Sophrony, whose *Nedelnik* (*Sunday-Book*, 1806) is the first modern Bulgarian printed book, and N. Gerov, compiler of the first major dictionary of Bulgarian. Together their efforts created an awakening of Bulgarian national consciousness.

The period also saw the development of a Slovak literary language. The Catholic priest Ján Hollý (1785–1849) was the first Slovak writer to use the Slovak language successfully in his poetry. At the same time, however, the Slovakian people persisted in reading texts in Czech dialects. Even *Ján Kollár's Slávy dcera* (*The Daughter of Sláva*, 1824), considered a principal work of Slovak literature, was written in Czech. However a group of young Slovak Lutheran writers, headed by Ľudovít Štúr, abandoned Czech in favour of Slovak. Later poets, such as Andrej Sládkovic (Andrej Braxatoris) and Janko Král', used a refined form of literary Slovak to produce nationalistic, Romantic works.

The trend for investigating and codifying indigenous cultures led Czech scholars (in what was then known as Bohemia and Moravia) to investigate their country's earlier literature and history. Patriotism revived in reaction to the authoritarianism of the Habsburg government. Combined with the currents of Romantic Movement interest in a national literary revival surged. The revival of the Czech literary language, carried out by the scholar Josef Dobrovský (1753–1829), was cemented by Josef Jungmann's publication of a Czech-German dictionary in 1835–1839. Their efforts were cemented in the lyrics of the great Romantic poet Karel Hynek Mácha (1810–1836), which revealed the influence of Lord Byron, Walter Scott, and the Polish Romantics.

In Poland, the poet Adam Bernard Mickiewicz (1798–1855), a lifelong advocate of Polish national freedom, displayed the growing influence of folklore upon his own work. This was tempered, however by a Westernizing tendency. While Mickiewicz's first collection of poems, *Poezye* (*Poetry*, 1822), included ballads and romances, its preface described his desire to incorporate Western forms into Polish literature. However, by the second volume of *Poezye* (1823), he had moved toward a new kind of Romantic expression. The volume contained parts two and four of his *Dziady* (*Forefather's Eve*), in which he fused folkloric elements with a story of tragic love. The third part of *Dziady*, published in 1833, envisaged the important role Poland might play within the nations of Western Europe. Mickiewicz's masterpiece *Pan Tadenz* (1834), an epic poem that describes the life of the Polish gentry in the early 19th century, appeals to Napoleon's forces, and to the Polish troops under his command, to liberate Poland from Russian rule.

RUSSIA

The literary critic Vissarion Belinsky (1811–1848) proposed 1739 as the exact year in which Russian literature began. Although recent criticism has refuted this thesis—which ignored the indigenous writings that had existed in Russia for hundreds of years—Russian literature certainly gained international influence during the 18th century. Throughout this period, and into the 19th century, Russian writings can be characterized by a concern with their relationship with Western cultures. It is perhaps not surprising, then, that texts that defied "Western" literary conventions, such as Laurence Sterne's *Tristram Shandy*, enjoyed commercial success in Russia, as writers looked for ways to challenge Western traditions in their works.

Under the influence of Peter the Great, who ruled Russia until 1725, Western culture was so pervasive that by the 19th century the first language of the nobility was French. As a result of this cultural interference, Russian critics began to see literature as a foreign import. Under the rule of Catherine II "the Great" (1762–1796), however, Russian poets began to develop an indigenous poetic voice. The most successful was Garvila Derzhavin (1743–1816), known for his panegyric *Oda K Felitse* (*Ode to Felitsa*, 1782), and his odes *Bog* (*God*, 1784) and *Vodopad* (*The Waterfall*, 1791–1794). Meanwhile, the prose writer Nikolay Karamzin (1766–1826) was emerging as the dominant figure of the Russian sentimentalist movement. His most notable achievement was his 12-volume work *Istoriya gosudarstva rossiyskogo* (*History of the Russian State*, 1818–1826). However, this work did little to assert the language of the Russian people, using instead a Gallicized, rarefied vocabulary to narrate the country's history.

The 19th century began with what is now referred to as the "Golden Age" of Russian poetry. The period, characterized by aristocratic sensibility, is exemplified by the verse translations of Vasily Zhukovsky (1783–1852) and the alternately playful, erotic, and melancholic poems of Konstantin Batyushkov (1787–1855). However the most remarkable poet to emerge during this period was Aleksandr Sergeyevich Pushkin (1799–1837), who is often regarded as the founder of modern Russian literature, and as the man who gave shape to a literary language in Russian. As a writer of a philosophical bent, evaluating the validity of culture in general, Pushkin adopted a parodic mode, composing erotic and often sacrilegious mock-epics including *Gavriiliada* (*The Gabrieliad*, 1821), a daring retelling of the Annunciation, and *Ruslan i Lyudmila* (*Ruslan and Ludmila*, 1820), a parody of epic, folk tale, ballad, and romance. His lyrics include self-conscious works on the double identity of the poet as artist and man; political poems that veer between praise and

**THE POETS
ALEKSANDR PUSHKIN, IVAN KRYLOV, VASILY ZHUKOVSKY, AND NICOLAI GNEDICH,** Oil on canvas, Hermitage, St Petersburg, Russia

Russian culture was invaded with West European values from the 17th century onward. This led to the cultural crises of the 18th century, when Russian writers tried to establish their national identity in literature. Finally, the Russian language found its definite form in the creations of V.A. Zhukovsky and A.S. Pushkin.

mockery of the Tsar and his treatment of the Poles; daring compositions, such as *Vospominaniye* (*Remembrance*, 1828) and *Elegiya* (*Elegy*, 1830); remarkable love poems, such as *Ya vas lyubil* (*I Loved You Once*, 1829); and, *Anchar* (*The Upas Tree*, 1828) and *Ne day mne Bog soyti s uma* (*God Grant I Go Not Mad*), meditations on human evil.

Because of their vast array of subplots and their multi-layered parodic structure, Pushkin's works do not read well in translation. This is a particular issue in his complex narrative poems *Tsygamy* (*The Gypsies*, 1824) and *Medny vsadnik* (*The Bronze Horseman*, 1833). Pushkin pushed the boundaries of narrative verse to compose the quasi-Shakespearian drama *Boris Godunov* (1824–1825), and four *Little Tragedies* in 1830, each of which deals with a philosophical problem. However, the culmination of his efforts in this form is reflected in his verse novel *Eugene Onegin* (1825–1832), which is now seen as the first significant Russian novel. Influenced by the precociousness of Sterne's *Tristram Shandy* and Byron's *Don Juan*, it tells the story of Onegin, a "superfluous man," through an endless succession of digressions, narrative voices, and self-parodies. The work's serial publication over several years enabled it to incorporate the author's changing perspectives.

The most significant prose writer during this period was the comic author and nonsense writer Nikolay Vasilyevich Gogol (1809–1852). His short stories include *Nos* (*The Nose*, 1836), a satire on the failure of explicable systems, *Shinel* (*The Overcoat*, 1842), possibly the most influential Russian short story, and *Zapiski sumasshedshego* (*The Diary of a Madman*, 1835), a daring mixture of empathy and insult. Meanwhile the inherent absurdity of language, and even of existence itself, is challenged in the stories *Nevsky prospekt* (*Nevsky Avenue*, 1835) and *Povest o tom, kak possorilsya Ivan Ivanovich s Ivanom Nikiforovichem* (*The Tale of How Ivan Ivanovich Quarrelled with Ivan Nikiforovich*).

NIKOLAY VASILYEVICH GOGOL

Gogol, with his bright satire, specified the religious and moral topics in Russian culture. He is best known for his short stories, for his play *Revizor* (*The Inspector General*), and for *Myortvye dushi* (*Dead Souls*), a prose narrative that is subtitled a "poem."

Gogol's famous play *Revizor* (*The Inspector General*, or *The Government Inspector*, 1836), a satire written in critique of the corruption of Tsarist Russia, is notable for its absence of sympathetic characters and its awareness of its own artifice. It is unsurprising that the absurdist modern playwright Samuel Beckett acknowledged Gogol as an influence. Another significant work is *Myortvye dushi* (*Dead Souls*, 1842), a prose narrative that purports to be a poem, which exposes the falsities of bureaucracy as a means of allegorizing humanity's fruitful search for meaning. An undercurrent of despair runs throughout Gogol's work, manifesting itself, through comedy, in the cruelty of the revelation that existence is a mere fabrication. Whether this revelation marks Gogol as a realist, exposing the truths of life to man, or as an absurdist, mocking man's incessant and fruitful search for meaning, is open to (ongoing) interpretation.

Chapter 7
REALISM TO NATURALISM

CONGRES DE VIENNE.
SEANCE DES PLENIPOTENTIAIRES
DES HUIT PUISSANCES SIGNATAIRES
DU TRAITE DE PARIS.

JEAN JACQUES ROUSSEAU WITH THE PANTHÉON, PARIS

Rousseau, one of the dominant thinkers of the Enlightenment in the 18th century, tried to grasp the emotional and passionate side of humans in his general philosophy. His novel *Julie; ou la nouvelle Héloïse* impacted the late 18th century's movement of Romantic Naturalism.

FACING PAGE: Congress Of Vienna, 1815, By Jean-Baptiste Isabey, Louvre, Paris, France. European statesmen at the Congress of Vienna, where the territorial divisions of Europe were decided after the Napoleonic and French revolutionary wars.

Between September 1814 and June 1815, at the end of the Napoleonic wars, the Great Powers (Austria, France, Prussia, Russia, and Britain) met at the Congress of Vienna in order to agree on the new map of Europe. The guiding principle of their discussions was the restoration of pre-Napoleonic boundaries. However, one of the results of the wars had been to crystallize questions of allegiance and national identity. Nations such as Hungary and Romania were gaining a new self-awareness (often referred to as a "National Awakening"), even though they were still satellites of imperial powers. Other territories, including what we now know as Italy and Germany—at that time merely collections of princely states—started to conceive of themselves as coherent wholes.

This rise in nationalism was mirrored in the Romantic literature of the period, which celebrated nations' mythical and folkloric origins. The Romantic vision of the homeland was used to give legitimacy to the nationalist cause, developing the idea of a return to one's true roots and destiny. This was given its fullest expression in the works of the philosophers Rousseau, Herder, and Hegel, the writings of Ossian and Goethe, and the paintings of artists such as Caspar David Friedrich, Delacroix, and Goya.

Yet despite capturing the mood of the times, elements of the Romantic Movement were giving way to new concerns. While the Romantic creed provided some escape from the challenges of the modern world—the Industrial Revolution, population explosion, and urban sprawl—its tendency toward melodrama and fantasy, its championing of heroic isolation, and its recourse to lofty modes of expression seemed to many to be inappropriate in a society where the communal whole and cross-class interplay were of growing importance.

And so, a new realism was asserted in Romanticism's wake. Striving to reflect everyday existence just as it was (rather than escape it), Realist literature developed a no-nonsense approach, effacing embellishment and interpretation from its texts, and concentrating on the depiction of often-mundane situations. Mirroring the contemporary expansion of matter-of-fact reportage in newspapers and periodicals, literary writers had a new purpose—as social critics or commentators.

Science too was to have an important effect on cultural endeavors. The pioneering work on photography by the likes of Louis Daguerre (1787–1851) meant that real subjects in

TOP: *STILL LIFE,* 1837, Daguerreotype by Louis-Jacques-Mandé Daguerre, Société Française de Photographie, Paris, France

RIGHT: THÉOPHILE GAUTIER

The French writer, whose influence was strongly felt during the transition from Romanticism to Naturalism in France, achieved his first major success with his epistolary novel *Mademoiselle Maupin*. In the introduction to this novel, Gautier explained his theory of "l'art pour l'art," a purpose-free art.

everyday situations (including all the incidental detail in the background) were now taking the place of the romanticized visions of painters, who edited out the mundane and the trivial in their pursuit of the Platonic ideal. In the fields of biology, chemistry, and geology, scientists were observing the real world under the microscope and also making discoveries with far-reaching implications. From the 1830s, Charles Darwin (1809–1882) worked on his theory of evolution, which eventually bore fruit in his book *On the Origin of Species* (1859). This provided great ballast to the growing belief that science rather than religion held the answers to understanding the universe. It also bolstered confidence in the idea of progress and that problems in any sphere—social, political, economic— could be solved with expertise, empirical study, and application. Whereas the substance of everyday life had previously been considered unworthy, now it fascinated, and, for art as much as anything else, was deemed to have immense relevance and moral value.

The Realist Movement in literature gained credence steadily throughout the first half of the 19th century and blossomed in the 1850s, particularly in France. Some writers, of course, bridged the gap between the Romantic and Realist Movements, and others continued writing in the Romantic vein until late in the century. Other philosophies gained currency too—the idea of "art for art's sake," for example (generally accredited to the poet Théophile Gautier, 1811–1872)—but the belief that art ought to address society's problems, however ugly their forms, remained a widely held one, such that literature became a valuable engine for change.

1815 End of the Napoleonic Wars.	(later part of the united Italy), and the Ottoman Empire.	**1869** Leo Tolstoy's work *War and Peace* is published.
1815 The Treaty of Vienna is signed.	**1856** Gustave Flaubert writes *Madame Bovary*.	**1870-1871** Franco-Prussian War, resulting in French defeat.
1834 End of the Spanish Inquisition (founded in 1478).	**1861** Foundation of the united Kingdom of Italy under Victor Emmanuel II.	**1871** George Eliot writes *Middlemarch*.
1837-1901 Reign of Queen Victoria, one of the most progressive periods in British history.	**1861-1865** American Civil War.	**1890** Henrik Ibsen publishes *Hedda Gabler*; poems of Emily Dickinson are published posthumously.
1848 Year of revolutions across Europe.	**1863-1865** Polish uprising against Russia.	**1898** Émile Zola writes *J'accuse* in support of Alfred Dreyfus.
1848-1851 War of Independence in Hungary.	**1866** Austro-Prussian War; Prussia is victorious, taking control over the German states.	**1903** Henry James's novel *The Ambassadors* is published.
1853-1857 Crimean War between Russia and the (eventually triumphant) combined forces of France, Britain, the Kingdom of Sardinia	**1866** Dostoyevsky writes *Crime and Punishment*.	**1907** August Strindberg pens *The Ghost Sonata*.

Stendhal

One writer often considered a Realist amongst Romantics was Stendhal. He was born Marie-Henri Beyle, in Grenoble in 1783, the son of a lawyer. In 1799 he took up a post at the Ministry of War, where he developed an ardent admiration for Napoleon and took part in most of the Emperor's campaigns. After Napoleon's defeat, Beyle moved to Italy, where he adopted the pseudonym Stendhal and turned to writing. From this time on, he spent periods either in Italy or Paris—in later life as Consul at Civita Vecchia. He died in 1842.

His output consists of writings on art, music and travel, essays (notably *Racine et Shakespeare*, 1822 and 1825, in which he writes in favor of Romanticism) and novels. His two principle novels *Le Rouge et le Noir* (*Scarlet and Black*, 1831) and *La Chartreuse de Parme* (*The Charterhouse of Parma*, 1839) received little acclaim during his lifetime, although he correctly predicted that they would be appreciated in due course: he was, in many ways, a writer ahead of his time.

Certainly there are many Romantic elements in his work. The heroes of both *Le Rouge et Le Noir* and *La Chartreuse*

de Parme are rebels fighting against oppressive political and social regimes. Like his creator, Julien Sorel, the hero of *Le Rouge et Le Noir*, is a fervent (although clandestine) supporter of Napoleon and aspires to climb the social ladder, just as his war-mongering hero had done. And, also characteristic of Romantic literature, fact is often embroidered for creative effect, and readers are shown only a biased version of events in order to win their sympathy for the protagonist.

STENDHAL,
1840, By Johan Olaf Soedermark, Musée National du Château, Versailles, France

The writings of Stendhal mark the transition in French literature from Romanticism to Realism. Though he celebrated emotions like other Romantic writers, Stendhal wrote in a straightforward, realistic style, critically examining the social climate and manners of his time.

But there are also many elements of Realism in Stendhal's writings. The subtitle of *Le Rouge et le Noir* is "Chronique de 1830," and it is prefaced by a quotation from Danton, "the truth, the bitter truth." Stendhal also vividly evokes the image of a mirror to indicate how his novel is a reflection of glimpses from real life; it portrays characters from all walks of life, not just the higher echelons (although class barriers are still rigid), and it provides snapshots that can be pieced together to form a true depiction of the greater world at a decisive historical moment in time. In his psychological analysis of his characters, too, he is well in advance of many of his contemporary writers.

Hugo

Also spanning the transitional period from Romanticism to Realism is the novelist, poet, and dramatist Victor Hugo (1802–1885). Born in Besançon, Hugo was the son of a general in the Napoleonic army and a staunchly conservative, royalist mother. After spending his early years on the campaign trail with his father, at the age of 10 he moved to Paris. His mother's political stance perhaps explains his own early conservatism—his concentration on translating the classical poets and his devotion to king and country. His first collection of poems, entitled *Odes et Poésies Diverses* and published in 1822, earned him early acclaim and a pension from Louis XVIII. It was in this year, too, that he married Adèle Foucher.

It is in Hugo's early plays, however, that a shift away from the established classical tradition is first apparent. In the preface to his early historical drama *Cromwell* (1827), he called for a break with classical drama. In *Hernani* (1830), now little read or performed, he dared to put his support for the Romantic Movement into practice on stage. Brave in its disrespect of the classical unities of time and place, the play stunned too with its ground-breaking move away from the use of the pure Alexandrine verse form that had long been standard in French drama. Its first night was dubbed the "Battle of Hernani" since the performance precipitated a riot among the theatergoers, between the horrified conservatives and the bohemian Romantic crowd who had flocked there in support.

LEFT: VICTOR HUGO

The best-known works of Hugo are the novels *Les Misérables* and *Notre Dame de Paris*.

TOP: QUASIMODO, From *The Hunchback of Notre Dame*, By Antoine Wiertz of Brussels, Belgium

Although Hugo wrote a total of seven novels, 21 plays, and 18 volumes of poetry (much of this, too, is highly Romantic, such as the exotic *Les Orientales*), it is for two novels that his reputation retains its high position. *Notre-Dame de Paris* (*The Hunchback of Notre Dame*), published in 1831, cemented his reputation as a master of the Romantic style—it is melodramatic, emotional, written in a French that was much closer to the spoken French than to the elevated language of classical French literature, and has a highly unconventional hero. Although the novel was less than successful with the critics, it proved hugely popular with the reading public and secured Hugo's reputation abroad. Another legacy widely credited to the book is the restoration of Notre Dame itself. Hugo's lengthy, lovingly crafted description of the crumbling Gothic building inspired the architect Viollet-le-Duc to restore the cathedral to its former glory.

In later life Hugo became increasingly involved in politics, and this is marked by a shift in his writing, which he increasingly used to express his humanitarian views on society. He was a staunch supporter of the Republic, and spent years in exile on the islands of Jersey and Guernsey after the restoration of the monarchy under Louis Napoleon. His greatest work, *Les Misérables* (1862) dates from this period. It is an epic on social injustice and misery among the lower classes in the 19th century, and its characters are used to symbolize issues such as social degradation, subordination of women, and child poverty. Hugo intended his great tome to encourage social awareness and change. After the Paris Commune of 1870–1871, Hugo returned to Paris, and was elected to the Senate. Despite his wishes, his burial, in 1885, was a grand state affair. A humanitarian to the last, Hugo left 50,000 francs to the poor.

Flaubert

While Stendhal and Hugo covered the transitional period between movements, Gustave Flaubert (1821–1880) is

GUSTAVE FLAUBERT

The French novelist and short story writer was regarded as a leader of the Realist school of French literature. His masterpiece *Madame Bovary*–a realistic novel, portraying bourgeois life–led to his trial (and narrow acquittal) on charges of immorality.

generally considered the father of the Realist Movement—although the author himself loathed the label. Born in Rouen in 1821, the son of a doctor, he himself trained and practised as a lawyer until nervous attacks (possibly epilepsy) forced him to return to the family home. He then devoted himself to writing.

He is best known for his novel *Madame Bovary* (1857), a work that took him five years to complete as a result of an obsessive dedication to achieving purity of style. He is considered the champion of the Realist Movement for his minute attention to detail, his ability to capture the mundanity of everyday (in this case, bourgeois) life, his unemotional and unsentimental approach, his avoidance of metaphors, and his aim for zero authorial intervention. Yet not even Flaubert could escape this last feature to some degree, if only because every writer presents reality as he or she sees it, projecting his or her mind into the characters. Hence, he famously declared, "Madame Bovary, c'est moi" ("Madame Bovary, that's me").

The book was serialized in the Revue de Paris, reflecting the publication trend at the time for serializations of works of fiction, with cliff-hanging endings to each installment. The

LEFT: MADAME BOVARY

BELOW: THE DEATH BED OF MADAME BOVARY, Before 1889, Oil on canvas

Emma Bovary typifies the psychological make-up of the French bourgeoisie in the 19th century. Unhappy in her marriage, she nurtures romantic fantasies, which she fulfills through two adulterous relationships. When Emma finds that her dream world is falling apart, she prefers death to accepting a world not consonant with her fantasies and commits suicide.

Madame Bovary is the story of a self-centered bourgeois woman who, bored by her marriage to a dull provincial doctor, takes two lovers, racks up debt, and eventually commits suicide. The book caused a scandal, and both Flaubert and his publisher were tried for an "outrage to public morals and religion." The case, however, was eventually dropped and the book sold well, cementing Flaubert's reputation.

Flaubert's other works include the historical novel *Salammbô* (1862), documenting the war between Rome and Carthage, *Sentimental Education* (1869), set during the 1848 Revolution and the Second Republic, and recounting a love affair between a young man and an older woman—a highly regarded novel that is stylistically as refined as *Madame Bovary* in its careful attention to detail and highly controlled composition—and the more exotic work *The Temptation of St Anthony* (written in the 1840s but not published until 1874), inspired by Breughel's painting of the same name.

In his personal life, Flaubert cut a lonely figure. He never married, and although he had a mistress—the poet Louise Colet—his relationship with her was largely conducted by post. In later life he also wrote extensively—and platonically—to George Sand. He died of a stroke in 1880. His literary legacy was enormous, however, and he can be credited as a crucial influence on younger writers such as Guy de Maupassant.

Balzac

While Hugo had used his later novels as vehicles for social and political comment, other realist writers went a stage further and developed a keen interest in the science behind the events they were describing. Science was making the headlines by the mid-19th century, and the most fundamentally challenging development was the theory of evolution formulated by the English naturalist Charles Darwin (1809–1882), whose *On the*

introduction of primary education for all in France in the 1830s had resulted in significant growth in the literacy rate by the mid-century, and the middle classes in particular soon developed a voracious appetite for fiction. Advances in printing technology and the growing availability of cheap books and periodicals fed this demand.

Origin of Species was published in 1859. Naturalism in literature was a refinement of Realism, maintaining the latter's keen attention to detail and unbiased presentation of characters, but attempting to scientifically explain the social and hereditary reasons for their behavior. It is also often possible to discern among naturalist writers a shift in stance on the question of free will. Writers increasingly saw individuals' destinies as the product of their physical and social environment rather than the result of their own choices and moral qualities.

Although Émile Zola (see below) is hailed as France's leading exponent of Naturalism, some critics consider Honoré de Balzac (1799–1850) to be one of the earliest and greatest French writers to adopt this approach. Certainly, he is a champion of Realism, and certainly he presents his work in a way that is highly influenced by science. His legacy is a vast body of work—almost 100 finished novels and essays—entitled *La*

Comédie Humaine (in reference to Dante's *Divine Comedy*), in which he chronicled the turbulent, post-Bonaparte French society (roughly 1815–1848) in minute detail.

His writing, with extensive description, intricately recorded detail of the mundane, and unromanticized, frank, in-depth character analysis, is almost like that of a historian. Many of his characters occur in more than one novel, heightening the sense of reality across the body of work, and there is movement between cross-sections of society, from the poorest boarding-houses to the grandest salons, which presents a fuller picture of the society which Balzac described. Mirroring scientific analysis, he subdivided his *Comédie Humaine* into "studies," or series, of manners, philosophy, and analysis, and therein classified works as documenting scenes of life, whether "Parisian," "provincial," "country," "private," "military," or "political."

The works were initially published as a collection in 1842, although Balzac's plans to expand it were cut short by his death in 1850. In the preface to the collection, Balzac states that he applied zoological techniques to his analysis of the human race and credits biologists such as the Comte de Buffon (1707–1788) and Étienne Geoffroy Saint-Hilaire (1772–1844) as having influenced his approach.

Many of Balzac's novels were initially serialized in periodicals to feed the growing appetite among the wider public for fiction. He stated that "these books are written for everybody," reflecting the increasing trend for the novel to serve some democratic purpose. His books deal with issues pertaining to class and social success, money, power, the corruption of the middle and upper classes, the situation of women in society, family relationships, and the struggle of the individual against society. And his extensively described backdrops are central to a full understanding of his characters—the city of Paris is often lauded as one of the greatest characters of the *Comédie*

HONORÉ DE BALZAC

The French author is best known for his magnum opus *La Comédie Humaine* (*The Human Comedy*), which consists of over 90 short stories, novellas, and novels. The work—presenting a cohesive overview of French life in the years after the fall of Napoléon Bonaparte in 1815—went through various stages of editing and revision before taking its final shape. Due to his keen observation of detail, Balzac is regarded as one of the founders of Realism in European literature.

Humaine, while the author himself described the city as having "human qualities." Of the finished works, the most notable are *Les Chouans* (1829), *Eugénie Grandet* (1833), *Père Goriot* (1834–1835), a reworking of Shakespeare's *King Lear*, *Illusions Perdues* (1843), *Le Cousin Pons* (1847), and *La Cousine Bette* (1848).

Balzac's personal life was almost as colorful as that of many of his characters. He attempted suicide in his teens, before then training unhappily as a clerk of law. As a writer he was dogged by financial problems and demanding creditors and frequently worked through the night, legendarily fuelled by strong black coffee. His almost obsessive approach included painstakingly revising his writing—time-consuming, considering his hugely prolific output. He married his long-term love, the Polish noblewoman Ewelina Hauska, in March 1850, but died the following August.

Zola

As the century progressed, France's leading exponent of Naturalism, Émile Zola (1840–1902) came to dominate the literary scene. His novels, on such themes as poverty, alcoholism, the working-classes, heredity, and sex and prostitution, proved hugely appealing to the public, and his works sold in the high thousands. The expansion of the field of science, notably in the work of Charles Darwin, also heightened the public's interest in Zola's naturalistic project. The author's notoriety was cemented by his involvement in one of the biggest political scandals of the 1890s, the Dreyfus Affair.

The son of an Italian engineer, Émile Zola was born in Paris in 1840. He worked as a clerk, then for a publisher before moving into journalism, and finally writing fiction. Like Balzac, he grouped many of his novels into a series (*Les Rougon-Macquart*), with the same characters appearing in several works—a "social and natural history" (Zola) of five generations of a family in the French Second Empire. Of the 20 novels in the series, the first, *Thérèse Raquin* (1867; also adapted by Zola into a play, first performed in 1873), brought Zola immediate acclaim. In its preface he states that he wishes to study "temperaments and not characters." His success in portraying his characters as representative types has led the work to be considered a classic example of naturalist writing.

Other renowned works include: *Le Ventre de Paris* (*The Belly of Paris*, 1873), *L'Assommoir* (*The Drunkard or Dram Shop*, 1877) on poverty and alcoholism—and highly regarded for its smooth translation of street slang onto the page; *Nana* (1880), the sequel to *L'Assommoir*; *La Bête Humaine* (1890), a psychological thriller, and *La Débâcle* (1892), a novel on the Franco-Prussian war. However, it is *Germinal* (1885)—which documents a miner's strike in northern France—that is widely considered to be his masterpiece, for its gripping plot, its championing of working-class causes (the inhumane conditions under which miners were expected to work) during the Industrial Revolution and Zola's subtle scientific analysis.

In 1898, Zola wrote what was his most politically influential piece—*J'accuse* (*I accuse*), an open letter to the then president Félix Faure. Published on the front page of the Parisian daily paper *L'Aurore*, the letter accused the French army and government of anti-Semitism and gross miscarriage of justice over the conviction for treason (for spying) of the Jewish captain Alfred Dreyfus. This highly controversial letter proved Zola's commitment to his belief in the social responsibility of the writer, but was personally very risky. In 1899 he was convicted of libel and sentenced to jail, but he fled to England to avoid incarceration. Following the fall of Faure's government, Dreyfus was pardoned and Zola was allowed to return to France, where he continued writing. He died in 1902. Dreyfus was completely exonerated by the French High Court in 1906.

Maupassant

Among the many writers influenced by Zola was Guy de Maupassant (1850–1893). Born near Dieppe, Maupassant was a family friend and protégé of Flaubert, whose artistic circle the former joined on returning from the Franco-Prussian war of the 1870s. Like Flaubert, Maupassant laid strong emphasis on purity of style—on economical plots, the importance of simplicity in writing, and on painstakingly considered style. Such a careful approach was well suited to short-story writing, and Maupassant is arguably the finest French exponent of this genre.

He first made his name by writing the short story *Boule de Suif* (*Ball of Fat*) in a collection of stories on the Franco-Prussian War. The book, published in 1880, was the brainchild of Zola, whose short story *L'Attaque du Moulin* (*Attack of the Windmill*) also featured in the collection. It was young Maupassant's contribution, however, that proved an overnight success—thanks to its clean plot, seemingly simple style, and its novel, unexpectedly undramatic ending.

GUY DE MAUPASSANT

Maupassant was a Naturalist author, generally considered the greatest French short story writer. The themes of Maupassant's short stories and novels are mainly based on the bourgeois way of life, the Franco-Prussian War, and the fast and fashionable life of Paris. His characters are driven by feelings of lust, greed, and ambition, and he has no place for any higher feelings or emotions.

Guy de Maupassant

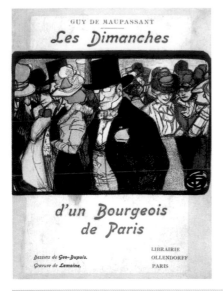

Paul Verlaine (1844–1896), and Stéphane Mallarmé (1842–1898) wrote symbolist works that harked back to Romanticism and were characterized by metaphor, evocation, heady sensory images, and free verse form. Baudelaire scandalized with (and was prosecuted for) his heady and nostalgic symbolist collection *Les Fleurs du Mal* (*The Flowers of Evil*, 1857), which shocked with its themes of sex and death. These poets saw their artistic purpose as burdensome —in 1884 Verlaine coined the expression *"poète maudit"* ("accursed poet") for writers including Rimbaud and Mallarmé who, he said, suffered from the curse of genius.

BRITAIN

In Britain, the Victorian period (1837–1901) was one of great expansion and development. Population growth, increasing urbanization, wealth creation, better education among the middle classes, burgeoning industry, and great advances in science and engineering all led to a widespread challenging of old systems and beliefs. In literature, it was a particularly rich period for the novel, which fed the growing demand for fiction—as entertainment, knowledge, and sometimes even moral instruction—from an increasingly literate public.

An isolated parsonage in Haworth, West Yorkshire, was the unlikely source of some of the period's most acclaimed novels. The daughters of a clergyman (their mother died at an early age), the Brontë sisters—Charlotte (1816–1855), Emily (1818–1848), and Anne (1820–1849)—fired their imagination and their love of literature by devouring works from their father's library. From an early age, they produced stories under the pen-names Currer, Ellis, and Acton Bell.

Of the three, Charlotte achieved the greatest success among contemporary readers for *Jane Eyre* (1847), a partly autobiographical story of a plain young orphaned governess

In the decade that followed, Maupassant's output—used to finance a playboy lifestyle—was considerable. It included journalism, around 300 short stories (most notably *La Parure/ The Necklace*, of 1885), and six novels, of which the most highly regarded are *Une Vie* (*A Woman's Life*; 1883), *Bel-Ami* (1885), *Mont-Oriol* (1887), and *Pierre et Jean* (*Pierre and Jean*, 1888).

Towards the end of his life, syphilis took hold, and he suffered increasingly from mental illness and paranoia. In 1891 he attempted suicide and was committed to an asylum, where he died in 1893.

Some writers, however, were tiring of the scientific, highly self-conscious nature of Realism and Naturalism in literature, and a number of them began to shift towards a more esthetic, sensory goal. The novelist Charles-Marie-Georges (Joris-Karl) Huysmans (1848–1907), influenced in his early realist writing by Zola, produced works such as the unofficial manifesto of estheticism, *À Rebours* (*Against Nature*, 1884). Poets including Charles Baudelaire (1821–1867), Arthur Rimbaud (1854–1891),

LEFT: THE BRONTË SISTERS, c. 1834, Painted by their brother Branwell, Oil on canvas, National Portrait Gallery, London, UK

From left to right: Anne, Emily, and Charlotte. There is a shadow of Branwell in the painting, which appeared after he painted himself out. The sisters grew up in gloomy surroundings, so their stories deal with themes such as violence, suffering, endurance, or rebellion against fate.

TOP: HEATHCLIFF RETURNS, 1993, Jonathan Barry, oil on canvas, Bridgeman Art Library

who falls in love with her employer and becomes betrothed to him, only to discover on her wedding day that he is already married. Although there is ultimately reconciliation, this does not come without tragedy and moral torment. The novel's other themes include social class, madness, the Gothic (hugely popular during the Victorian period), and the status of women in society. Charlotte's other notable works include *Shirley* (1849) and *Villette* (1853). The only sister who married (to her father's curate, Arthur Bell Nicholls), Charlotte died during pregnancy.

The second sister, Emily, wrote just one novel, *Wuthering Heights* (1847). Set on the bleak, wild Yorkshire Moors, the novel concerns the tempestuous, destructive, elemental relationship between Catherine Earnshaw and the orphan Heathcliff—a couple portrayed as two parts of one soul, like good and evil. Passionate, tragic, littered with Gothic and supernatural motifs, at times melodramatic, and with an impressively mature structure, it was less popular than *Jane Eyre* when first published, but is now generally considered to be the greatest of all the novels written by the sisters.

Anne, the least acclaimed of the three, yet still not without merit, wrote the novels *Agnes Grey* (1847) and *The Tenant of Wildfell Hall* (1848). Her novels are in a more realistic, less romantic style than those of her sisters.

Another important female English novelist from the Victorian period—one who enjoyed considerable contemporary success—was George Eliot, the pseudonym of Mary Ann Evans (1819–1880). Her works include *Adam Bede* (1859), *The Mill on*

BECKY SHARP AND SIR PITT CRAWLEY, From *Vanity Fair* by William Makepeace Thackeray

In the given picture, Becky Sharp turns down Sir Pitt Crawley's proposal because she's just married his son!

where his father worked for the East India Company. He returned to England in 1817. After writing articles for periodicals for several years, he published his first major novel, *Vanity Fair* in 1847–1848, initially in serialized form. The book is a caustic satire of the increasingly corrupt upper echelons of society. It follows the attempts of the intelligent, attractive and resourceful heroine Becky Sharp to navigate her way in society when all its rules discriminate against her. Thackeray's other works include *The History of Henry Esmond* (1852) and *The Virginians* (1859).

Perhaps the most famous figure in 19th-century literature was Charles Dickens (1812–1870). His gift for biting satire and perceptive description of people and places made him one of the most influential critics of the social conditions of Victorian England. In addition, his gift for comic characterization and gripping plots made him popular with the reading public and a very wealthy man. His reputation was established early with his first novel, *Pickwick Papers* (1836), and cemented by his second, *Oliver Twist* (1838). The latter is a sentimental, melodramatic story of an innocent child caught in the harsh world of the workhouse. The success of the story was followed up with *Nicholas Nickleby* (1839), a typically Dickensian world of fools, snobs, and villains, who condemn themselves with their every utterance.

the Floss (1860), *Silas Marner* (1861), *Middlemarch* (1874), and *Daniel Deronda* (1876). These novels, in which she considers issues that were hugely pressing at the time, such as the role of women, marriage (Eliot herself lived openly with the married critic G.H. Lewis, despite her religious upbringing), class, religion and morality, political reform and education, are admired for their realism. Eliot is famed for her authentic depictions of provincial life, but was also highly adept at writing convincing dialogue and often praised for her penetrating characterizations.

A child of imperial times, William Makepeace Thackeray (1811–1863) was born in Calcutta,

GEORGE ELIOT,
1849, François D'Albert Durade,
Oil on canvas,

After a trip to the United States, Dickens wrote *Martin Chuzzlewit* (1844), a critical examination of the profit motive as he saw it in operation in the US. His moral fairytale *A Christmas Carol* (1843) introduced Ebenezer Scrooge, one of his most famous characters and a warning against avarice for all times. More mature, complex works followed, such as *Dombey and Son* (1848) and *David Copperfield* (1850), which both feature the innocence of youth at the hearts

LEFT: CHARLES DICKENS

A prolific author of the 19th century, Dickens is famous for his remarkable characters and the way he presented them and the social classes of his times. He particularly talked about the plight of the poor and down-trodden in his works.

RIGHT: OLIVER TWIST "ASKING FOR MORE," by H. Devine, From the *World of Charles Dickens*, later made as a Spode plate, W/c on paper, Dickens House Museum, London, UK

of their stories. Dombey—a symbol of industrialization and commerce—is contrasted with the soft human qualities of his daughter Florence. Dickens' favorite and most autobiographical work, *David Copperfield*, charts the growth of the optimistic, diligent, and persevering hero from childhood to maturity.

The 1850s brought continued success with *Bleak House* (1853), *Hard Times* (1854), and *Little Dorrit* (1857). Social criticism is central to these novels, which portray a society mired in legal complexities, *laissez-faire* practices, and corruption. During the last phase of his career, Dickens published *A Tale of Two Cities* (1859), set in London and Paris at the time of the French Revolution; *Great Expectations* (1861), a novel about coming of age and social mobility; *Our Mutual Friend* (1865), which returns to the theme of the dangers of the pursuit of wealth; and the unfinished *The Mystery of Edwin Drood* (1870), a murder mystery.

Whereas the works of Dickens predominantly feature urban life in Victorian Britain, the novels of Thomas Hardy (1840–1928) take as their province the changing rural landscape (Dorset or "Wessex" in particular). Hardy's most acclaimed works—*Far from the Madding Crowd* (1874), *The Return of the Native* (1878), *The Mayor of Casterbridge* (1886), *Tess of the D'Urbervilles* (1891), and *Jude the Obscure* (1895) are set in the early Victorian period and explore themes such as social mobility, sexual inequality (Hardy's female characters are often portrayed with greater depth than his male characters), Victorian morals, and religion. Many of the novels also combine careful description of ordinary life with an underlying sense of the inevitability of fate and the indifference of the greater forces that govern the world, with repeated reference to the fates of Classical literature. This is an original adaptation of the Naturalist vision of man at the mercy of his environment. A feeling of pessimism is compounded by a sense of nostalgia for the dying old

THOMAS HARDY,
At his home at Max Gate, early 1920s

The English naturalist author and poet shocked Victorian readers' sensibilities with his *Tess of the d'Urbervilles* (1891) and *Jude the Obscure* (1895), which focused on social evils like sin, the class system, and the vagaries of religion and marriage. His tragic characters were termed "immoral" and "obscene." In his Preface to the 1912 edition of *Jude*, Hardy talks about a bishop who burned a copy of his book "probably in his despair at not being able to burn me." The controversy led to a sharp rise in the demand for Hardy's novels, but he turned his attention to plays and poetry.

world and the fear engendered by the rapid change and advancement of the Victorian period.

In addition to his novels, Hardy also published more than 40 short stories and more than 10 volumes of poetry (including the collection, *Wessex Poems*, and the verse drama, *The Dynasts*). In fact, he considered himself a poet rather than a novelist, even though he is now perhaps more famous for his novels.

Victorian Poets

When the Romantic poet William Wordsworth died in 1850, Alfred Tennyson (1809–1892) was made Poet Laureate, a post he held for most of the Victorian period. A prolific writer, he was popular with his contemporary audience and boasted Queen Victoria among his readers. She made him a baron in 1884, the first English writer to be granted such an honor. T.S. Eliot later described Tennyson as "the great master of metric as well as of melancholia" and it is widely acknowledged that he had a magnificent command of rhyme, meter, and rhythm, and created beautifully musical poetry. Recurrent themes in his work include classical myth, medieval legend, the conflict between religion and science, and nature and domesticity. Typically, though, Tennyson's work concentrates more on conveying sensation and experience, rather than providing comment or criticism.

Among Tennyson's most famous works are *The Lotos-Eaters* and *The Lady of Shalott* (from *Poems*, 1833), *Tithomius, Ulysses, Morte d'Arthur,* and *Locksley Hall* (from *Poems*, 1842), the magnificently elegiac *In Memoriam A.H.H.* (1849), *Maud* (1855), *Enoch Arden* (1864), and *Harold* (a work of dramatic verse, 1876). Fitting his position as the queen's poet, he also wrote patriotic verse such as *The Charge of the Light Brigade* (1854), in which he pays tribute to British soldiers fighting in the Crimean War.

Another prominent poet of the time was Robert Browning (1812–1889), considered the most famous English exponent of the dramatic monologue form in poetry. Born in London, he fled to Italy in 1846 after secretly marrying the poet Elizabeth Barrett in defiance of her father's wishes. In 1853, Browning published his great work, *Men and Women* (1853), consisting of 51 poetic monologues by different narrators. The work is now considered to be one of the most important collections of poetry of the Victorian period, but received little attention at the time. After his return to England in 1861, Browning published *Dramatis Personae* (1864), followed in 1868–1869 by the four-volume blank-verse poem *The Ring and the Book*,

LEFT: THE LADY OF SHALOTT, 1858, By William Maw Egley, Sheffield Galleries and Museums Trust, UK

This painting depicts Tennyson's poem of the same name. It shows the Lady having turned from her work and her mirror to gaze on Lancelot's actual form, thus triggering her death.

TOP: ALFRED LORD TENNYSON

RIGHT: ROBERT BROWNING, Woodbury, UK

which cemented his reputation. Common themes in Browning's poetry include the nature and purpose of art, the artist's responsibility for exerting moral judgment over his subjects, the grotesque, the Middle Ages and Renaissance Europe, and time unfulfilled.

The medieval and Renaissance periods were of particular fascination to many artists and writers in England during the second half of the 19th century. In furtherance of this enthusiasm, the poet, painter, and translator Dante Gabriel Rossetti (1828–1882)—brother of the poet Christina Rossetti (1830–1894)—founded the Pre-Raphaelite Brotherhood, along with the painters John Everett Millais (1829–1896) and Wiliam Holman Hunt (1827–1910). The Movement, which lasted from 1848 to the early 1920s—and also included William Morris among its members and the art critic John Ruskin among

its supporters—was intended to revitalize art and literature by harking back to the period prior to Raphael (particularly the medieval period), when less academic observation and a more earthy approach facilitated better, more authentic creativity.

The poet Algernon Charles Swinburne (1837–1909) was a close friend of Rossetti and the Pre-Raphaelites. He is often viewed as a decadent poet, whose controversial themes include irreligion, sadomasochism, a desire to die, and lesbianism. The medieval is also a common subject. His personal life was troubled, marred by alcoholism and mental breakdown. His collections include *Atalanta in Calydon* (1865), *Poems and Ballads I, II,* and *III* (1866, 1878, and 1889) and *A Century of Roundels* (1883), dedicated to Christina Rossetti, in which he showcases a new verse form, the roundel, similar to the French rondeau.

conviction for gross indecency and subsequent imprisonment for hard labor from 1895 to 1897. The trial scandalized Victorian society, and fascinated generations to come—Wilde's arrest was later immortalized by the poet John Betjeman. On his release, Wilde fled to France, where he wrote the ballad *The Ballad of Reading Gaol* (1898).

The other most famous playwright of the late 19th and early 20th centuries was George Bernard Shaw (1856–1950), who had much in common with Wilde. Both were born in Ireland but soon left Ireland to settle in England. Both wrote plays known for their witty dialogue. However, Shaw is also remembered for dealing with social problems of the day in his plays. A socialist spokesman who protested against all social evils, Shaw was particularly angered by the exploitation of the working class and condemned it vociferously. He added a distinct vein of

Drama

In drama, meanwhile, the most eminent playwright of the era was Oscar Wilde (1854–1900). Born in Dublin, Ireland, and the son of a Peer, Wilde is best known for his witty satirical plays as well as the novel *The Picture of Dorian Gray* (1891). The latter draws upon the decadent esthetic of Huysmans, Aubrey Beardsley, and others, as well as the tradition of Gothic horror in telling the story of a man who sells his soul for his vanity and the gift of eternal beauty.

In the period that followed, Wilde wrote his most successful plays: *Lady Windermere's Fan* (1892), *A Woman of No Importance* (1893), *An Ideal Husband* (1895), and *The Importance of Being Earnest* (1895). His flourishing career and his famously decadent lifestyle were put on hold, however, after a homosexual affair with Lord Arthur Douglas led to his

comedy to his plays to present their hard-hitting messages in a light and effective way.

Shaw's earliest plays were appropriately called *Plays Pleasant and Unpleasant* (1898). Among these, *Widower's Houses* and *Mrs. Warren's Profession* severely attack social hypocrisy, while *Arms and the Man* and *The Man of Destiny* are milder. In his later plays, discussion sometimes envelops the plot, as in *Back to Methuselah* (1921), but he also wrote his masterpiece *Saint Joan* (1923) in this period. Other important plays by Shaw are *Caesar and Cleopatra* (1901), *Major Barbara* (1905), *The Doctor's Dilemma* (1906), *Androcles and the Lion* (1912), and *Pygmalion* (1912).

RUSSIA

In Russia, in the second half of the 19th century, two figures stood out above all others in the field of prose: Count Leo Tolstoy (1828–1910) and Fyodor Dostoyevsky (1821–1881). Tolstoy's most famous works, *War and Peace* and *Anna Karenina*, are often held as constituting the highest expression of realism, depicting the broad sweep as well as the minute detail of 19th-century Russian life. Dostoyevsky, on the other hand, created characters that were more often symbolic of particular ideas, and as such is sometimes considered (by the great Russian critic Alexander Blok, for example) as one of the forerunners of literary symbolism. Dostoyevsky's novels are also more limited in timeframe than Tolstoy's and so their characters are less apt to be dwarfed by the immensity of time and history. This again is a departure from the realist vision, enabling Dostoyevsky to embody his characters with spiritual values, sometimes even prefiguring existentialism.

Tolstoy and Dostoyevsky are also often seen as representing old and new approaches to characterization. The literary theorist Mikhail Bakhtin (1895–1975) and the Russian Formalist school

ANNA KARENINA

Anna Karenina, the tragic story of a fashionable married woman, is hailed as a greater achievement of tragedy and of the novel form than *War and Peace* had been the decade before.

of criticism saw in Dostoyevsky a new "polyphonic" approach to fiction. Here, characters have their own independent voices and the author makes no attempt to homogenize them or privilege one point of view over the other. As Bakhtin notably explained, "Dostoyevsky brings into being not voiceless slaves...but free people, capable of standing alongside their creator, capable of not agreeing with him and even of rebelling against him." Tolstoy, by contrast, assumes the monophonic approach, where the general outlook is that of the author and the characters' points of view are arranged to articulate his vision.

While Dostoyevsky's novels may now have critically eclipsed Tolstoy's, in their own time however, it was Tolstoy who enjoyed the greater success. His reputation was first established with three autobiographical novels, *Childhood*, *Boyhood*, and *Youth* (1852–1856), which depict a rich landowner's son coming to terms with the differences between himself and his peasants. These social and political questions continued to be central to his search for moral purpose and a rational justification for his life. Also during this period, Tolstoy served in the Russian army. His experiences during the Crimean War found expression in

Sevastapol Sketches (1855), and were later to serve him well for his realistic portrayal of the horrors of war in his mature work.

His first great work, *War and Peace* (published serially 1865–1869), is often considered one of the greatest novels ever written. Gustave Flaubert, the master of realist fiction, compared Tolstoy to Shakespeare on reading it for the first time. This epic story features 580 characters, and encompasses Napoleon's headquarters, Emperor Alexander I's court, and the battlefields of Austerlitz and Borodino. The novel embodies Tolstoy's theory of history—in which even actors of the caliber of Napoleon and Alexander are ultimately insignifican—and also espouses some of his lesser-profound beliefs, e.g. that humans have no free will, but need to believe that they do. It is, however, Tolstoy's ability to conjure up a whole world so vividly and believably that keeps readers enthralled to the very end.

Interestingly, Tolstoy considered *War and Peace* as a prose epic rather than a novel, and it was his second great work, *Anna Karenina* (published serially 1873–1877), that he considered to be his first true novel. This is the story of an aristocratic woman who pursues an adulterous affair and becomes a victim of society's rigid codes and hypocrisy. It is also the parallel story of Konstantin Levin, a landowner (much like Tolstoy), who works alongside the peasants in the fields and seeks to reform the social order. Tolstoy's final novel, *Resurrection*, was published in 1899. It recounts the story of a nobleman, Neklyudov, who seeks redemption for a sin committed years earlier, when a brief affair with a maid resulted in her losing her job and ending up in prostitution. The book aimed to expose the injustices of the legal system and the hyprocrisy of the Orthodox church. Unsurprisingly, Tolstoy's later Christian anarchist views and his literal interpretation of the ethical teachings of Jesus (not to mention his advocation of many communist ideas) brought him into conflict with the church. He was finally excommunicated in 1901, and when he died, a few years later, in 1910, he was buried in a simple peasant's grave near his country estate.

LEO TOLSTOY

The Russian novelist was tormented with doubts about self-worth and regret over past actions in his last years.

Dostoyevsky's life and work followed a very different course. While he achieved early success with the short novel *Poor Folk* (1845), any prospects he may have had evaporated when he was arrested and imprisoned in 1849 for his membership in a liberal intellectual group, the Petrashevsky Circle. Following the revolutions in Europe in 1848, Tsar Nicholas I took action against any political organization that he thought could threaten the status quo in Russia. Dostoyevsky was initially given the death sentence, though this was then commuted to four years of exile with hard labor at a prison camp in Siberia. Moreover, on his release in 1854, Dostoyevsky was then required to serve in the Siberian Regiment, which he did for a period of five years.

The effects of his experiences in prison and in the army were to strengthen his Christian faith and to undermine his trust in the value of "Western" ideas—in particular, socialism and nihilism. Dostoyevsky's post-prison fiction revolved around the belief that utopias and positivist ideas were unrealizable. Instead, his complex stories were populated by angst-ridden characters who agonized over existential themes of spiritual regeneration through suffering, mental breakdown, suicide, and psychological conflict caused by the clash of traditional Russian culture with modern Western philosophies.

Among Dostoyevsky's most famous works are *Notes from Underground* (1864), often held as a precursor of philosophical existentialism, and *Crime and Punishment*, published serially in 1866. The latter introduced to literature the character of Raskolnikov, a rebellious intellectual who murders a pawnbroker for the dual purpose of solving his own financial difficulties and ridding humanity of an evil parasite. A few years later came *The Idiot* (1869), the story of the Christ-like Prince Myshkin, who vies with the unscrupulous Rogozhin for the hand of the beautiful Nastasya. The story ends in tragedy as Myshkin's "idiotically" good intentions

PORTRAIT OF FYODOR DOSTOYEVSKY, 1872, By Vasily Perov, Oil on canvas, Tretyakov Gallery, Moscow, Russia

prove powerless against society's norms in averting disaster. Perhaps Dostoyevsky's greatest work, though, is *The Brothers Karamazov* (1880). This novel recounts the murder of a father and the varying degrees of culpability each son bears for the killing. It also manages to bind in many of the spiritual and moral struggles of the day, providing a ready case study for philosophers and psychologists on the subjects of faith and doubt, rationality, and free will.

Whereas Tolstoy and Dostoyevsky both reacted decisively against Western cultural influences in Russia, the novelist and playwright Ivan Turgenev (1818–1883) was the epitome of the progressive Westernizer. As a consequence, despite his vocal admiration for his two contemporaries, Turgenev was mercilessly satirized by Dostoyevsky in his novel *The Devils* (1872) and was even challenged to a duel by Tolstoy. Nevertheless, by virtue of his most famous novel, *Fathers and Sons* (1861), and his many short stories, he is recognized as one of the greatest Russian writers.

Turgenev's cosmopolitanism was, in fact, not due to any dislike of his mother country. He had studied at the University of Berlin and admired many of the European ideals of the Enlightenment, but he was also passionate about Russia, despite having fallen foul of its censors. On one occasion, he was even imprisoned and then exiled to the country for two years for the slightest of infringements. He was also drawn away from Russia

IVAN TURGENEV,
Unlike his contemporaries Dostoyevsky and Tolstoy who wrote about church and religion, Turgenev focused his attention on Russia's movement toward social reform. His works offer realistic portrayals of the Russian peasantry and insightful studies of the Russian intelligentsia who were leading the country into a new age.

by his long affair with the opera singer Pauline Viardot.

Turgenev achieved his first literary success with *A Sportsman's Notebook* (1852), a collection of short stories based on rural life on his mother's country estate. The book is believed to have played a part in persuading the public in favor of the abolition of serfdom in 1861. Following the accession of Alexander II in 1855 and a relaxation of the censors' activities, other notable works followed, including the novel *On the Eve* (1859) about a Bulgarian revolutionary, Insarov, and the novella *First Love* (1860) about the tangled love affairs of youth. Turgenev's finest work, however, is the novel *Fathers and Sons* (1862), concerning the character of Bazarov, whose story demonstrates without parallel the predicament of the would-be reformer in Russia. Critics at the time were divided as to whether Bazarov constituted a glorification or a parody of the "new men" of the 1860s.

Another notable exponent of shorter fiction was Anton Chekhov (1860–1904). Chekhov had initially begun writing short stories to pay his way through medical school and support his family, after his father's bankruptcy. However, as his confidence grew, he became a master at recording apparently trivial events, and with a mixture of humor and pathos transforming them into some of the greatest realist fiction ever written. Through stories such as *Rothschild's Violin* or *The Lady with the Lapdog*, he is also credited with having transformed the short story form, and foreshadowed

CHEKHOV BROTHERS

Here Anton Pavlovich Chekhov, aged 20, is seen with his brother, the painter N.P. Chekhov.

CHEKHOV'S *THREE SISTERS,* Performed by Moscow Arts Theater, 1940

This was the first play that Chekhov wrote specifically for the Moscow Art Theater, having experienced success in his collaboration on *The Seagull* and *Uncle Vanya*.

modernist writers in pioneering a version of the stream-of-consciousness technique, while eschewing conventional plot closure.

GERMANY

In German-speaking Europe, the period between the end of the Napoleonic Wars and the failed March 1848 revolution in the German Confederation is often referred to as the *Vormärz*, or pre-March era. It was a period characterized by attempts by the state to curb the ideals of the Enlightenment and the liberal disposition of the rising middle classes—a process begun in 1819 with Metternich's Carlsbad Decrees, which introduced censorship of the press. Some writers—including those often classed as Biedermeier—responded to the situation by addressing non-political subjects in their works. Others—notably those associated with the *Junges Deutschland* (Young Germany) movement—adopted a more activist stance, and concerned themselves with issues such as human rights, political freedom, and social justice.

The term Biedermeier derives from the pseudonym used by Adolf Kussmaul (1822–1902) and Ludwig Eichrodt (1827–1892) in poems satirizing the depoliticized literature of earlier 19th-century bourgeois culture. The label came to be applied to architecture and the decorative arts as well as literature, and denoted a taste and sensibility that typified the new urban middle class. Whereas Romantic literature—or at least its production—had tended to be associated with the nobility (often writing about idealized peasants), Biedermeier literature was usually by and for the emerging commercial and professional classes. In terms of subject matter, the new writing usually featured with non-political themes; historical fiction and scenes of rural life were popular.

Among the best writers associated with the Biedermeier culture were the poets Annette von Droste-Hülshoff (1797–1848) and Eduard Mörike (1804–1875). The former achieved success with poems about her native Westphalian landscape and on religious themes. She is also notable for

ANNETTE VON DROSTE-HÜLSHOFF

As a woman of the 19th century, Annette von Droste-Hülshoff had problems being accepted as a serious poet and author. Her first book (1838) met with disrespect and indifference; merely 74 copies were sold. Although later editions of her work sold better, at the time of her death she was still virtually unknown. Today Annette von Droste-Hülshoff is regarded as the most significant poet of her era.

EDUARD MÖRIKE

Primarily a lyric poet, Mörike also produced prose works that are significant in their contribution to modern German narrative. His poetry marks the transition in lyric poetry from the classical and romantic tradition around 1800 to the flourishing of modernist lyric around 1900. His novel *Maler Nolten* (1832) forms a link in the shaping of the German *Bildungsroman*.

her novella, *Die Judenbuche* (*The Jew's Beech*, 1842), which foreshadows realist literature in its explanation of a murder by reference to the social context and the perpetrator's psychology. Eduard Mörike's works included *Lieder* (songs), idylls, and sonnets, as well as folk tales, many written in simple, unelevated language, and leavened with his Swabian humor. He also wrote *Maler Nolten* (*The Painter Nolten*, 1832)––a *Bildungsroman* (novelistic genre centering on a person's formative experiences) that achieved considerable popular success)—and a witty novella, *Mozart auf der Reise nach Prag* (*Mozart on the way to Prague*, 1856).

The *Junges Deutschland* movement was, by contrast, a more confrontational affair. Those associated with it were united by a progressive outlook and a belief in political and social engagement. Its proponents—including Ludwig Börne (1786–1837), Georg Büchner (1813–1837), Karl Gutzkow (1811–1878), and Heinrich Heine (1797–1856))—also, in varying degrees, reacted against the introspection and otherworldiness of Romanticism in their work. Heine, for example, in addition to his Romantic lyric poetry on themes such as death, love, and folk legends, produced reams of newspaper articles, literary reportage, and satire. He made himself so unpopular with the authorities in Germany that publication of his works was banned and he was forced to move to Paris to avoid risk of arrest. Georg Büchner's course was even more dramatic. After organizing a secret society and writing a revolutionary pamphlet, he had to flee into exile (the pamphlet's publisher was less fortunate and died in prison after having been extensively tortured). Using Strasbourg as a base, he produced his famous plays, *Dantons Tod* (*Danton's Death*, 1835), a work of psychological realism on the theme of the French

Revolution; *Leonce and Lena* (1836), a satire on the aristocracy; and the unfinished *Woyzeck* (reworked for publication in 1879), a tragedy about the moral predicament of a working-class man exploited by his social superiors. This last work would later have a significant influence on naturalistic and expressionistic writers.

Many of the achievements and concerns of the progressive *Vormärz* writers were taken forward by Theodor Fontane (1819–98), who adapted many of the developments in French fiction to the depiction and criticism of contemporary Germany. After serving as an apprentice and an apothecary, and later joining the army, he took up writing full time from 1849, working as a journalist (with periods as a foreign correspondent in England and later covering Prussia's wars with its neighbors). He published poetry and books about his foreign travels in the 1850s and 1860s, but it was not until the late 1870s that he turned his attention to the novels for which he would be remembered. In works such as *L'Adultera* (*The Woman Taken in Adultery*, 1882), *Cécile* (1887), *Frau Jenny Treibel* (1893) and, most notably, *Effi Briest* (1895), Fontane combined subtle characterization with social observation.

Important novelists from elsewhere in the German-speaking world include the Swiss writer Gottfried Keller (1819–1890), who is best known for *Der grüne Heinrich* (*Green Henry*, 1854–1855), a *Bildungsroman*, inspired by his own early life and training as a fine artist. Also hailing from Zürich was the poet and novelist Conrad Ferdinand Meyer (1825–1898), who is noted for novellas such as *Der Heilige* (*The Saint*, 1879) that draw on medieval and Renaissance history. Another master of the novella was Theodor Storm (1817–1888), who found particular acclaim with *Immensee* (1852) and *Der Schimmelreiter* (translated either as *Rider of the White Horse* or *The Dykemaster*, 1888), both taking inspiration from the bleak North Sea Plain of his native Schleswig-Holstein (which Germany annexed from Denmark in 1864). Storm also produced poetry, which was strongly influenced by the works of Mörike.

ITALY

In Italy, too, by the second half of the 19th century, Romanticism began to cede ground to other literary creeds. After 1850, a new classicism gained currency, with Giosuè Carducci (1835–

FAR LEFT: THEODOR FONTANE

Fontane, initially a journalist, turned to writing in his later life. His *Before the Storm* (1878) is considered a masterpiece of historical fiction. Novels such as *Effi Briest* (1895) marked Fontane as a master of modern realistic fiction. He was famous for his distinct conversational style, his insightful societal portraits, and non-judgmental stance towards social transgression.

LEFT: GIOSUÈ CARDUCCI

Regarded as the unofficial national poet of modern Italy, Carducci was the first Italian to win the Nobel Prize in Literature (in 1906). Carducci's later poetry is his finest. His collections *Rime Nuove* (*New Rhymes*) and *Odi Barbare* (*Barbarian Odes*) contain his greatest works.

ANNA MAGNANI IN *LA LOUVE*, By Giovanni Verga, Production by Franco Zeffirelli, June 1965, Théâtre of Nations, Paris, France

the *Verismo* movement. Although inspired by French realism, it differed crucially in that it took a deeply pessimistic view of any scientific or social value to be derived from realist literature. Instead, Capuana and Verga emphasized the impersonality of their works, taking pains to eliminate any trace of authorial opinion or moral message. The value of the project lay in its documentation of social conditions—which had the effect of highlighting disparities in standards of living between the industrializing north and the neglected south of the newly unified country.

Luigi Capuana was a novelist, playwright, poet, and critic. In 1860, at the age of 21, he abandoned his law studies and joined Garibaldi's *Risorgimento* movement as secretary of the revolutionary committee in his hometown, Mineo, in the Sicilian province of Catania. A year later, these experiences bore fruit in his first literary success—the verse drama *Garibaldi*. In 1864 he moved to Florence, where he mixed in literary circles, published essays, worked as a theater critic, and developed his skills as a novelist. On his return to Sicily four years later, he took up a position as a school inspector (later becoming a town councilor and mayor) and continued to produce plays, novels, poems (in Sicilian), and journalistic essays. The works for which he is best known today are the novels *Giacinta* (dedicated to Zola and published in 1879) and *Il Marchese di Roccaverdina* (1901).

Giovanni Verga's career mirrored Capuana's in many ways. He was also born in Catania, just a year later than Capuana. He also abandoned his law studies to become a writer, joined Garibaldi's movement, and settled in Florence in the late 1860s. In 1872, however, Verga moved to Milan, and concentrated on honing his distinctive narrative voice, combining literary language with style and idiom from everyday speech, and developing his skills of characterization. He achieved lasting fame with the short story collection *Vita dei Campi* (*Life in the Fields*, 1880), which included many stories set in rural Sicily,

1907) as one of its chief exponents. Sometimes considered modern Italy's national poet, Carducci was also a critic, historian, and translator (having done some of the works of Goethe and Heine into Italian). He was, nevertheless, fiercely critical of Romanticism, and instead advocated resurrecting Italy's classical heritage—both its meters and its spirit—for the purpose of attacking the church, and, at times, the monarchy as well. His most famous poem is the *Hymn to Satan*, composed in 1863, which stoked revolutionary zeal against papal political authority. His reputation was sealed by his later collections, *Rime Nuove* (*New Rhymes*, 1861–1867) and *Odi Barbare* (*Barbarian Odes*, 1873–1889). Other important poets in Carducci's mold were Guido Mazzoni (1859-1943) and Giovanni Marradi (1852-1922).

Realist literature also flourished in Italy in the wake of Romanticism. Its main exponents were Giovanni Verga (1840–1922) and Luigi Capuana (1839–1915), who wrote a manifesto for the most notable of which is *Cavalleria Rusticana*. This story was later adapted as a libretto for the opera of the same name by Pietro Mascagni. The successful premiere of the work in 1890 spawned a new tradition of post-Romantic Italian opera, which looked to the naturalism of Zola and Ibsen, as well as Verga and his imitators, for inspiration in depicting the sordid and sometimes violent realities of everyday life. The most famous composers in this vein are Ruggero Leoncavallo (1857–1919), Umberto Giordano (1867–1948), and Giacomo Puccini (1858–1924)—whose *Tosca* and *La Bohéme* are most clearly in the *Verismo* tradition.

After his success in the short story genre, Verga himself achieved even greater success with two novels (the only ones completed out of a projected series of five): *I Malavoglia* (1881) and *Mastro-Don Gesualdo* (1889), which again documented contemporary social conditions. The first of these was later, in 1923, translated into English—along with Verga's most important short stories—by D.H. Lawrence. Verga moved back to his native Sicily in 1894, but produced no other major works before his death in 1922.

EASTERN EUROPE

In Poland, writers' adherence to Romanticism waned as a pragmatic reaction to political realities, following the disastrous January Uprising in 1863 in the Russian-controlled portion of the country. The uprising had taken inspiration, in part, from the successes of Garibaldi in Italy, but in the face of vastly superior numbers and equipment, the Polish revolt failed to gain any major victories. Severe reprisals followed, with public executions, and deportation of up to 70,000 people to Siberia. Any participation granted the Polish people in their own government ended and Russian became the country's official language. In response to this situation, many Poles abandoned the idea of armed insurrection in favor of "organic work." This was a movement—in many ways successful—initiated by positivist intellectuals to counter the pressures of Russification (and Germanization in the Prussian-controlled sector of the country) through economic and cultural self-improvement. The Polish nation's energies were now channeled into the education of the masses, modernization, and economic development in place of vain armed struggle.

POLISH UPRISING AGAINST RUSSIA

The January Uprising was a revolt in the former Polish-Lithuanian Commonwealth (present-day Poland, Lithuania, Belarus, Latvia, parts of Ukraine, western Russia) against the Russian Empire. It began on 22 January 1863 and lasted until all insurgents were captured in 1865. The uprising began as a spontaneous protest by young Poles against conscription into the Russian Army, and was soon joined by high-ranking Lithuanian officers and various politicians. The insurrectionists, severely outnumbered and lacking serious outside support, were forced to resort to guerrilla warfare tactics. They failed to win any major military victories or capture any major cities or fortresses. But they did manage to blunt the effect of the Tsar's abolition of serfdom in the Russian partition.

JAN NERUDA

Poet, writer, and journalist, Jan Neruda is recognized as one of the outstanding figures of 19th century Czech literature. He is best known for his masterpiece *Tales of Little Quarter* (1878), which comprises stories about the loves, lives, and small failures of petty bourgeois inhabitants of Mala Strana.

As a new positivist outlook replaced the Romantic conception of nationalism, so prose came to predominate over poetry. New periodicals such as *Tygodnik Ilustrowany* (*Illustrated Weekly*, founded in 1859) found a ready market with the emerging urban middle classes. One of the most noted journalists writing in these publications—and a leading advocate of "organic work"—was Bolesław Prus (1847–1912). As a teenager, he had fought in the 1863 Uprising and suffered serious injuries and then imprisonment. Having turned to writing as a means to address his nation's problems, he became a leading exponent of Polish realist fiction, producing novels such as *The Doll* (1890), which portrays romantic idealism frustrated by the inertia of bourgeois Polish society within the closely observed setting of Warsaw.

In Bohemia and Hungary too, a reawakened sense of nationhood led to failed attempts to gain autonomy from their overlords (in this case, the Habsburgs). Revolutions took place in both countries in 1848: in Bohemia, the uprising was contained, but in Hungary, it led to the War of Independence, which lasted until 1851. The repression that followed, though severe, was fortunately not on the scale of the mass deportations organized by the Russians in Poland, and indeed, as the power of the Habsburg Empire declined, in subsequent years political concessions were made. In 1861, elections were held once again for a new Bohemian Diet (or parliament), and in 1867, a year after Austria's defeat in the Austro-Prussian War, the famous Austro-Hungarian Compromise was reached with Hungarian politicians. This accorded the Hungarian half of the empire equal legal status to the Austrian half, with the emperor becoming a dual monarch and retaining authority over the armed forces and foreign policy. In both Bohemia and Hungary the reforms heralded periods of industrialization, increasing prosperity, and a revitalization of romantic nationalism.

In Bohemia, the most celebrated representative of the age was the journalist, short story writer, and poet Jan Neruda (1834–1891). He was a leading member of the May School, a group of writers that took its name from Karel Mácha's (1810–1836) poem *Máj* (1836)—a Romantic work about the

SÁNDOR PETÖFI

Petöfi (1823-1849) was the author of exquisite Hungarian lyrics. He composed the national poem *Talpra Magyar* (1848), and several epics, including *Janos Vitez* (1845). Active in the Hungarian revolution of 1848-1849, he was recognized as Hungary's national poet with his patriotic songs. Petöfi's poetry served as inspiration to the patriots of the revolution, in which he was killed.

execution of an outlaw, which dealt with themes of alienation, individualism, and man's relationship with Nature. The writers of the May School—including the novelist Karolína Svetlá (1830–1899) and the journalist and poet Vítezslav Hálek (1835-1874)—were united by their resolve to achieve a new status for Czech culture by breaking away from the provincialism of the past, embracing themes of universal significance, and bringing literature up to date with the latest developments elsewhere in Europe. In doing so, the May School came to dominate Czech literature in the 1860s and 1870s. Neruda's contribution took the form of a stream of influential essays, poems in everyday Czech language that promoted the renewed patriotism, and, his most famous work, a collection of short stories called *Tales of the Little Quarter* (1877). This last pioneered realism in Czech literature, took the reader on a tour of the streets, presenting local characters, and human follies of Neruda's native district in Prague.

In Hungarian literature too, a romantic conception of national identity was adapted to a growing market for prose—in the form of both novels and periodicals—and gradually came under the influence of foreign realist writers. The novelist Mór Jókai (1825–1904) was perhaps the most famous writer of the period and also participated in many of the great events of the time. He had fought in the War of Independence and only narrowly escaped imprisonment thereafter; following the settlement of 1867, he was to serve as a member of parliament for over 20 years. His writing career originally took inspiration from Victor Hugo, though his more than 100 volumes of fiction showed far more partiality to melodrama and escapism than those of his model. Nevertheless, with novels such as *A Hungarian Nabob*

(1853–1854) and *The Man with the Golden Touch* (1873), he was highly successful in developing a popular market for Hungarian language literature and sometimes even influencing public opinion on important social and political questions.

SCANDINAVIA

While in 1860 Scandinavia was still on the cultural fringes of Europe, by the 1890s—just 30 years later—writers such as Henrik Ibsen and Bjørnstjerne Bjørnson in Norway, and August Strindberg in Sweden, were influencing the course of literature

LEFT: IBSEN'S *DOLL'S HOUSE*

A Doll's House (1879) was the second in a series of realist plays by Ibsen, the first being *The Pillars of Society* (1877). Charged with the fever of the 1848 European revolutions, *A Doll's House* represented a new modern perspective in literature that challenged the romantic tradition.

in the rest of Europe. This cultural bloom was also experienced in the fields of music—with Edvard Grieg and Jean Sibelius —and the visual arts—most notably with Edvard Munch and Gustav Vigeland.

The Industrial Revolution and the herewith associated economic growth, urbanization, emerging middle classes, and social problems came late to the Scandinavian countries. Intellectually too, Scandinavia was a late developer, and the influence of philosophies such as liberalism, utilitarianism, positivism, socialism, and anarchism was felt no earlier than the 1870s. While political and social development had taken decades to unfold elsewhere in Europe, in Scandinavia the

PORTRAIT OF BJØRNSTJERNE BJØRNSON

period of catching up was short and hectic. In literature too, the progression from folk-inspired Romanticism to Naturalism at the end of 19th century was concentrated and intense; it is often referred to as "The Modern Breakthrough."

One of the leading promoters of realism and naturalism in Scandinavia was the Danish scholar Georg Brandes (1842–1927), whose critical writings played a central role in cultural thinking from the 1870s onward. He was instrumental in bringing the works of foreign writers, from Hugo to Nietzsche (and even Disraeli), to the attention of Scandinavian writers. In addition, his academic reputation abroad was such that his studies of Scandinavian writers introduced foreign readers to literary developments at home. Many writers and artists, however, spent extended periods overseas, establishing colonies of writers and artists in Paris, Berlin, and Rome. Ibsen himself was away for 27 years, mostly in Germany and Italy, before returning to Norway as a famous old man. In this way, continental literary techniques, styles, and preoccupations were combined with Scandinavian settings and landscapes in revitalized national literatures.

In Norway, "The Great Four" writers—Bjørnstjerne Bjørnson, Henrik Ibsen, Alexander Kielland, and Jonas Lie—are often considered the greatest literary representatives of the period. After Ibsen, it is perhaps the novelist, poet, playwright, and journalist Bjørnstjerne Bjørnson (1832–1920) who is most widely read today. In his own time, his nationalist, independentist political stance vis-à-vis the union with Sweden made him a popular spokesman for Norwegian language. He remained politically active throughout his life, agitating for social justice, gender equality, and the universal right to vote. His most famous early novels, *Synnøve Solbakken* (1857) and *En glad Gut* (*A Happy Boy*, 1860), are written in a simple everyday language, portraying rural peasant life in the new realist manner. He also wrote what is considered Norway's first realist drama, *En fallit* (*A Bankruptcy*

DON JUAN, By Alexander Pushkin, Actor Konstantin Stanislavski as Don Juan, 1889.

DRAMA

Before the advent of realism, theater in the 19th century had consisted largely of melodramas and farces, each with their limited range of stock characters. Realist drama is often held to have begun with the works of Henrik Ibsen (1828–1906), but the tradition of psychological realist theater in Russia—exemplified by the plays by Alexandr Ostrovsky, Aleksey Pisemsky, Tolstoy, and Turgenev—was also influential. The director and theorist, Konstantin Stanislavsky (1863–1938) was also instrumental in developing and disseminating new ideas and techniques.

The aim of realist theater was to replace the stylized and often sentimental repertory that had gone before with portrayals of life that audiences could recognize from their own experiences. Objectivity and the avoidance of artifice were central to the movement, with the "fourth wall" convention (a term coined by Denis Diderot, 1713–1784, to denote the boundary between actors and audience) strictly followed. Actors' showing their awareness of the audience (or "breaking the fourth wall") through asides or soliloquies or removing the "mask" of character was forbidden. Stage sets were realistic and everyday language reinforced the notion that audiences were observing a reflection of themselves. The subject matter of plays was highly psychological, revealing those morals and emotions that are often not shown in public, and placing them within their social and physical context.

Ibsen's plays also followed their own development within the framework of realist theater. His early play, the philosophical verse-drama *Brand* (1866), shows the influence of the Danish philosopher and theologian Søren Kierkegaard (1813–1855). Its plot consists of a priest who struggles with inertia in the face of doing the right thing. Ibsen followed up the success of this with *Peer Gynt* (1867), about a young man at odds with the norms of bourgeois life. This play—again written in verse—is full of symbolism, drawing heavily on Scandinavian and German folk legend. Both *Brand* and *Peer Gynt* show a clear debt to Romanticism in their poetic visions of lonely heroes in search of the truth.

The second stage of Ibsen's career benefited from the influence of Georg Brandes, who inspired the playwright to develop his work in the direction of realism and naturalism and employ the use of prose rather than verse. Ibsen's first political and social play was *The Pillars of Society* (1877) and it heralded the period of Ibsen's greatest success, yielding works such as *A Doll's House* (1879), *Ghosts* (1881), *An Enemy of the People* (1882), and *The Wild Duck* (1884). Many of the plays of this period

Strindberg is recognized as Sweden's greatest author. While working as a journalist, he wrote the historical drama *Mäster Olof* (1872), which was rejected by the national theater and not produced until 1890. It is now considered the first modern Swedish drama. Strindberg became famous with his novel *The Red Room* (1879), which satirized the Stockholm art world.

MISS JULIE, A 2001 production of Strindberg's play at Vienna's Oesterreich Theater.

followed this up with a satirical short-story, *The New Country* (1882), and a collection of poetry, *Poetry in Verse and Prose* (1883). These works' attacks on the Establishment—including political institutions, bureaucracy, the press, business, the church, and the cultural elite—made Strindberg so unpopular at home that from 1883 to 1889 he chose to live in exile.

Plays from Strindberg's early period—such as *Miss Julie* (1888)—are often compared to Ibsen's. Strindberg continued to evolve, however, abandoning the "science" of naturalist theater in favor of symbolist and expressionist dramas, most notably, *The Dance of Death* (1900), *A Dream Play* (1901), and *The Ghost Sonata* (1907).

The Russian author Anton Chekhov (1860–1904) also was influenced by Ibsen in his plays. His reputation as a playwright rests on four late plays, *The Seagull* (1896), *Uncle Vanya* (1897), *Three Sisters* (1901), and *The Cherry Orchard* (1904), all of which were staged with great success by Stanislavksy's Moscow Art Theater. Chekhov's plays eschew complicated plots and satisfying endings in favor of psychological insight, mood, and even lyricism. They can also be difficult to interpret; the playwright himself was disappointed with many productions of his works, insisting, for example, that his plays were comedies and not tragedies.

deal with the traditional roles of men and women in late 19th-century life. *A Doll's House*, in particular, caused a scandal with its portrayal of a housewife and mother of three small children who leaves her husband and children in the interests of self-realization.

The final stage of Ibsen's career brought the plays *Hedda Gabler* (1890) and *The Master Builder* (1892), in which the emphasis was transferred from criticism of the conventions of society to the study of characters' inner psychological conflicts.

His last plays, especially perhaps *When We Dead Awaken* (1899), also exhibited a move towards naturalism, and even expressionism, maybe as a result of the influence of August Strindberg.

August Strindberg (1849–1912) represents the modern breakthrough in Swedish literature. His naturalistic novel *The Red Room* (1879)—a tale about hypocrisy and corruption—is regarded as the first Swedish modern novel and exhibits the influence of authors such as Charles Dickens and Mark Twain. Strindberg or *An Admission of Failure*, 1875). Seven years before his death in 1910, he was awarded the Nobel Prize for literature.

Besides The Great Four, Amalie Skram (1846–1905) holds a high reputation in Norwegian literature. A controversial writer in her time, she became known as a feminist writer for novels that explore themes such as female sexuality. However, her reputation has endured as one of the foremost Norwegian naturalist authors. Chief among her works is the tetralogy of novels, *The People of Hellemyr* (published between 1887 and 1898), which charts the fortunes of a family over several generations. Also important are her four novels about the institution of marriage: *Constance Ring* (1885), *Lucie* (1888), *Mrs Ines* (1891), and *Betrayed* (1892). These debate the sexually subservient status of women in marriage and were considered highly provocative when first published.

In Sweden, the breakthrough of realism arrived with Strindberg's satirical novel *Röda Rummet* (1879). Johan August Strindberg (1849–1912) dominated Swedish literature for the next 30 years, though other writers worthy of mention include the poet Ola Hansson (1860–1925) and the novelist Selma Lagerlöf (1858–1940).

HENRIK PONTOPPIDAN

The Danish novelist's realistic and pessimistic novels depicted the social evils and the miserable situation of the peasant proletariat of his country. His major novels include the semi-autobiographical *Lucky Peter* and the five-volume cycle *The Realm of the Dead*. He shared the 1917 Nobel Prize for Literature with Karl Gjellerup.

AMALIE SKRAM

The Norwegian author and feminist spoke for women's rights through her naturalist writings. Skram's stand against repression of women in marriage and family made her a highly controversial author, and she was eventually forced to abandon Norway for Denmark as her literary homeland. Skram was also known for her studies of contemporary bourgeois life. Her famous works include *Constance Ring*, *Lucie*, and *The People of Hellemyr*.

19TH-CENTURY BOSTON ACADEMICIANS

The engraving depicts a group portrait of
Boston authors and intellectuals. Left to
right, standing: Author Oliver Wendell Holmes
(1809–1894), diplomat James Russell Lowell
(1819–1891), naturalist Louis Agassiz (1807–
1873). Left to right, seated: Poet and essayist
John Greenleaf Whittier (1807–1892), poet and
essayist Ralph Waldo Emerson (1803–1882),
historian John Lothrop Motley (1814–1877),
author Nathaniel Hawthorne (1804–1864), and
poet Henry Wadsworth Longfellow (1807–1882).

The most significant Danish writers of the period
included Herman Bang, Holger Drachmann, Jens
Peter Jacobsen, and Henrik Pontoppidan. Herman Bang
(1857–1912) was one of the first novelists in Scandinavia
to write about the neurotic life of modern cities. The
novel *Stuk* (*Stucco*, 1887) uses the budding modernization
of Copenhagen, with its shallow capitalism and social
flux, as the background for the inexplicable demise of a
young man's love affair. Also of particular importance
is Holger Drachmann (1846–1908), who adapted the
naturalistic ethos to poetry, as well as producing fine
examples in the medium of the short story, especially in
his 1877 collection, *Sange ved Havet; Venezia* (*Songs of the
Sea; Venice*).

AMERICAN LITERATURE

The cultural background of American literature is quite different
from that of Europe. With the United States' declaration of
independence from Great Britain in 1776, a distinctive American
literature came to flourish, built on a unique cultural background
that stretched back to the original settlement of the New World.

America had been founded in its modern form by religious refugees—the "Pilgrim Fathers"—who emigrated from Europe in the 1620s. Their Calvinist Puritanism became one of the formative influences on American culture. Its central tenets included a belief in the inherent evil of man, the salvation of the elect few, predestination, and a general distrust of sexuality, excess, and pleasure together with an emphasis on guilt and orthodoxy. Gradually, of course, strict adherence to Calvinism waned, but its cultural influence nevertheless remained. Other competing creeds also made their mark, not least Evangelical Christianity, the emotional, fervent attitude, which contrasted strongly with the sombre stoicism of Calvinism. Enlightenment ideas also enjoyed wide influence. Its faith that all things were answerable to reason, and that science and rational thought provided the path to a new Utopia generated a new optimism and provided a secular equivalent to the Protestant work ethic—that with hard work, anything can be achieved.

American culture is also indelibly stamped with the mark of individualism. Many people came to the New World to find freedom from oppression, and the concept (if perhaps not always the reality) of the frontier kept this hope alive. As immigrants moved west from their points of arrival in North America, the frontier came to be seen as the fabled place where man lived closest to Nature, and where success or failure depended on skill, courage, and determination rather than social standing or inherited wealth. Unsurprisingly, the values of Romanticism found fertile ground in America. Philosophically, though, America's particular brands of individualism and liberty found notable expression (and criticism) in *Democracy in America* (two volumes, 1835 and 1840) and *The Old Regime and the Revolution* (1856) by the French political historian, Alexis de Tocqueville (1805–1859).

The full implications of the frontier concept found articulation in 1893, in the *Frontier Thesis* of Frederick Jackson Turner (1861–1932), written significantly, only three years after the frontier had officially been declared closed. The Thesis provided a useful explanation as to why American attitudes and politics were so different from European ones. It argued that the more the frontier moved west, the more European characteristics and institutions—established churches, social class, and government interference, for example—were discarded, and the more people became American, democratic, and individualistic. The closing of the frontier prompted much debate about the end of "American Exceptionalism" and about the possibility of transforming North America into an imperial power. In the event, it seems that the frontier spirit has been replaced by the "American Dream," a vaguer—and therefore more resilient—vision of the world where individuals enjoy full liberty and reap the just reward for their efforts.

In literature, many aspects of the American character were crystallized in the famous essay, *Nature* (1836) by Ralph Waldo Emerson (1803–1882). Therein, Emerson, a former minister,

RALPH WALDO EMERSON

Emerson was the chief exponent of the American Transcendentalist Movement. He presented the ideas and values of Transcendentalism in *Nature* (1836), which was a result of at least 10 years of intense study in philosophy, religion, and literature. Almost everything that Emerson wrote afterward was an extension, amplification, or amendment of the ideas he first affirmed in *Nature*.

HENRY DAVID THOREAU

Thoreau is best known for his book *Walden*, a reflection upon simple living in natural surroundings—one of the main principles of Transcendentalism—and his essay *Civil Disobedience,* an argument for civil liberties, or individual resistance to civil government in moral opposition to an unjust state.

Holmes—one of the so-called New England Brahmins (together with the poets Henry Longfellow and James Lowell)—as America's "Intellectual Declaration of Independence."

One of Emerson's most famous followers was the writer and thinker Henry David Thoreau (1817-1862). Thoreau is best known as the writer of *Walden* (1854), a memoir of the years 1845 to 1847, when he lived alone in a cabin he had built on land lent to him by Emerson beside a pond in the woods of Massachusetts. The book celebrates individualism, self-sufficiency, and the simple life that allowed humans to live close to nature without the interference of civilization, modernity, and authority. While *Walden* was essentially a book about withdrawal from society for the purposes of personal spiritual development, Thoreau's later work was about engagement. He was a staunch opponent of the Mexican-American War—which he saw as cynical land-grabbing—and in protest he refused to pay federal taxes, suffering brief imprisonment as a result. He was also a supporter of Native American rights and participated in anti-slavery activities. His radical views on resisting overbearing government found expression in 1849 in an essay that came to be known as *Civil Disobedience* (in pointed opposition to European ideas of civil obedience advocated by Locke, Paley, and others). Thoreau's principles eventually came to influence figures as diverse as Tolstoy, Gandhi, and Martin Luther King.

urged readers to study the natural world for spiritual guidance rather than relying on conventional religious practice. He also championed free will as opposed to predestination and personal conscience against authority. Predictably, the establishment denounced him as an atheist—a view reinforced by Emerson's support for the Unitarian view that Jesus was not a divine being—though his work did inspire a new movement of writers and thinkers who became known as the Transcendentalists. The following year (1837) Emerson made another highly influential statement on American culture, with his speech *The American Scholar* delivered at Harvard. In this, he advocated an American culture, free from European allegiances, and exhorted his fellow writers to achieve a distinctively American writing style. The speech was hailed by Oliver Wendell

Another important New England writer of the period was Nathaniel Hawthorne (1804–1864). His early interest in Transcendentalism gradually gave way to what critics have labelled "Dark Romanticism." This world view is much less positive about the moral character and spiritual aptitude of humankind, sees nature as a potentially malign—even if spiritual—force, and is pessimistic about individuals' capacity for effecting social change. Hawthorne's short stories, such as *The Minister's Black Veil* and *Mudkips of Fire*, exhibit a regression to a more Puritan outlook that sees man as inherently sinful and warns readers against the extremes of individualism. His most famous work is the novel *The Scarlet Letter* (1850), a melodrama about a woman ostracized for committing adultery. Significantly, this was one of the first mass-produced books in America and became a best-seller. Themes such as guilt, pride, and sexual repression struck a chord with American readers of the time.

Hawthorne, in his turn, was the mentor of Herman Melville (1819–1891), who became perhaps the greatest exponent of Dark Romanticism with his novel *Moby Dick* (1851), which he

MOBY DICK

In the given scene from Melville's *Moby Dick*, Captain Ahab and Tashtego sight the White Whale from the top of the foremast.

HUCKLEBERRY FINN

Here Huckleberry is seen holding up a rabbit he has just shot.

HENRY JAMES

Though James was born in America, he lived the majority of his life in Europe, becoming a British citizen in 1915 after the outbreak of World War I. The clash of the innocence and enthusiasm of the New World with the corruption and wisdom of the Old was a common theme in his works, such as *Daisy Miller* (1879), *The Portrait of a Lady* (1881), *The Bostonians* (1886), and *The Ambassadors* (1903).

dedicated to Hawthorne. This highly symbolic work about a whaling vessel's search for the great white whale explores themes of good and evil, humanity and nature, obsession and survival. At the time of publication, however, readers and critics were disappointed by the novel's concern for metaphysical speculation. They had instead been hoping for a rerun of the author's earlier exotic adventures on the high seas. *Moby Dick* was a commercial flop, and Melville's reputation withered, and was only resurrected some 30 years after his obscure death as a minor customs official in New York.

One of the first major American writers not to hail from the East Coast was Mark Twain (1835–1910), who was born in Missouri, a slave state in the Midwest. He developed a brand of realism that was quintessentially American and immensely popular with the reading public. His masterpiece is the novel *Adventures of Huckleberry Finn* (1884), which deals with themes of freedom, racism, and moral conflict with society's values, all set against the backdrop of the Mississippi River before the Civil War (1861–1865). It was the book's style, however, that had the greatest impact on American literature and indeed changed the way the language came to be written. Twain eschewed the conventional literary language in favor of an unadorned, everyday style, and he allowed his characters to speak like real people, using local dialects and accents. His other famous works include *The Adventures of Tom Sawyer* (1876) and *Life on the Mississippi* (1883).

America's values were confronted head-on by novelist and playwright Henry James (1843–1916). Although born in New York, he spent most of his adult years in England, and consequently accumulated ample experience of the differences between Old World and New World attitudes. Novels such as *The American* (1877), *The Portrait of a Lady* (1881), and *The Wings of the Dove* (1902) plunge American characters into European settings where their openness, assertiveness, and even brashness jar with the alluring beauty of a decaying, corrupt, almost feudal civilization.

In the field of poetry too, the 19th century saw a distinctively

EMILY DICKINSON

The American lyric poet experimented with poetic rhythms and rhymes and has been called "the New England mystic." Almost all her poetry was published posthumously. The subjects of Dickinson's poems, expressed in intimate, domestic figures of speech, include love, death, and nature.

American tradition established. The two greatest American poets of the era were strikingly different in temperament and style—though once again, the influence of Emerson and the Transcendentalists can be traced in both. Walt Whitman (1819–1892) came from a humble background and subsequently worked as a typesetter, itinerant schoolteacher, journalist, volunteer-nurse during the Civil War and, in later life, as a government clerk. He is famous as the author of *Leaves of Grass*, which he intended to be an American epic and which has since earned him the accolade of being America's first "poet of democracy" for its inclusion of personages from presidents to prostitutes. The work is also notable for its use of free verse, lines of irregular length, and unusual images and symbols.

Emily Dickinson (1830–1886), by contrast, lived her life in reclusive gentility in small-town Amherst, Massachusetts. She never married, and indeed in later life rarely even left her room, communicating, if at all, by letter. Instead, she seems to have reserved her emotional energy for the 1,800 poems she produced—though these remained private and only a dozen were published during her lifetime. The influence of Transcendentalism is clear, but her writing develops far beyond, exploring themes of death, melancholia, gender, and religion (drawing on New Testament stories in American colloquial language). In technique, her work was ahead of their time, perhaps even proto Modernist, employing idiosyncratic punctuation, capitalization, line lengths, and breaks, making full use of half rhyme and often leaving poems untitled.

DETECTIVE FICTION

The earliest examples of the genre of detective fiction can be traced to early Arabic literature (*The Three Apples*—one of the tales narrated by Scheherazade in the 9th-century collection, *One Thousand and One Nights*) and Chinese literature (such as the 18th-century novel *Di Gong An*, translated into English as *The Celebrated Cases of Judge Dee*). However, the genre's popularity in Western literature arose substantially in the second half of the 19th century.

Edgar Allan Poe's *The Murders in the Rue Morgue* (1841) is generally considered as the first true example of detective fiction. In this, and subsequent stories (*The Mystery of Marie Roget,* 1843, and *The Purloined Letter,* 1844), Poe cultivates the personality of the eccentric C. Auguste Dupin, whose brilliant intuition, logic, and powers of observation lead him through an intricate plot towards discovering the truth behind a mystery. This detective formula has remained more or less constant ever since.

In Great Britain, Charles Dickens took up the genre for one of the sub-plots in his novel *Bleak House* (1853). Inspector Bucket of the Metropolitan Police is charged with investigating the murder of the devious lawyer Tulkinghorn. Initial suspicion falls on Lady Dedlock, who is overcome with

THE MURDERS IN THE RUE MORGUE, By Edgar Allan Poe

This is a short story by Edgar Allan Poe, published in Graham's Magazine in 1841. It has been claimed as the first detective story, in which a ferocious orang-utan commits horrific murders. Poe referred to it as one of his "tales of ratiocination."

SHERLOCK AND MORIARTY, From Holmes' *The Final Problem*, by Sidney Paget, 1893

Here Holmes and Moriarty are seen struggling at the Reichenbach Falls; apparently, both are killed. Though it was intended to the last story about Sherlock Holmes, Doyle brought Holmes back because of tremendous unrelenting pressure from fans.

guilt at a secret love affair, but eventually the real killer, her French maid, Hortense, is "uncovered"—though not before numerous false accusations have led to tragedy.

Wilkie Collins (1824–1889) continued to develop detective fiction where Dickens, his mentor, left off. His *The Woman in White* (1860) is often cited as the first great mystery novel, and *The Moonstone* (1868) firmly established the genre with several of its classic conventions, including the country house robbery, the "inside

job," the bungling local constabulary, the "locked room" murder, and a final twist in the plot. With these novels, Collins achieved considerable commercial success on both sides of the Atlantic. Over the following 20 years he wrote another 15 novels, and despite a gradual decline in quality, he came to be revered as the "grandfather of English detective fiction."

Even Collins's success was eclipsed, however, by Arthur Conan Doyle (1859–1930), whose creation, Sherlock Holmes, has become perhaps the most celebrated fictional detective of all time. His very first mystery, *A Study in Scarlet* (1887), makes mention of Poe's Dupin, and although Holmes refers to him as "a very inferior fellow," the debt to Poe is clear, owing much to his style of analysis, reliance on forensic detail, and understanding of psychology. Alongside Holmes, Conan Doyle perfected the plot device of the detective's less able foil—"here in the person of Dr Watson"—who provides an excuse for explaining the intricacies of the mystery for the benefit of the reader.

In continuation of Conan Doyle's Sherlock Holmes stories, notable successes in the genre included the Father Brown stories of G.K. Chesterton (1874–1936), and *Trent's Last Case* (1913) by E.C. Bentley (1875–1956). These ushered in the so-called "Golden Age" of the genre in the 1920s and 1930s, during which period the genre came to be dominated by four so-called "Queens of Crime": Margery Allingham (1904–1966) and her Albert Campion stories, Agatha Christie (1890–1976) with the Miss Marple and Hercule Poirot mysteries, Ngaio Marsh (1895–1982) and the Roderick Alleyn stories, and Dorothy Sayers (1893–1957) with the Lord Peter Wimsey series.

At this time, efforts began to codify the conventions and best practice in the genre. Notable among these was the *Decalogue* (1929) of ten commandments

THE A.B.C. MURDERS, By Agatha Christie

The book—featuring Hercule Poirot, Arthur Hastings, and Chief Inspector Japp—employs a combination of first and third-person narrative. Christie had previously experimented with this approach (famously pioneered by Charles Dickens in *Bleak House*) in her novel *The Man in the Brown Suit*. However, in *The A.B.C. Murders*, the third-person narrative is supposedly reconstructed by the first-person narrator, Hastings.

by Ronald Knox (1888–1957), which stipulated, among other things, that "no accident must ever help the detective, nor must he ever have an unaccountable intuition which proves to be right" and that "no Chinaman must figure in the story." The American writer S.S. Van Dine produced a similar catalogue in his *Twenty Rules for Writing Detective Stories* (1928). More than anything else, though, the Golden Age of detective fiction was characterized by a comforting atmosphere, in which law

and order were always vindicated, crime was punished, and a happy innocence prevailed.

This era of moral confidence ended with World War II. Thereafter, the American school of "hard-boiled" detectives took over the classic British genre and the moral divisions between the agents of justice and the perpetrators of crimes became blurred. Chief among the exponents of this development in the genre were Raymond Chandler (1888–1959) with his Philip Marlowe investigations, Dashiell Hammett (1894–1961) with the Sam Spade stories, and Erle Stanley Gardner (1889–1970) with his Perry Mason novels. This was the era of the wise-cracking private eye, who trawled the mean streets and dark alleys of American cities for gangsters, corrupt businessmen, gold-digging women, and amoral chancers.

In the later 20th century, detective fiction retained its popularity and found new innovations. There is Sara Paretsky's female private investigator, V.I. Warshawski, Patricia Cornwell's forensic expert, Kay Scarpetta, not to mention Umberto Eco's philosophical friar, William of Baskerville in *The Name of the Rose* (1980), and Philip K. Dick's science fiction classic, *Do Androids Dream of Electric Sheep?* (1968). Seemingly, for all its conventions, the detective genre is malleable enough to reflect all times and ethics.

Chapter 8
MODERNISM
AVANT-GARDE

Librairie moderne.

Véritable Extrait de Viande Liebig.

THE BATTLE OF PARDERBERG, The Second Boer War (1899–1902)

The Boer Wars (1880–1881) and (1899–1902) were fought between the British and the descendants of the Dutch settlers (Boers) in South Africa. The Second Boer War was an example of the worst excesses of imperialism. It involved large numbers of troops and ended the conversion of the Boer republics into British colonies. This inspired other colonies to fight for independence.

FACING PAGE: Well-dressed French men and women frequent an up-market book shop in the early 20th century.

By the end of the 19th century, social, political, and cultural trends that had been more or less evident for several decades reached the critical mass to bring about dramatic changes. In the most developed European countries, the pre-industrial economy and way of life had almost disappeared. By the early 1900s, the process of urbanization was well advanced, with almost 80 percent of the population of Britain and around 60 percent of the populations of France and Germany living in towns and cities. As a result, regional differences became less important and nation states more cohesive. In France, for example, while in the early 19th century local dialects and languages of entirely different groups had made it impossible for people of different regions to understand each other, by the end of the century, the French language truly had national currency and was a unifying force.

Moreover, as the concept of the nation state achieved greater credibility, the idea of an empire was coming under increasing criticism. The Second Boer War (1899–1902) in South Africa, although won by the British, inspired other colonies to rebel. Authoritarian rule and cultural hegemony seemed more and more at odds with liberal ideals and less and less practicable on the ground.

At home as well, the power of the traditional ruling classes—often based on holdings of agricultural land—was being undermined by the growth of trade in towns and cities and the concomitant emergence of the middle classes and organization of the working classes. In some countries, increased electoral suffrage and rights for women were dividends of this process in the early decades of the new century. World War I, however, was a catalyst for more extreme redistributions of political power. In Russia, the revolution of October 1917 heralded government along Marxist lines. Fascism, on the other hand, took hold in Italy in the 1920s, and in Germany and Spain in the 1930s.

The growth and density of population in recently industrialized towns and cities also made the dissemination of ideas and texts (of all kinds) much easier. The wider availability of education brought increased literacy, which in turn created a mass readership and a popular press to supply it. Literature (and culture generally)

LUMIÉRE CINEMATOGRAPHY, 1890s

The advent of movies at the beginning of the 20th century provided a means to reach out to masses.

DEFINING MODERNISM

Modernism as a cultural phenomenon or movement constitutes writers' and artists' response to the new conditions of the 20th century, when the old certainties in religion, ethics, and social order were radically challenged. Different writers confronted modernity in different ways. Some responded with feelings of alienation from the new world and with a sense of loss for the traditions that were being discarded. And although some of these chose, therefore, to address their efforts to like-minded members of the cultural and intellectual elite, they also found wide sympathy among ordinary people for many of their views. Traditional community life was being subsumed into the urban sprawl and individuals from all social strata felt

became, therefore, more important politically. Governments could use it to unify, to mobilize, and to manipulate. But, in the right conditions, mass literacy could also have a democratizing effect—leveling, bringing ordinary people new educational opportunities and employment prospects, and allowing the debunking of all kinds of lies and half-truths, whether from propaganda, advertising, or religious dogma. It is often noted that in World War I, for the first time, rank and file soldiers were able to write letters home describing their experiences.

The new century and its advances in technology also brought a new range of cultural media. Cinema, radio, gramophone, and later, television offered the means for mass dissemination of culture and information across classes and across borders, while providing mass entertainment at the same time. Not surprisingly, the possibilities of reaching a mass audience led to a vast expansion in cultural production. In addition to movies, popular music, and commercial art and design, the 20th century saw the production of considerably more literature than any previous period in history.

CAFÉ DE LA PAIX, Paris, 1919

Proximity to Palais Garnier attracted a lot of famous men to Café de la Paix. Some visitors were Jules Massenet, Émile Zola, and Guy de Maupassant.

1899–1902 Second Boer War in South Africa.	**1916** Franz Kafka's *The Metamorphosis* and James Joyce's *A Portrait of the Artist as a Young Man* are published.	**1927** Virginia Woolf publishes *To the Lighthouse*.
1902 Joseph Conrad writes *Heart of Darkness*.		**1928** W.B. Yeats publishes *The Tower*.
1910–1911 Mexican Revolution; Post-Impressionist Exhibition is held in London.	**1917** T. S. Eliot writes *Prufrock and Other Observations*.	**1929** William Faulkner's work *The Sound and the Fury* is published.
1912 Thomas Mann publishes *Death in Venice*.	**1919** League of Nations formed.	**1929** Beginning of world economic crisis; Great Depression lasts until 1937.
1912–1913 Balkan wars.	**1922** T. S. Eliot writes *The Waste Land*; James Joyce publishes *Ulysses* in Paris.	**1939–1945** World War II.
1913 D. H. Lawrence writes *Sons and Lovers*.	**1922** USSR is formed.	**1942** Albert Camus publishes *The Stranger*.
1914 James Joyce publishes *Dubliners*.	**1924** André Breton brings out the First Surrealist Manifesto.	**1948** Ezra Pound brings out *Pisan Cantos*.
1914–1918 World War I.		

uncertain about their new anonymous roles in the emerging fragmented society.

The idea of the avant-garde became a prominent feature of artistic endeavor during the modernist period. Originally a military term meaning "vanguard," it denotes an attempt to break new ground, to push the boundaries of existing cultural activity. The rise of the avant-garde at this time had much to do with the need for artists, writers, and composers to redefine their roles in order to distinguish their work from the new mass culture. Painters, for example, who had previously had a monopoly as image-makers, now had to prove that there was still a place for them beside photographers. Indeed, the role of the artist became a common theme in modernist literature, and the tension between the popular, conventional, and commercial on the one hand, and the rarefied, iconoclastic, and anti-commercial on the other, became a constant drone in the background.

FRANCE 1880–1920

In many ways, Paris was the epicenter of modernism. From its beginnings in the late 19th century until the 1940s—when Europe became engulfed in war and the focus of cultural activity shifted to New York—modernism grew and flourished in Parisian soil. In poetry, the writings of Rimbaud, Baudelaire, Laforgue, and others signified a departure that would eventually lead to the works of Ezra Pound, T.S. Eliot, and Wallace Stevens, among many others. In terms of the novel, Proust's *In Search of Lost Time* would influence a whole generation of modernist writers, which included James Joyce, Ernest Hemingway (both of whom also lived in Paris for long stretches), and Virginia

WAITING FOR GODOT

A 1956 production at New York's Golden Theater of Samuel Beckett's *Waiting for Godot*, arguably the 20th century's most famous play.

Charles Baudelaire is in the foreground, with other early 19th century literary figures—Charles Augustin Sainte-Beuve, Henri Murger, and Jules Barbey D'Aurevilly—in the background.

Symbolists—Rimbaud, Verlaine, Laforgue, Mallarmé, Valéry, and others. Literary symbolism was a reaction against Realism and Naturalism in favor of the spiritual plane, the imagination and dreams. As Charles Baudelaire (1821–1867) put it, "I should like the fields tinged with red, the rivers yellow and the trees painted blue. Nature has no imagination." Baudelaire was the author of the movement's seminal work, *Les Fleurs du mal* (*The Flowers of Evil*, 1857), a collection of poems that scandalized France and led to subsequent prosecution and fining of both the author and publisher. The subject matter that caused such a brouhaha mostly related to sex (including lesbianism). Other important themes included death, *ennui*, melancholia, the attractions of vices such as sex and alcohol, as well as—with particular significance for modernism—the corruption of the city, feelings of alienation, and lost innocence. The poems also employ imagery related to the sense of smell and fragrances, which are used to evoke feelings of nostalgia and past intimacy. Fifty years later, this would crucially influence Proust's *In Search of Lost Time*.

Woolf. In drama, the works of Alfred Jarry proved seminal for the surrealist theater of the 1920s and 1930s and, beyond, for Samuel Beckett, whose *Waiting for Godot* is perhaps the most famous modernist statement in the medium.

Of course, modernist tendencies could be seen (and major works were produced) across Europe, and notably also in the United States. But Paris became not just a center for French culture, but also for Western art and culture in general. Many of the greatest artists of the time—including Pablo Picasso from Spain, Igor Stravinsky from Russia, and James Joyce from Ireland, for example—settled in Paris and brought elements of their native cultures with them to enhance the creative ferment.

In literature, one of the pivotal movements that prepared the ground for modernism was that of the French

Baudelaire died in 1867 (of illness precipitated by drink, drugs, and syphilis), but during the subsequent decades Verlaine, Rimbaud, and others would continue to develop his esthetic of otherworldly decadence. Paul Verlaine (1844–1896) popularized the term *poète maudit* ("accursed poet") to refer to poets who fought against poetic conventions and suffered the scorn of critics and society. In 1886, though, Jean Moréas (1856–1910) published his Symbolist Manifesto, and the term "symbolism" achieved wider currency.

The Symbolists saw the material world, in Baudelaire's expression, as a forest of symbols for another world—a

LEFT: CARICATURE OF PAUL VERLAINE, From *Les Hommes d'Aujourd'hui*, By Emile Cohl

French poet Verlaine was a leader of the Symbolist movement in poetry. With Stéphane Mallarmé and Charles Baudelaire, he formed the so-called Decadents.

PORTRAIT OF ARTHUR RIMBAUD, AT THE AGE OF 17 1872, By Étienne Carjat

world of transcendent reality. They turned away from the mere physicality of the world, abandoned any efforts to influence it or get the better of it, whether through scientific or mercantile calculation, and rejected positivism and the idea of human progress. They also cultivated an otherworldliness, a mysticism, an obsession with mortality and a fascination with the possibilities of altered consciousness caused by eroticism and by drugs, alcohol, dreams, and delirium.

In terms of literature, they turned against the declamatory attitude and lofty rhetoric of the public poets of the preceding era as well as the sentimentality, the matter-of-fact language and pseudo-scientific documentation of its novelists. Instead, they aimed to suggest and evoke feelings and moods through the sounds of words, through the cadence of verse and metrical innovation. Their discarding of the rigid verse conventions of the recent past placed poetry on a trajectory via Jules Laforgue (1860–1887) and Gustave Kahn (1859–1936) toward the free verse of Ezra Pound and other arch-modernists.

Among the most important works of this group of writers are the poems of Arthur Rimbaud (1854–1891), all of which he wrote by the age of 19. Many—such as *Le Bateau ivre* (*Drunken Boat*, 1871), where the speaker is the boat itself—attempt to achieve a vatic state through disorientation of the senses. Rimbaud is also famous for his tempestuous love affair with fellow poet Paul Verlaine (1844–1896), which ended with Verlaine's shooting and injuring the younger man. The whole episode is evoked in Verlaine's collection of poems, *Romances sans paroles* (1874).

Also highly influential was the poet, Stéphane Mallarmé (1842–1898), whose most famous work, *L'après-midi d'un faune* (*The Afternoon of a Faun*, 1876), is an extended metaphor for the idea that the attainment of a higher state is only possible through the renunciation of possession and realization. In pursuit of

STÉPHANE MALLARMÉ, 1876, By Édouard Manet, Oil on canvas, Musée d'Orsay, Paris, France

intimation of greater truths rather than comprehension of lesser ones, Mallarmé took the musical potential of poetry to its limit, often letting the meanings of words take second place to their sound relationships. Moreover, his innovative use of typography and page layout to modify the meanings of the words would prove influential for the Futurist, Dadaist, and Surrealist poets and artists of the 1910s, 1920s, and 1930s.

After Mallarmé's death, his protégé, Paul Valéry (1871–1945), carried the symbolist vision into the new century. Under Mallarmé's tutelage, he achieved some early success as a poet (he later revised and published these works as *Album des vers anciens*, 1920), but in 1892 underwent a personal intellectual crisis and, disaffected with literature in general, ceased wrtiting poetry for about 20 years. From 1912 onward, however, under the encouragement of André Gide and others, he began working on poetry again, though it was not until 1917 that his attempts bore fruit, with the success of *La Jeune Parque*. Valéry's last major contribution to poetry came in 1922 with *Charmes*, a collection that includes

the celebrated poem, *Le cimetière marin*; this confirmed his reputation.

While symbolism found its ideal means of expression in poetry, its mystical reveries were less adaptable to the length of a novel. Joris-Karl Huysmans' (1848–1907) *À rebours* (*Against Nature*, 1884)—the story of the attitudes and cultivated tastes of a reclusive dandy—includes many of the concerns of symbolism. It is, however, a difficult read, as so little happens, and not a strong candidate for a sequel or emulation (although Gustave Kahn did try, with his *Le Roi fou* of 1896).

Many novelists, however, found other avenues in their departure from naturalism and rejection of philosophical positivism. Some turned back to religion. This included Huysmans himself, whose literary career took him from naturalism and then symbolism to Satanism (*Là-bas*, 1891) and finally Catholicism (*La Cathédrale*, 1898). André Gide (1869–1951), on the other hand, managed to combine an obsession with the interior life with social criticism. His early works—in particular, *Les Nourritures*

PAUL VALÉRY (1871-1945)

Valéry's 512-line *La Jeune Parque* (1917) is often regarded as the finest French poem of the 20th century, though it is the most difficult. Its shifting modes of expression attempt to portray the different moods and feelings of a young woman contemplating love and death during the course of a night. The result is more akin to a tone poem in music than a traditional verse form with tidy logic and singularity of attitude.

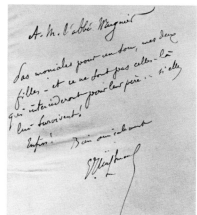

TOP LEFT: JORIS-KARL HUYSMANS

TOP RIGHT: LETTER FROM HUYSMANS TO THE MUGNIER ABBOT WHO DETERMINED HIS CONVERSION TO CATHOLICISM

Huysman's works reflect his development from naturalism (*Marthe*, 1876) to the style of Decadents (*À rebours*, 1884), to a fascination with Satanism (*Là-bas*, 1891), to his full acceptance of Roman Catholicism (*La Cathédrale*, 1898).

war. Also published in 1913 was the first installment of Marcel Proust's vast work, *À la recherche du temps perdu* (*In Search of Lost Time*). Subsequent volumes incorporated World War II, and Combray, the village at the center of the story, is depicted as being divided by opposing armies, as Paris is bombarded and the narrator's boyhood haunts become battlefields. Of those novels that make the conflict their main subject, *Le Feu* (1916) by Henri Barbusse (1873–1935) is undoubtedly the most famous.

In contrast to the English literature of the period, however, French poetry developed no distinctive movement in the manner of Wilfred Owen and Siegfried Sassoon. Instead, in France, it was the experimental poetry of the avant-garde that most convincingly took up the issues of war. Of particular importance is the collection *Calligrammes* (1918) by Guillaume Apollinaire (1880–1918, injured in World War I and then died

terrestres (1897) and *L'Immoraliste* (1902)—advocated, along symbolist lines, the life of the senses, free from the strictures of conventional moral and social codes. Over the subsequent decades, however, this interest in self-exploration became a quest with wider implications—moral, social, and political. *La Porte étroite* (1909) examined the themes of self-indulgence and self-denial while *Corydon* (1924) defended homosexuality (to public outrage), *Voyage au Congo* (1928) attacked European colonialism, and *Retour de l'U.R.S.S.* (1936) described his personal experiences of Communism.

Themes of personal identity, memory, and their relation to modern life became all the more pertinent in the context of the mechanized slaughter of World War I. This emphatic break with the past is nowhere better symbolized than by the novel *Le Grand Meaulnes* (1913)—a nostalgic tale of adolescent love and innocence—by Alain-Fournier (pseudonym of Henri Alban-Fournier, 1886–1914), who was an early fatality in the

ANDRÉ GIDE

Gide's voluminous writings include plays, stories, and essays, and show a great diversity of subjects and literary techniques. He was a psychological novelist, an innovative modernist, a major literary critic, a social crusader, and a spokesman for homosexual rights. But he is primarily known as a moralist and thinker, whose search for self (the theme for most of his works) is essentially religious. In 1947 Gide was awarded the Nobel Prize in Literature for his contributions to literature.

from the flu epidemic). While the work of Mallarmé twenty years earlier had precipitated a crisis of language and meaning, finally, in *Calligrammes*, the same techniques, taken a stage further (unstable word definitions, disjunctures in logic, unexpected juxtapositions, and pictorially used typography), found a context and subject matter that suited them perfectly.

During the second decade of the 20th century Apollinaire was at the center of the modernist movement in France. A close friend of Picasso, he was an important art critic, helping to define the Cubist movement and coining the term "orphism" to describe some painters' tendency to absolute abstraction. He also coined the word "surrealist" and wrote the earliest surrealist play, *Les Mamelles de Tirésias* (written in 1903, first performed in 1917). Among his most important literary co-conspirators were Max Jacob (1876–1944) and Blaise Cendrars (1887–1961), whose poems and novels share Apollinaire's appreciation of chance, experimentation, and the need to break with tradition, while also exhibiting his collage-like techniques and reliance on irony, parody, and often manic humor.

In the field of drama, the wellspring of the avant-garde was *Ubu Roi* (1896) by Alfred Jarry (1873–1907). Apollinaire knew Jarry toward the end of his life and, in agreement with his rejection of the belief in the progress of humanity, drew on the anarchic humor and ferocious satire of his plays for his own work. Beyond Apollinaire, Jarry's influence can also be detected in the surrealist works of the 1920s and 1930s, and the Theater of the Absurd of Ionesco and Beckett thereafter. It is important, indeed, not to understate the cultural shift that *Ubu Roi* represented. Around the time of its first performance, French theater was a largely commercial and conventional affair, with the formulaic farces of Feydeau, the *pièces à theses* of the likes of Augier, and the neo-Romanticism of Rostand. Among the most interesting works of the last decades of the 19th century were the plays of Auguste Villiers de l'Isle-Adam (1838–1889)—especially *Axel* (1890)—and Maurice Maeterlinck (1862–1949)—most famous for *Pelléas and Mélisande* (1892). These combine the reliance on myth seen in Wagner operas with an emphasis on the psychic and otherworldly qualities in the Symbolist poets.

TOP: WORLD WAR I FRENCH LIST OF THE DEAD

LEFT: MONUMENT TO APOLLINAIRE, Stone head of Dora Maar by Picasso topping monument to Apollinaire in village square at Vallauris, France.

HENRI BARBUSSE

Le Feu (1916) by Henri Barbusse is typical among French war novels in its revival of realist description and moral revulsion to events in World War I.

PROUST

Marcel Proust (1871–1922) is famous as the author of the monumental novel *À la recherche du temps perdu* (usually translated as either *In Search of Lost Time* or *Remembrance of Things Past*), published in seven volumes from 1913 to 1927. Unquestionably a landmark in the development of the modern novel, *In Search of Lost Time* influenced many great writers of the 20th century, including James Joyce and Virginia Woolf.

Although there is debate about how much the narrator of *In Search of Lost Time* can be identified with its author, it seems that the book is at least partly autobiographical. Proust was born into a wealthy family in Auteuil in the west of Paris in 1871, just after the end of the Franco-Prussian War. As a child, he suffered from asthma and other ailments and was therefore dispatched for long holidays in the village of Illiers. This, combined with elements of Auteuil, became the model for the fictional town of Combray, where much of *In Search of Lost Time* takes place. As a young man, he lived the life of a social butterfly in fashionable Parisian circles, but gradually withdrew and devoted himself to literature. In the late 1890s he came out on the side of Dreyfus in the scandal that absorbed France (his mother's family, incidentally, was Jewish). Also around this time, he discovered Ruskin and began a translation of *The Bible of Amiens*.

A pivotal event in his life came in 1905 with the death of his mother, to whom he was extremely close. Thereafter, Proust applied himself to his fiction writing, and by 1912 had completed the first volume of *In Search of Lost Time*.

Increasingly suffering from illness, Proust lived out his last years as a recluse, confined to his cork-lined bedroom and working at night to complete his great work. He died before finishing the revisions, but his brother Robert edited the last three volumes, which were published posthumously.

A central theme of the novel is the arresting of time through memory. Proust developed the concept of involuntary memory, whereby happenings in everyday life—often fleeting sensations of smell, taste, touch, and so on—trigger unexpected memories of the past. A famous example of this phenomenon occurs with the book's narrator tasting a morsel of a madeleine cake dipped in tea; it awakens vivid memories of the past in a kind of epiphany that the Symbolist poets would no doubt have appreciated. Voluntary memory, by contrast, is where memories of the past are summoned up by conscious effort.

The theme of memory is made all the more important by the period covered by the novel. The Third Republic encompassed enormous political and social changes, from the Franco-Prussian War and the Commune to the period of new wealth created by industrialization and empire, from the Dreyfus Affair to the disasters of World War I. Proust's observation of the instability of modern life and the mysteries of flux and time echoes in many ways the work of his cousin, the philosopher Henri Bergson (1859–1941). Another important influence was undoubtedly John Ruskin (1819–1900), particularly in his views about the nature and role of art.

Other major themes of *In Search of Lost Time* include the society and the individual, social mobility, homosexuality, artistic and analytic intelligence, and the nature of love. Of course, Proust's work is as much about form and language as it is about content. It is an exploration of the possibilities of the novel, breaking new ground in its treatment of characterization and plot, and evolving a literary style all of its own.

ENGLAND: VICTORIAN TO MODERNIST

It is often remarked of English culture in the 20th century that it failed to produce an avant-garde movement of its own. There is some truth in this, and among the reasons suggested are the relative political stability of the country, the moderate temperament of its people, and the reliance on other English-speaking nations for new cultural ideas. This last factor is probably the most credible and significant. While there were many important English writers during this period—not least Lawrence, Woolf, and Auden—generally, however, writers from elsewhere were at the vanguard of iconoclasm and experimentation. Yeats and Joyce from Ireland; Pound, Eliot, Faulkner, and Hemingway from the United States; even Conrad (who wrote in English) from Poland. Nevertheless, radicalism and experimentation are not the only criteria of literary value, and English writers of the period were not only highly productive but also created a body of work that has been of lasting interest.

One quintessentially English writer who also represents the shift from 19th to 20th centuries is Thomas Hardy (1840–1928). His career as a novelist (see previous chapter) came largely to an end with *Jude the Obscure* (1895), and thereafter he devoted himself to his poetry. His most famous poem, *The Darkling Thrush*, was written in the last days of the 19th century and is often seen as the death knell of Romanticism. The use of the rare word "darkling" links the poem to that high expression of Romanticism, Keats's *Ode to a Nightingale* (1819). However, whereas its predecessor depicts a landscape full of the promise of early summer, Hardy's poem portrays a funereal winter, with the thrush flinging its "soul upon the growing gloom," while humanity finds itself adrift, without the certainty of God.

As well as in outlook, Hardy's poems (of which he wrote some 900) also exhibit the transition in poetic style from the Victorian to the modern age. Although the forms of his poems are largely

JUDE THE OBSCURE, 1896, By Thomas Hardy

The last of Hardy's novels began as a magazine serial and was first published in book form in 1895. It is the story of Jude Fawley, a lower-class young man who dreams of becoming a scholar.

traditional, he introduces colloquialisms, dialect words, and even neologisms. This fits the personal subject matter of his work—the individual's attempt to make sense of the baffling course of life, love, and death—and emphasizes its departure from the confident public declamations of Victorian poetry.

During Hardy's lifetime, poetry had a much greater readership than it does today. Some poets (Rupert Brooke and Robert Bridges, for example) became bestsellers, and the practice of writing verse was a relatively common pastime among the general public. A lot of popular verse looked back to the 19th century for its form, tone, and content, and much of it now receives little critical attention. Even historical categorizations such as "Georgian" (for English poetry written during the reign of King George V, 1910–1936) have become derogatory terms. There were poets, however, who achieved both popularity in their own time and lasting renown. Rudyard Kipling (1865–1936) was one such poet. His *Barrack-Room Ballads* (1892), which included poems such as *Gunga Din* and *Mandalay,* drew on the vernacular language and attitudes of the British in India. His poem *If* (published 1910) summed up the stoic virtues that supposedly helped Britain build its empire; it became hugely popular during World War I. Despite later criticism for his imperialist views and possible racism, Kipling's works do at least show great awareness of the problems of the British Empire. Moreover, much of his writing (*Plain Tales from the Hills*, 1888, for example) aims to portray realistically the psychology and predicament of the colonizers, rather than present his own analysis.

Another poet whose popularity has endured is A.E. Housman (1859–1936). His *Shropshire Lad* (1896) became a *vade mecum* for soldiers in World War I. This war, however, also bred a new kind of poetry of its own—one that was unsentimental, uncompromisingly at odds with establishment values, and that confronted modernity instead of looking to the past. Many soldiers found that the patriotic idealism of poetry written early in the war (such as that of Rupert Brooke, 1887–1915, for example) did not reflect the real conditions of the conflict. The tactics of the often-elderly upper-class generals proved out of date. The military leadership was also out of touch with the thoughts of ordinary conscripted soldiers, and generally appeared uncaring toward their predicament. In addition, standards of organization were poor, physical conditions appalling, and there was a lack of understanding of the mental trauma suffered by soldiers. The wider significance of this was that the war highlighted problems inherent in society in general. Poems such as *Anthem for Doomed Youth* by Wilfred Owen (1893–1918) brought to poetry a new realism coupled with a technical armory to hammer home the message of protest. Colloquial language gave voice to the ordinary soldier, half-rhyme suggested a rejection of harmony and platitude, and alliteration evoked the sounds of mechanized warfare. Moreover, poems such as *The General* by Siegfried Sassoon (1886–1967) added to the mixture of bitter irony and caustic satire.

In terms of the novel, the first decades of the 20th century were a time of great formal development, yielding a number of

TOP: *THE JUNGLE BOOK,* 1903, By Rudyard Kipling, Stapleton Collection, UK

LEFT: RUDYARD KIPLING

Kipling enjoyed early success with his poems but soon became a master short story teller, presenting intriguing portrayal of the people, history, and culture of his times. He celebrated the heroism of British colonial soldiers in his works, but his fame rests on *The Jungle Book*, which has inspired many literary works and adaptations to television and film.

TOP: *HOWARDS END*

Howards End was Forsters' first critically acclaimed novel and success-fully adapted to the screen. Here Director James Ivory is seen at AMPAS's "Great to be Nominated" series, honoring *Howards End* at the Academy Theater on 20 August 2007 in Beverly Hills, California.

LEFT: E.M. FORSTER

literary terms, this translated into a giving way of narrative, plot, and rational argument in favor of the individual's stream of consciousness, reliance on imagery, a new use of mythology, and the fragmentation of space and time. This was the age of the pessimistic outsider.

One subject with which novelists found themselves increasingly at odds was the idea of the British Empire. Although Kipling was seen as an upholder of imperialist values, he did, however, highlight the ethical and social problems of one nation ruling over and living with people of a quite different culture. Other writers would take this much further. Joseph Conrad (1857–1924) had also experienced the colonial enterprise first hand. Novels such as *Lord Jim* (1900) explore the limits of English codes of behavior beyond the bounds of the home country. *Nostromo* (1904) develops the themes of loyalty, innocence, self-knowledge, corruptibility, and moral growth in conditions of extreme stress and danger in South America. Perhaps Conrad's most famous work, though, is the novella *Heart of Darkness* (1899). Its central character is the notorious Kurtz, who is a symbol of the evil that European civilization has wreaked on its colonial lands and how that evil has rebounded, corrupting its perpetrator.

One of Conrad's many novelistic innovations is to show characters and events from several different viewpoints—from those of the narrator, the protagonist, and other characters. He also employs shifts of time to bring additional perspectives to the events at hand. For Conrad, there is no objective set of rules from which to judge, no hegemonic value system, no shared ethical code. Instead, there is moral complexity, conflict, misunderstanding, a sense of impending anarchy, loneliness, and pessimism.

Another novelist concerned with the theme of clashing values was E.M. Forster (1879–1970). His most important work is *Passage to India* (1924), which again portrays the complexities

landmark works. Part of the impetus behind this era of literary experimentation was the feeling among some writers that the prevailing conventions and values were alien to life as they saw it. With the ending of the religious and social certainties of the Victorian period, writers searched in vain for what critical theorists refer to as a metanarrative—an all-encompassing explanation of history and culture. New developments in the fields of psychology by Sigmund Freud (1856–1939) and in anthropology by J.G. Frazer (1854–1941) only emphasized how wrong-headed, or at least inadequate, the old creeds were. In of the colonial situation and eschews simplistic judgment. His earlier novels explore the confrontations brought about as the rigid divisions of the Victorian social order dissolve in the wake of modernity's process of change. *A Room with a View* (1908), for example, throws together repressed English gentlefolk, American-inspired free-thinkers, and sexually uninhibited Italians in a *pensione* in Florence. *Howards End* (1910) mixes together progressive esthetes, mercantile empire builders, and working class people against the background of the "progress" of the new suburbs into rural England. *Maurice* (published posthumously in 1971) examines the personal conflicts faced by homosexuals living in a society that is in denial.

The novels of D.H. Lawrence (1885–1930) also depict the problems of a country trying to face up to modernity. The son of a coal-miner and a former school-teacher, Lawrence was alive to the conflicts of social change from an early age. His first major novel *Sons and Lovers* (1913) is in many ways a *Künstlerroman* (an artist's coming-of-age novel). It drew heavily on his family life and contrasts an uneducated working-class father with a genteel and socially ambitious mother. He followed this up with *The Rainbow* (1915)—which was suppressed following a court case for obscenity—and its sequel, *Women in Love* (1920). By today's standards the sexual content of Lawrence's books is unremarkable. His particular interest in sex and physicality was in part a reaction to English codes of behavior and the sexual and emotional repression they engendered. It also had to do with Lawrence's belief that modern European civilization had placed too much emphasis on the mind and not enough on the body. He saw his parents as a case study for this phenomenon: the honest vitality of his working-class father as opposed to the materialism and middle-class aspirations of his mother.

These themes are taken a stage further in Lawrence's other famous novel, *Lady Chatterley's Lover* (1928). The book was first published in Italy, owing to the censorious attitude of the

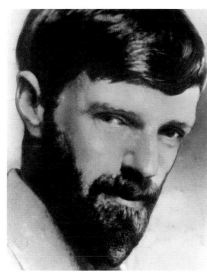

TOP: *LADY CHATTERLEY'S LOVER*

Printed in Florence, Italy, in 1928, the novel was not printed in the United Kingdom until 1960. Here two women are seen outside a book shop in Leicester Square, London, with paperback copies of *Lady Chatterley's Lover*, after a jury at the Old Bailey decided that it was not obscene.

RIGHT: D.H. LAWRENCE

British authorities, and was only released in Britain in 1960. It depicts a variety of relationships, several bridging social classes. Death is now associated with gentility and convention, while sexuality is shown as having the potential to bring emotional fulfillment or destruction, depending on whether it is based on instinct or calculation.

Lawrence's novels exhibit the influences of the realist and naturalist traditions. They combine vivid depictions of the physical environment with subtle observations of psychology.

In addition, however, there is also a strong poetic quality and an extensive use of symbolism. Lawrence was indeed a prolific poet as well as a novelist, short story writer, and playwright. From 1919, he also turned his attention to travel writing; he spent almost all of the rest of his years living and traveling overseas. The results—books such as *Sea and Sardinia* (1921) and *Mornings in Mexico* (1927)—underline the contrast between the treadmill of life in the industrialized northern countries and the more instinctive, simple life of warmer countries.

One of Lawrence's early supporters was the novelist, critic, and editor Ford Madox Ford (1873–1939). Ford exerted a major influence on modernist literature through his editorship of *The English Review* and the *Transatlantic Review*, which published works by Hardy, Yeats, and Conrad (Ford also co-authored two novels with him) and first brought Lawrence and Wyndham Lewis to public attention. Ford's reputation is also founded on one of his novels, *The Good Soldier* (1915). The book is noteworthy for its unreliable narrator and its use of flashbacks, which leave the reader unsure as to the true version of events and leave the story open to interpretation. The concepts of time and consciousness were indeed central concerns of modernist writers. The works of Freud and

Jung suggested that past events had the potential to merge with the present through memory, whether consciously or subconsciously. A truthful portrayal of a character therefore required the depiction of the jumble of their perceptions, memories, and feelings in a continuous flow. Events could no longer be presented in a neat and tidy sequence and, as a consequence, the novel became a more fluid, less logical, and less contrived form.

Many of these ideas reached their fullest expression in the novels of Virginia Woolf (1882–1941). The daughter of an eminent Victorian literary critic, Sir Leslie Stephen, Woolf was at the center of a clique of artists and intellectuals in London known as the Bloomsbury Group. Members included the novelist E.M. Forster, the biographer Lytton Strachey, the economist J.M. Keynes, the painter Duncan Grant, and Woolf's husband, the publisher Leonard Woolf.

After producing a couple of fairly conventional early novels, Virginia Woolf began experimenting with form and technique in her third book *Jacob's Room* (1922). She developed an intense, lyrical style and used poetic rhythms and imagery to evoke emotions and impressions without requiring that her

TRANSATLANTIC REVIEW MEMBERS, *c.* 1925

From left to right: Writers Ford Madox, James Joyce, and Ezra Pound, with lawyer John Quinn, standing in front of doorway.

VIRGINIA WOOLF, 1902, George Charles Beresford

Woolf was a significant figure in London literary society and a member of the Bloomsbury Group in the interwar period.

sentences denote concrete meanings. In novels such as *Mrs Dalloway* (1925), the humdrum, even drab settings are elevated by the author's poetic vision. In a manner that perhaps owes something to Proust, commonplace things are infused with life and significance through the way the characters perceive them.

Woolf is often credited with the development of the stream of consciousness technique. This is where the reader enters the mind of a character and shares their experience of fictional events. Mrs Dalloway, for example, gives a monologue of her interior life over the period of a single day in London. The reader receives her subjective impressions, thoughts, and feelings in a continuous flow. Of course, memories play a part and there are frequent flashbacks. The subconscious also plays

a role. The effect can be illogical and disorienting, but then a coherent narrative with a logical sequence of events would not be consistent with an individual's real experience. Often, the novelist breaks the conventions of grammar, syntax, and punctuation in order to accommodate the irrational flow of consciousness.

After *Mrs Dalloway*, Woolf's next novel, *To The Lighthouse* (1927), develops her poetic technique further with the use of symbolism (not least in the lighthouse of the title). Symbols are also used as a means of emphasizing multiple perspectives; symbols have different meanings for different characters in the novel. *The Waves* (1931) also concentrates on subjectivity and the instability of meaning, as six characters reveal very different responses to the death of a mutual friend.

In addition to formal innovation, Woolf's work also has special significance for feminist criticism. Her essay, *A Room of One's Own* (1928), is a landmark in feminist thought, as it examines the role of women in literary history and asks whether a woman could have produced work of the quality of Shakespeare. Woolf's answer seems to be that they would have been denied the opportunity.

IRELAND

In the last years of the 19th century, Irish literature underwent a major revival, and over the succeeding decades, it would make an enormous contribution to the development of modernism in English-language literature. The revival initially took the form of an upsurge of interest in Celtic myths together with a concern for national identity. Literary histories became popular alongside sentimental narrative poetry and collections of fairy stories. The revival is sometimes referred to as *The Celtic Twilight* after the title of a collection of stories by W.B. Yeats (1865–1939) published in 1893.

While the writers of the Celtic Twilight movement re-established Irish identity, a sense of place and the importance of the Irish vernacular, W.B. Yeats took the revival movement several stages further. His early work, in the last decades of the 19th century, is perhaps best represented by his famous poem, *The Lake Isle of Innisfree* (1890), in which the speaker yearns (from his urban setting) for an idealized simple life in rural Ireland. Gradually, though, Yeats moved away from the Pre-Raphaelite-inspired lyrics of his earlier poetry to incorporate elements of the mysticism of the French poets of the time. A book by his friend Arthur Symons, *The Symbolist Movement in Poetry* (1899), proved highly influential, as it would later to T.S. Eliot as well.

Greater engagement with the Irish nationalist cause, however, eventually led Yeats to make a more decisive break with his earlier romantic attitudes. His youthful idealization of the Irish peasant classes was replaced with a more realistic and direct approach. His poem, *September 1913,* announces "Romantic Ireland's dead and gone / It's with O'Leary in the grave." Other poems, such as *The Second Coming* (1921), develop one of Yeats's signature themes, that of the cyclical nature of history

and its significance in explaining the decline of civilization as he saw it. Later works, notably the collection *The Tower* (1928), combine these theories about eternity and the patterns of history with his earlier interest in mysticism. His tone once more becomes more personal as he attempts to reconcile the events of the outside world with the spiritual life.

W.B. YEATS, Photogravure from *Men of Mark*, 1913

Yeats was one of the founders of the Irish Literary Revival, along with J. M. Synge, Sean O'Casey (1880–1964), and Padraig (Padraic) Colum (1881–1972). He had an inclination toward mysticism and visionary traditions and drew heavily from Irish folklore. Both these interests were sources of poetic imagery for Yeats.

JAMES JOYCE (1882–1941)

While T. S. Eliot's *The Wasteland* and Samuel Beckett's *Waiting for Godot* are often considered the greatest modernist works in the fields of poetry and drama respectively, James Joyce's *Ulysses* achieves a similar status in respect of the novel. In terms of content, its vast range of impressions and thoughts dramatically enlarged the scope of the novelistic form, and in respect of technique, it proved a radical departure from the hackneyed modes of expression of the preceding era.

Joyce was born and brought up in Dublin, but spent almost all his adult life abroad, in Trieste, Zürich, and Paris. Nevertheless, his works are all set in Ireland and are thematically anchored in Irish culture. His first major work of fiction was *Dubliners* (1914), a volume of short stories portraying ordinary townspeople trapped by the strictures of a stagnant society and religion. He followed this with *A Portrait of the Artist as a Young Man* (1916), a *Künstlerroman* (or artist's coming-of-age novel) that introduces Joyce's alter ego, Stephen Dedalus (who would later also feature in *Ulysses*).

By far his most important work, however, is *Ulysses*, first published in book form in Paris in 1922, after encountering censorship problems on grounds of alleged obscenity in the United States and Britain.

The book takes place on a single day, 16 June 1904, and transposes the characters and events of Homer's *Odyssey* to modern Dublin—which is faithfully depicted in all its detail and squalor. The characters of Odysseus, Penelope, and Telemachus are represented by their less heroic modern counterparts, Leopold Bloom, Molly Bloom, and Stephen Dedalus. The book has a highly schematic structure: each chapter covers approximately one hour of the waking day, corresponds to a particular episode of Homer's *Odyssey*, has its own distinct literary technique, and is even associated with a particular art or science, color, and bodily organ.

As well as experimenting with form and structure, Joyce also plays with the full gamut of techniques at the level of the sentence. He employs puns, parodies, jokes, nonsense, allusions, and neologisms as well as making full use of the stream-of-consciousness technique to depict his characters' interior lives. The effect is a dizzying cacophony without resolution, offering the reader as much of a sensory overload as the modern metropolis itself.

Joyce's final work, *Finnegans Wake* (1939), took the principles of *Ulysses* even further. Indeed, some critics (and even earlier supporters such as Ezra Pound) felt that these ideas had been extended beyond tolerable bounds. Many readers find the wordplay alone so complex as to make the book almost unreadable. The book's difficulty is then compounded by the mélange of techniques (notably free dream associations, allusions, and stream of consciousness) and philosophical ideas, including Giambattista Vico's cyclical view of history.

JAMES JOYCE

Dublin's main thoroughfare O'Connell Street, is closed and turned into an outdoor eatery for the Bloomsday Centenary breakfast, Sunday June 13, 2004, in commemoration of Leopold Bloom's famous morning meals in James Joyce's 'Ulysses' almost 100 years ago. Bloomsday falls on June 16.

AMERICAN LITERATURE

The period from 1880 to 1950 saw American literature come of age, as the country's growth in cultural influence matched its enormous economic expansion. Yet, despite achieving the status of a world superpower, the period was not one of complete and unbridled confidence. Even during the boom times, many questioned the narrow-minded pursuit of wealth they saw all around them. Many artists and writers (including Pound, Hemingway, Dos Passos) emigrated to Europe in the hope of finding a deeper set of cultural values there. They converged on Paris and set up an expatriate colony, earning themselves the sobriquet, the "Lost Generation." Back home, by the 1930s, boom had turned to bust, and the soul searching of the Great Depression found eloquent expression in the works of William Faulkner, John Steinbeck, and others. The 1940s, however, brought a kind of renewal, as America gained relative strength politically and economically as Europe was devastated by war. Cultural life was invigorated by an influx of artists, writers, and intellectuals fleeing domination by the Nazis.

In the field of poetry, by the end of the 19th century, Whitman and Dickinson had already laid the foundations of a distinctive American poetic tradition. Writers such as Robert Frost (1874–1963) continued the New England tradition of nature poetry into the next century. In comparison with Emily Dickinson, however, Frost was much less experimental in his technique.

Another quintessentially American poet was William Carlos Williams (1883–1963). He set out to develop an entirely American form of poetry, believing—as he put it in his volume of essays, *In the American Grain* (1925)—"all art begins in the local." To this end, he eschewed the worn-out language of British culture in favor of the idioms and expressions of the kind of ordinary Americans he met in his day job as a medical doctor. He experimented with poetic form in an attempt to

ROBERT FROST

Frost was a master of traditional meters, and revived the use of blank verse (un-rhymed iambic pentameters), managing to combine it with the rhythms of colloquial speech. On occasions, he wrote in free verse (*After Apple-Picking* for example), though unlike Whitman, he generally found the lack of metrical constraint artistically unsatisfying. On one occasion he said, "I'd sooner write free verse as play tennis with the net down."

capture the rhythms of everyday speech, formulating the concept of the variable foot (which he claimed was suited to the newly relativistic world) and developing the "stepped triadic line" (see *To Elsie* for example). The culmination of his development as a poet came with the arch-modernist five-part free-verse collage, *Paterson* (published between 1946 and 1958), which evokes the people and culture of an industrial city in New Jersey and the role of the poet therein.

Earlier in his career, in the first decades of the 20th century, Williams had been associated with the Imagist movement and contributed to its first anthology, *Des Imagistes* (1914), edited by Ezra Pound. Imagism derived in part from the critical writings of T.E. Hulme (1883–1917) who, in turn, owed much to the French Symbolist tradition. Imagist poetry was characterized by economy of expression, emphasis on musical cadence rather than metrical regularity, and direct treatment of "things" rather than suggestion or abstraction (Pound: "The natural object is always the adequate symbol"). Most of those associated with the movement, including Williams and Pound,

EZRA POUND

Pound was a central figure in the modern movement in the English and American literature. He promoted and shaped the work of his contemporaries such as W.B. Yeats, Robert Frost, William Carlos Williams, Marianne Moore, H.D., James Joyce, Ernest Hemingway, and especially T.S. Eliot. He founded Imagism, a movement in poetry which focused on clarity, precision, and economy of language, as against traditional rhyme and meter.

antipathy toward his home country. He was influential in bringing literature from other cultures to the attention of English-language readers, producing, for example, free verse recreations of early Italian, Provençal, and even Chinese poetry (*Cathay*, 1915). Allusions to foreign languages and literatures pepper his own original poems. After working in a variety of styles inspired variously by medieval Romance, mystical philosophy, classical Latin, and Imagism, Pound embarked on his great work, the *Cantos*, in 1915. He continued working on this project, publishing sections as he went along, until the final *Drafts and Fragments of Cantos CX to CXVII* came out in 1970. This kaleidoscopic and often fragmented work embraces a vast array of themes and sources, including myth, history, the relationship of modern life to cultural tradition, and even economics and the banking system (*Cantos XLII–LI*, for example).

moved on to develop their work in their own directions, but the Imagist project was nevertheless influential for modernist poetry in general and clearly marked out an opposing camp to the Georgian poets (see above).

The figure at the center of the modernist camp of poets was Ezra Pound (1885–1972). He had studied with Williams at the University of Pennsylvania; he later worked as Yeats's secretary; he coined the name "Vorticism" for Wyndham Lewis's avant-garde movement; he edited T.S. Eliot's *The Waste Land*; he became an important member of the American expatriate community of artists in Paris; and he was also on close terms with many of the Dadaists and Surrealists. In fact, he seems to have known almost every major modernist writer, and encouraged and promoted many of them, including James Joyce, D.H. Lawrence, Marianne Moore, and Rebecca West.

Pound's own significant output includes poetry, essays, and translations. Unlike Williams, he looked outside the United States for the material for his poetry, and indeed, had a notable

Perhaps the most celebrated (and notorious) section of the work is the *Pisan Cantos* (*LXXIV–LXXXIV*) written during Pound's imprisonment in a United States Army detention camp in Italy at the end of World War II. Pound had been a vocal supporter of Mussolini and an active participant in fascist propaganda activities. Following an aborted trial for treason, he was detained in a mental hospital in Washington DC until 1958. Although the *Pisan Cantos* were written in circumstances of personal mental and wider cultural collapse, they are nevertheless the most coherent and self-contained parts of the *Cantos* as a whole. In the absence of access to libraries and other sources, Pound drew on his own memories of Europe's shattered culture and his own role therein. Controversially, the poems were awarded the first Bollingen Prize from the Library of Congress in 1949.

Alongside the *Cantos*, the other definitive work of modernist poetry is *The Waste Land* by T.S. Eliot (1888–1965). Eliot was born, raised, and educated in the United States, but shared with Pound an allegiance to European culture over American. He emigrated to Britain in 1914, took British nationality in 1927, and saw his poetry as operating largely within European cultural traditions. Again, like Pound, Eliot filled his poetry with cultural allusions, his early work drawing in particular on the French Symbolists, J.G. Frazer's *The Golden Bough*, Wagner's operas, as well as religious texts, and classical authors such as Dante, Chaucer, Shakespeare, and Milton.

The Waste Land was published in 1922 and was immediately acclaimed for capturing the spirit of the times. Like the poets of World War I, Eliot discarded the hackneyed poetic idioms of the past in favor of styles and forms more appropriate to the modern world. The contrast between past and present, romanticism and modernity, is nowhere better expressed than in Eliot's earlier poem, *The Love Song of J. Alfred Prufrock* (1915): "Let us go then, you and I,/ When the evening is spread out against the sky/ Like a patient etherised upon a table."

T.S. ELIOT, On his honeymoon in the Bahamas, 1957, At Love Beach, New Providence Island, "A Wonderful Time," *Slim Aarons Holiday Magazine,* March 1960

The Waste Land takes the themes and techniques of *Prufrock* even further. Written as a dramatic monologue in five sections, it presents a vision of a barren world where the cultural and spiritual values of civilization have dissolved, leaving behind just the empty formalities of a life on auto-pilot. The poem features many different voices, spliced together almost like a radio play. Some voices seem almost disembodied and gnomic, others gabble away colloquially. None of the voices engage with each other. Sometimes it appears that someone is speaking in the first person, but then, confusingly, the speech shifts to other people. The fragmentation of voices, narratives, and forms, and the use of discordant images create a collage, which initially seems almost randomly put together. Eliot, however, deliberately never allows direct connections between the poem's elements; there is no comforting logic or metanarrative. Instead, it is incumbent upon the reader to try to rebuild some kind of civilization from the fragments and reconnect with spiritual values. Indeed, the poetry Eliot would write later in his career—particularly the *Four Quartets*—pursues just this quest for the spiritual life.

Back in the United States, the problem of re-accessing the spiritual life was also the preoccupation of Wallace Stevens (1879–1955). Poems such as *Final Soliloquy of the Interior Paramour* (1954) develop the notion of the *Supreme Fiction,* suggesting that even if God is a fiction, a person still has the potential to access the feeling of rightness associated with the idea of God. Other poems, including the celebrated *The Idea of Order at Key West* (1936), make us actively engage the imagination to try to piece together the fragments of our understanding of the world into a coherent whole.

Many of the same concerns can also be traced in the novels of the time. As well as the problem of coming to terms with modernity, issues faced by novelists such as Fitzgerald, Faulkner, Hemingway, and Steinbeck included the relative status of American culture against European, the challenge of finding

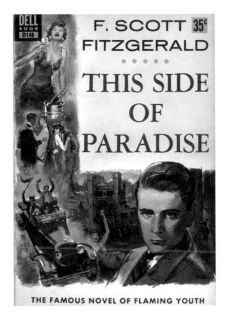

LEFT: *THIS SIDE OF PARADISE,* Cover of a paperback reprint

Fitzgerald's remarkable debut novel is an insider's satire of the American aristocracy and the social hierarchy of Ivy League universities.

RIGHT: *THE GREAT GATSBY,* Movie based on the novel by Fitzgerald and directed by Jack Clayton, 1974, American actors Robert Redford as Jay Gatsby and Mia Farrow as Daisy Buchanan

a new language and style for the novel, and the difficulty of negotiating the period's stark political choices.

The marked shift in sensibility between the modernist novelists and their predecessors is summed up by Edith Wharton's remark to F. Scott Fitzgerald: "To your generation, I must represent the literary equivalent of tufted furniture and gas chandeliers." Wharton (1862–1937), and Henry James before her (see previous chapter), had crafted well-wrought narratives, mostly concerning the lives and loves of the upper echelons of American society at the turn of the century. The novels of Fitzgerald (1896–1940), however, deal with what he called the "Jazz Age," a time of social and moral flux that gave new life to the American Dream yet harbored a latent sense of impending disaster.

Fitzgerald won literary acclaim early in life with his first novel *This Side of Paradise* (1920), which portrayed the sea change in moral and social codes after World War I. In many ways, the thematic material of Fitzgerald's novels reflects the circumstances of his own life. While his early success promised

the possibility of realizing the American Dream, his next novel, *The Beautiful and Damned* (1922), echoed his fears that it was too good to be true. The story concerns a beautiful young couple, whose innocence, hopes, and capabilities degenerate as they wait to inherit a fortune. In an attempt to escape the burden of expectation in his own life, Fitzgerald moved to France with his wife Zelda in 1924. It was there that he completed his most famous work *The Great Gatsby* (1925), often hailed as the quintessence of the "Great American Novel" (an idealized concept in American culture equivalent to the tradition of the national epic in Europe). Set on America's Eastern Seaboard, the book depicts a world of hedonism, selfishness, materialism, hypocrisy, and amorality. Yet its central character, Jay Gatsby, despite being immersed in this culture, and despite having enriched himself through bootlegging, emerges with his innocence intact. He is almost heroic in preserving his faith in the platonic ideal of the American Dream.

By the 1930s, however, Fitzgerald's own life was crumbling, as he descended into alcoholism and his wife suffered repeated

Rises (1926) focuses on the expatriate community in France and Spain in the early 1920s (it also popularized the expression, the "Lost Generation"). *For Whom the Bell Tolls* (1940) is set during the Spanish Civil War. Many of his short stories and much of his journalism also deal with Europe's wars.

Hemingway's themes do, however, have more universal significance. The idea of a man alone against a great enemy recurs in many of his works. Whether it is the matador against a bull (*Death in the Afternoon*, 1932), hunting for big game (*The Green Hills of Africa*, 1935), or the individual against the forces of war, Hemingway portrays a hard-boiled character who must demonstrate what he referred to as "grace under pressure." It seems that only through embracing individualism and testing oneself against elemental forces can one hope to escape from the effete culture, moral confusion, and impotence depicted in *The Sun Also Rises*. Hemingway sums up this philosophy in his last major work of fiction, *The Old Man and the Sea* (1952), a parable about an old Cuban fisherman's lonely, losing, but nevertheless heroic, battle with life.

nervous breakdowns. He completed one more novel, *Tender Is the Night* (1934)—about a psychiatrist who marries one of his patients—and half-finished another, *The Last Tycoon* (published posthumously in 1941), set in Hollywood, where he had taken a position as a scriptwriter. Despite an early death, his legacy was significant, and included many fine short stories in addition to his novels.

Although Fitzgerald is often considered a member of the Lost Generation, his most famous works are, in fact, set in the United States and concern American culture. The novels of Ernest Hemingway (1899–1961), on the other hand, have a much closer relationship to Europe even if many of their protagonists are American. His novel *A Farewell to Arms* (1929) drew on his work with the Red Cross in Italy during World War I. *The Sun Also*

Despite the machismo of many of Hemingway's characters, his fiction yields a poeticism of great subtlety. His writing style is spare and economical. Derived in part from his training as a journalist, it makes great use of short sentences and avoids rhetoric, embellishment, and cheap emotion. Through achieving a sense of objectivity, he opens up great scope for irony through understatement—which also suits his stoic characters. In addition, Hemingway had an ear finely tuned to dialogue and effects of rhythm and repetition. The overall concentration of expression equipped him perfectly for the short-story form.

In contrast with Hemingway, the works of William Faulkner (1897–1962) are fairly circumscribed in their geographical and cultural settings, being firmly rooted in the Deep South. Many of his novels and short stories are set in Jefferson and Yoknapatawpha County, based largely on his home terrain of Oxford and Lafayette County in Mississippi. Many of the same characters also reappear in successive works.

Yet despite the rural remoteness of his milieu and his avoidance of the society of other writers, Faulkner was, all the same, deeply engaged with modernist developments in literature. His first major work was the novel The Sound and the Fury (1929), which employs stream-of-consciousness, unrealiable-narrator, and time-shift techniques, and pointedly avoids neat resolution at the end. It tells the story of a once grand Southern family descended from a Civil War hero. Standing perhaps as a symbol for the degeneration of Southern values, the Compson family —greedy, racist, and effete—have lost their money, religious faith, and social position.

Faulkner's next published novel, As I Lay Dying (1930), is also set in Yoknapatawpha, though this time portraying a poor white family. It too employs the stream-of-consciousness technique and multiple viewpoints (through 15 different narrators). This was followed by Sanctuary (1931), which Faulkner claimed he had written to make money. In addition to being financially successful (in spite of its theme of rape), it also brought Faulkner critical attention. He followed up this success with Light in August (1932), about personal identity and race, and Pylon (1935), about a group of barnstorming pilots. Then in 1936 came Absalom, Absalom!, arguably his finest novel. It reintroduces the Compson family, and, like The Sound and the Fury, allegorizes Southern history. Different narrators give their own versions of events, and, in so doing, continue the Southern tradition of dwelling on the past and how it all went wrong. The different narratives also contribute to the process of myth-making, taking the story further and further away from reality and into the realms of the imagination. In this respect, the novel has something in common with the magic realist genre. It is significant that the downfall of the plantation owner at the center of the story is set in motion by his trying to rewrite his own past, by denying his marriage to a woman of mixed race and their son.

AS I LAY DYING, Dancer Valerie Bettis (left) rehearsing a ballet based on William Faulkner's novel

Other significant novels by Faulkner include *The Wild Palms* (1939), the "Snopes" trilogy (*The Hamlet*, 1940, *The Town*, 1957, and *The Mansion*, 1959), *Go Down, Moses* (1942) and *Intruder in the Dust* (1948). A number of his works—including *Absalom, Absalom!* and many of his short stories—contain elements of the Southern Gothic tradition. Another practitioner in the genre, Tennessee Williams, described it as a style that captured "an intuition of an underlying dreadfulness in modern experience." Faulkner's use of it was mostly restricted to the use of characters whose flaws are developed to an almost grotesque degree.

Another writer whose novels are closely associated with rural America is John Steinbeck (1902–1968). His most famous works, *Of Mice and Men* (1937) and *The Grapes of Wrath* (1939), are set in the context of the Great Depression and deal with the lives of migrant agricultural laborers escaping from the Dust Bowl. *Of Mice and Men* is the story of two workers—one small and shrewd, the other physically powerful but mentally retarded—who dream of saving enough money to buy their own smallholding, but whose plans end in disaster. The book touches on themes of racism, sexuality, loneliness, personal independence, and social equality. *The Grapes of Wrath* is about a family of poor sharecroppers who are driven from their home when their crops fail. They set out for California in the hope of finding work and a new life. Many of their efforts turn out to be futile—they encounter exploitation by big businesses, inadequate assistance from the government, and conflict with the trade unions. The publication of the book met with great controversy. It was ritually burnt, banned in some areas, and criticized by both the left and the right of the political spectrum. Steinbeck did have sympathy with many socialist ideas, but in fact, he had deliberately moderated his description of the deprivation he had witnessed in order not to distract from the story.

RIGHT: JOHN STEINBECK

Steinbeck won a Pulitzer Prize for his 1939 novel *The Grapes of Wrath*, and was awarded the Nobel Prize for Literature in 1962. The novel captured the desperation and yearnings of Depression-era migrant workers and galvanized support for New Deal social legislation.

BELOW : *THE GRAPES OF WRATH*, Play based on Steinbeck's novel, Actors (clockwise from top left): Sally Murphy, Mark Deakins, Jim True, and Gary Sinise

GERMAN LITERATURE

Literature in the German-speaking world during the modernist period was, of course, marked by the enormous upheavals of two world wars and the all-engulfing ideology of Nazism. It was a period, nevertheless, that helped foster several distinctive movements, including Expressionism, Dadaism, and Epic Theater.

Expressionism was an artistic tendency that found most currency in the visual arts—in particular, painting (Schiele, Kirchner, and Kokoschka for example) and early cinema (including Murnau, Wiene, and Lang). There were also notable exponents, though, within the fields of music, theater, and literature. The most obvious characteristic of the genre is the expression of intense emotion. To this end, it is anti-naturalistic, highly subjective, and has a tendency to distort reality, often to the point of the grotesque. There is sometimes also a strong element of satire.

Franz Kafka (1883–1924) was perhaps the most famous writer to work within the expressionist style. Among his most celebrated works is the novella *The Metamorphosis* (1915). Its extraordinary story tells from a man who awakes one morning to find himself transformed into an enormous insect. Although he retains his mind, he is no longer able to speak and is therefore utterly alienated. His family looks after him, but confine him to his room. Gradually, his size diminishes—in tandem with his personal identity—and eventually his family denies his existence altogether.

Another important work, *The Trial* (1925), continues the themes of alienation, disorientation, and guilt already seen in *The Metamorphosis*. It has one of the most famous opening lines of any novel ever written: "Someone must have slandered Joseph K., because one morning, without his having done anything wrong, he was arrested." The persecution Joseph K. feels at the hands of the malign and twisted state bureaucracy is compounded by a loss of humanity, as he slowly realizes the arbitrariness of society's codes and values. Other important works by Kafka include the novels *The Castle* (1926) and *Amerika* (1927), and the short stories *The Judgement* (1912) and *A Hunger Artist* (1924).

The apparent randomness and nihilism of modern life was also at the heart of the Dada movement. It began its activities in Zürich during World War I, and through its anarchic performances, cabarets, exhibitions, readings, and journals embraced a variety of arts and media. Although a relatively short-lived affair—as a coherent movement it was largely over by the mid-1920s—it nevertheless proved enormously influential. Spreading to Berlin and Cologne, New York and Paris, it provided inspiration not only to the Surrealists, but also to some degree to James Joyce, Absurdist theater, conceptual art, and even postmodernism. Among those who

FRANZ KAFKA

Kafka was born into a German-speaking Jewish family in Prague and lived there almost all his life. He published very little during his lifetime and never finished any of his full-length novels. It was left, therefore, to his friend and literary executor, Max Brod, to edit and prepare his works for publication posthumously, ignoring Kafka's wishes to have all his papers burnt. His most celebrated works include *The Metamorphosis* and *The Trial*.

A SCENE FROM *RISE AND FALL OF THE CITY OF MAHAGONNY* BY BERTOLT BRECHT, Roy Cornelius Smith as Fatty (left), Gwyneth Jones as Leokadja Begbick (center) and Wilbur Pauley as Trinity Moses (right), at the Salzburg Festival

Set in the mythical American West during the gold rush, this political-satirical opera from composer Kurt Weill and playwright Bertolt Brecht presents an ironic view of the capitalist society. *Rise and Fall of the City of Mahagonny* was first performed in Leipzig in 1930 and continues to attract audiences. Its music and songs are much acclaimed, especially the classic "Alabama Song."

produced Dadaist literature were the poet and author of the Dada Manifesto Hugo Ball (1886–1927) and the poet and painter Kurt Schwitters (1887–1948). Their works incorporated elements of chance, nonsense, and sound effects, as well as innovative typography.

An important part of the Dadaist mission was to attack the bourgeois artistic values of the era brought to an end by World War I. This political element was also central to the work of the playwright Bertolt Brecht (1898–1956), who befriended several of the Dadaists. Brecht's early plays show expressionist influence, but during the late 1920s, increasingly under the sway of Marxist ideas, he wrote the satirical musical, *The Threepenny Opera* (1928), with music by Kurt Weill. Adapted from John Gay's *The Beggar's Opera* (1728), it contains the immortal line, "What is robbing a bank compared to founding a bank?" Brecht and Weill followed up this success with *Rise and Fall of the City of Mahagonny* (1930), which was reviled by the Nazis.

On Hitler's coming to power in 1933, Brecht had to go into exile, heading first to Scandinavia, then from 1941 onward, to the United States. During these years, he wrote some of his most famous plays, including *Mother Courage and Her Children* (1941), *The Life of Galileo* (1943), *The Good Woman of Setzuan* (1943), and *The Caucasian Chalk Circle* (1948). In 1947, however, his communist sympathies meant that he had to leave the United States as well, and he returned to Europe, eventually settling in East Berlin in 1949. Here, he formed his own theater company, the Berliner Ensemble, and for the remainder of his life concentrated on developing the theatrical life of the city.

Brecht's legacy relates principally to his conception of theater. He rejected the idea that dated back to Aristotle—that the audience should identify emotionally with the action of the play. Instead, Brecht aimed to align drama with Marxist philosophy. In place of emotional catharsis, which left the spectator complacent, Brecht's plays aimed to stimulate the audience's rational faculties, which would spur them to effect change in the world outside. He called this type of drama "Epic Theater" since, similar to epic poetry, it made the audience aware that it was merely hearing an account of past events. Brecht hammered home this detachment of audience from dramatic action—or "alienation effect"—with the use of a number of devices such as explanatory signs, actors "breaking the fourth wall," and even stage directions being read aloud.

THOMAS MANN

One of the most important novelists working in German in the first half of the 20th century was Thomas Mann (1875–1955). The events that wrought havoc to his country during his lifetime provided the stimulus for the assessment of European culture that forms the overarching theme of his novels, stories, and essays.

His first major novel *Buddenbrooks* (1901), presents a bourgeois family (not unlike his own) and its business over four generations. As generation succeeds generation, the vitality and practical engagement with the world of the family's earlier members gradually gives way to more artistic sensibilities. It is progress of sorts, but, crucially, undermines the family traits that brought worldly success in the first place. Another famous work, *Death in Venice* (1912), takes the theme of degeneration further.

For many, World War I marked the end of an era of European culture. In Mann, it stirred his patriotic feelings as well as a sense of the artist's social responsibility. Initially, he attempted to rationalize the authoritarianism of the time (*Reflections of an Unpolitical Man*, 1918), but over the course of the 1920s he revised this outlook. His next major novel, *The Magic Mountain* (1924), suggests the dilemmas of his position. It recounts the story of a young man, who, before embarking on a career as an

engineer, visits a sanatorium in the rarefied climes of the Swiss Alps. He ends up spending seven years there among a group of patients who represent a cross-section of pre-war European culture. He indulges in a life of introspection alongside possibilities of love and death. In the end, however, he rejects this selfishness and re-engages with the world. On leaving the gilded cage of the sanatorium, he is drafted into the army to face death on the battlefield.

The late 1920s and early 1930s brought Fascism to Germany. Mann responded with the novella *Mario and the Magician* (1929), in which the character of Fascism is embodied in the person of the magician, who also represents the link between the artist and the charlatan. This work, and various essays and lectures opposing Nazism, meant that when Hitler came to power in 1933, Mann and his wife had to make a new home for themselves in Switzerland. In

1938, they emigrated to the United States. Mann continued producing important work throughout his period of exile. In 1933, he published the first of a four-part novel *Joseph and His Brothers* (1933–1943). This retells the biblical story of Joseph, with particular emphasis on the themes of myth and history, the individual and the tribe, and the emergence of monotheist religion. Then, in 1939, he published *Lotte in Weimar*, a response to Goethe's *The Sorrows of Young Werther* (1774). The evocation of the humanist civilization of Goethe's Weimar formed a poignant counterpoint to the extremism of the Nazis.

The novel *Doktor Faustus* (1947), however, provided a more explicit commentary on the events in Germany leading up to World War II. The story—a reworking of the Faust legend— concerns a German composer who enters into a pact to exchange the gift of love for 24 years of genius. When the 24 years are up, he suffers a complete mental collapse, though survives another 10 years before dying in 1940. His fate, from pride and temptation to loss of rational faculties, humanity, and life itself, reflects that of Germany's own soul. It also underlines Mann's belief in the inseparability of art and politics.

After World War II, Mann visited Germany regularly, though never lived there again. His last major work, *The Confessions of Felix Krull, Confidence Man* (Part I published in 1954), remained unfinished at his death.

FRANCE: FROM 1920s TO 1940s

In the interwar period, Paris continued as an artistic center at the forefront of modernism. It nurtured several new movements and attracted artists and writers from all over the world. World War II, however, marked the end of France's cultural pre-eminence. Many artists and writers emigrated—in particular, to New York—to escape the Nazi occupation. Moreover, the image of France was severely tarnished by the impotence of the defending French army, the collaborationist Vichy Regime, and later, by bitter colonial wars. Post-war France continued to foster important artistic achievements—including the writings of Beckett, Genet, Ionesco, Butor, and Perec—but all the same, it was soon clear that the cultural initiative had moved across the Atlantic.

The period began, however, with the inauguration of a new artistic movement. Surrealism developed from several sources. Tristan Tzara (1896–1963), one of the founding members of Dadaism, moved to Paris in 1919 to work with André Breton (1896–1966) and others on the magazine *Littérature*. Artistic and political disagreements, however, soon followed in abundance, and they went their separate ways, with Breton publishing the first issue of *La Révolution surréaliste* in 1924. The term "surrealism" had been coined by Apollinaire some years earlier, and the emphasis on attacking the absurdity of the old bourgeois order with the movement's own artistic absurdity came straight from Dadaism. In typical avant-garde style, Breton also issued several manifestoes for the new movement and incorporated in them ideas from Freud on the importance of bypassing the moderating influence of the conscious in order to access the subconscious. Through automatic writing, the use of alcohol and drugs, and the analysis of dreams, the Surrealists aimed to free themselves from the constraints of morality and convention and access the truth. The Symbolist poets provided ample inspiration for

this, and, in stripping away the effects of a bankrupt civilization, so too did supposedly "primitive" tribal art and culture. As the 1920s progressed, Breton became more and more interested in Marxism and attempted to reconcile it with Surrealism. This proved divisive within the movement, and caused many of its members to go their own way.

Apart from Breton, major literary figures associated with Surrealism included Paul Éluard (1895–1952), Louis Aragon (1897–1982), Antonin Artaud (1896–1948), and Jean Cocteau (1889–1963). As for Symbolism before it, poetry was the literary medium most suited to the aims of Surrealism. Perhaps the best works were those of Paul Éluard, in particular, *Capitale de la douleur* (1926), *La Rose publique* (1934) and *Les Yeux fertiles*

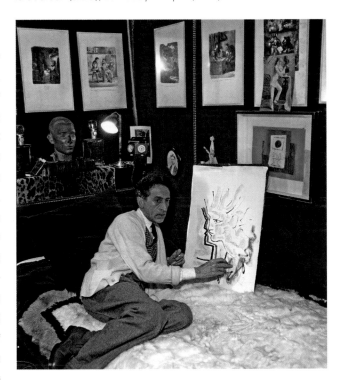

JEAN COCTEAU, 1946

Jean Cocteau was an artist, director, and writer, whose works reflect the influence of surrealism, psychoanalysis, Cubism, and Catholic religion. In his time Cocteau practised and promoted avant-garde styles and fashions.

(1936). In the theater, the plays of Cocteau and the theories of Artaud also proved influential. The latter developed the concept of the "Theater of Cruelty," which set out to shock the audience into apprehending the meaninglessness of life. It would later prove a source of inspiration to Genet, Ionesco, and Beckett. While there were also several Surrealist novels (Aragon's *Le Paysan de Paris*, 1926, and Breton's *Nadja*, 1928, for example), the most important works in the form in the interwar period were produced by writers working outside Surrealist circles, notably André Malraux (1901–1976), Antoine de Saint Exupéry (1900–1944), and Louis-Ferdinand Céline (1894–1961).

Toward the end of the 1930s, the nihilism of modernism found more philosophical form in Existentialism. Existentialist ideas

JEAN PAUL SARTRE AND SIMONE DE BEAUVOIR

Sartre was awarded the Nobel Prize for Literature in 1964, but he declined the honor in protest of the values of bourgeois society. Simone de Beauvoir was his longtime companion, whom he met in 1929.

had been articulated before, in the works of Kierkegaard, Dostoyevsky, Nietzsche, and Kafka for example. Its particular doctrines and emphases vary with different writers, but the unifying idea was to view the universe subjectively—from the point of view of the individual. For existentialists, there is no objective system of values, no god, no apparent meaning to the world. Man is therefore a solitary creature who is totally free and totally responsible. Jean-Paul Sartre (1905–1980) formulated his own brand of the philosophy in novels such as *La Nausée* (1938) and numerous plays—including *Les Mouches* (1943) and *La Putain respectueuse* (1946)—as well as in theoretical works. During the late 1940s, he became increasingly preoccupied with the implications of Communism and strove to reconcile it with his Existentialist ideas. The trilogy, *Les chemins de la liberté* (1945–1949), and the plays *Les Mains sales* (1948) and *Le Diable et le bon Dieu* (1951) chart the development of his thinking.

Another important writer of existentialist works was Simone de Beauvoir (1908–1986). Perhaps her most important novel is *L'Invitée* (1943), which depicts an individual discovering her freedom through a genuinely autonomous act—which just happens to be murder. Beauvoir is also renowned for her feminist writings, notably *Le Deuxième Sexe* (1949).

A third writer, Albert Camus (1913–1960), adopted a somewhat different approach to Existentialism (and indeed denied that he was an Existentialist at all). His most famous novel is *L'Étranger* (1942), which aimed to portray the absurdity of life, and the paradoxical honesty of amorality. In later works, such as the novels *La Peste* (1947) and *La Chute* (1956), and the essay *L'Homme Révolté* (1951), Camus increasingly attempted to challenge the nihilism of Existentialism through seeking out humanistic qualities. His writings also vehemently opposed Communist ideologies for the totalitarianism implicit in them.

POLITICS AND WAR: 1930s AND 1940s

The 1930s and 1940s are often portrayed as a period of stark political choices. The Wall Street Crash of 1929 and the economic depression suggested to many that the capitalist-democratic model had failed. Some therefore looked to Fascism, others to Socialism or Communism to provide the answer to poverty and social inequality. Yet over the course of the 1930s, these alternatives came to be tested, and previous allegiances were challenged as hopes were disappointed or fears confirmed.

Many writers, of course, saw it as their responsibility to take radical positions on the great political questions of the day. Some aligned with the extreme right. The Norwegian writer Knut Hamsun (1859–1952), for example, supported Germany through both world wars and even gave Joseph Goebbels the Nobel Prize medal he had won in 1920. Despite achieving international acclaim for his novels *Hunger* (1890)—often credited as the first modernist novel—and *Growth of the Soil* (1917)—which shows great sympathy for ordinary people and the vicissitudes of life—Hamsun's later works were, unsurprisingly, overshadowed by his political affiliations. Similarly, the literary reputation of Louis-Ferdinand Céline (1894–1961) has also been compromised by his fascist and anti-Semitic views. Nevertheless his novels—especially *Voyage au bout de la nuit* (1932)—have proved influential for their black humor, fragmentariness, nihilism, and use of vernacular language.

It was far more common, however, for writers to align with left-wing ideologies. Some, including Louis Aragon, André Breton, Tristan Tzara, Stephen Spender, and Arthur Koestler, actually joined the Communist Party. Many of these were soon disillusioned though, and even became vehement critics of the Party's ideology and activities. Arthur Koestler (1905–1983), for example, resigned from the Communist Party of Germany in 1938 after the Moscow show trials and wrote his most famous novel *Darkness at Noon* (1940) about the Stalinist purges. The 1939 Molotov-Ribbentrop Pact between Germany and Russia also did much to disabuse people of their trust in the principles of the communist leadership.

LEFT: ANNA AKHMATOVA, Photograph (1924) and line drawing (c. 1911, by Amedeo Modigliani)

Anna Akhmatova is best known for her works *Evening* and *Rosary*. She became a leader of Acmeism with her husband, a movement which praised the virtues of lucid, carefully-crafted verse and opposed the vagueness of the Symbolist style which dominated the Russian literary scene of the period.

FAR LEFT: ARTHUR KOESTLER, At his home in Alpbach, Austria

From 1937 Koestler was one of the main representatives of politically active European authors. He was a member of the German Communist Party from 1932 to 1938, but left the Party during the Moscow trials. Koestler is best known for his novel *Darkness At Noon* (1940), which marks his break with the Communist Party and his ideological rebirth.

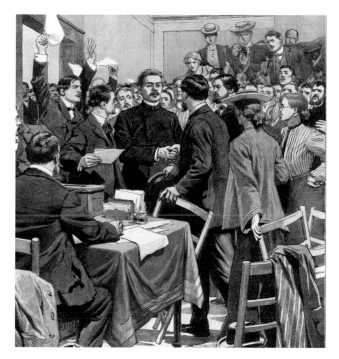

MAXIM GORKY, 1907

Russian writer Maxim Gorky attends a meeting of revolutionaries held in London.

For most writers within the Soviet Union, the idealism associated with the early years of the communist project dissolved far more quickly. Poets who had come to prominence before the Revolution as part of the Symbolist-inspired "Silver Age"—including Anna Akhmatova (1889–1966), Osip Mandelstam (1891–1938), and Boris Pasternak (1890–1960)—were now viewed as dangerous bourgeois elements. They could often only issue their work by *samizdat* (clandestine publication) and frequently suffered persecution (Mandelstam died in a prison camp). Even the radical avant-garde poet Vladimir Mayakovsky (1893–1930), who had promoted revolutionary principles so ardently throughout the 1920s, balked at the shift to Stalinism and committed suicide in 1930. In his wake, as the 1930s progressed, the officially-approved style of Socialist Realism became all-pervasive. The most artistically successful

exponents of the genre were the novelist and playwright Maxim Gorky (1868–1936), and the novelist and Nobel Prize-winner Mikhail Sholokhov (1905–1984). By contrast, novelists working outside the official ideology faced censorship or worse. A censored version of *The Master and Margarita* by Mikhail Bulgakov (1891–1940) was only published in 1966–1967, years after his death. Pasternak's *Doctor Zhivago* was smuggled out of the country and received its first publication in Italy in 1957.

In western Europe, though, under the threat of Fascism, writers were still prepared to flock to the cause. The Spanish Civil War (1936–1939) provided a rallying point, with some 30,000 foreign nationals volunteering to fight for the Republicans (an alliance of socialists, communists, and liberals) against the Nationalists (supported by extreme right groups, landowners, and most of the clergy). Among the volunteers were many writers, including George Orwell (1903–1950) and André Malraux, and more still gave moral and financial support, including W.H. Auden (1907–1973), Pablo Neruda (1904–1973), and Ernest Hemingway. The catalyst for involvement for many of them was the brutal murder of the poet and playwright Federico García Lorca (1898–1936) by Nationalist militia at the start of the war.

In the end, of course, the Nationalists prevailed, and Franco's regime instituted a policy of strict censorship. Many dissidents were imprisoned or went into exile. World War II broke out just a few months later, and, as European culture appeared to be disintegrating once and for all, many writers again questioned their role. For all the idealism at the start of the Spanish Civil War—Auden's poem *Spain* (1937) urged engagement—just a few years later, his poem *In Memory of W.B. Yeats* (1940) seemed to acknowledge impotence and withdrawal: "poetry makes nothing happen." It was indeed fitting, then, that Orwell's novel *1984* (1949) brought the period to a close with a warning of a nightmarish future.

Chapter 9
1950 TO PRESENT DAY
EXPERIMENTATION AND MASS MARKET

2004 BOOKER PRIZE NOMINEES
Five of the six Man Booker Prize 2004 nominees, left to right, Gerard Woodward, Colm Toibin, Achmat Dangor, Alan Hollinghurst, and Sarah Hall, pose for the media in London hours before the winner is announced. The sixth author, David Mitchell, was not present at the photocall.

FACING PAGE: A girl reads *Harry Potter and The Deathly Hallows* beside a poster of Harry Potter at a bookstore in Nanjing in China. China imported 50,000 copies of this bestseller, about half of its total imports of books.

The post-war world seemed, at least initially, to be one that had changed fundamentally. The old world order of dominant European colonial powers had been swept aside to be replaced by two nuclear superpowers—the USA and Soviet Union—who at times seemed bent on mutual destruction. Their enmity was played out across the globe in localized conflicts, but this overriding sense of menace found its way into much writing of the period. As the old European colonial powers saw their influence wane on the world stage, their former colonies, buoyed up by optimism and newly-forged identities stemming from their independence movements, began to engage on the global cultural stage through their authors, a movement that has been dubbed—albeit controversially—post-colonial literature.

Although there was a decline in the power and influence of Europe after the war, many people in the West saw great improvements in their quality of life as old social orders were challenged and a greater sense of equality and calls for a redistribution of the national wealth led to the setting up of welfare states, nationalization of key industries, and laws countering discrimination. These were patchy—with African Americans only gaining equal rights by the end of the 1960s—

and were, by the end of the century, being scaled down in many places, but they did at first give rise to a new confidence among working people, and writers responded to this with a new wave of social realism. Countering this was the rise of the post-war avant-garde. The champions of the new movement believed that World War II had done away with the old social and artistic conventions, and that the styles and ideas of the pre-war world were no longer relevant nor fully articulate. They sought to create new forms of expression that reflected what they saw as a new world of social dislocation and a technological-industrial complex that was both threatening (through the destructive power of nuclear weapons or environmental degradation) and controlling. Extreme forms of linguistic experimentation were explored, especially in poetry and theater, leading at times to an alienation of readers and audiences who struggled to understand the meaning behind the opaquely complex texts.

Toward the end of the century, writers began to look beyond the internal manipulation of linguistic structure and seek new ways of presenting the chaos and complexity of the world. Drawing on the ideas of post-modernist thinkers, writers began to present multiple viewpoints and voices within their texts, in a

1952 Ralph Ellison writes *Invisible Man*.

1956 First Congress of Black Writers meets in Paris.

1956–1957 Naguib Mahfouz writes the *Cairo Trilogy*.

1957 Samuel Beckett publishes *Endgame*; Albert Camus brings out *Exile and the Kingdom*.

1958 Chinua Achebe writes *Things Fall Apart*.

1960–1962 Belgian Congo, Uganda, Tanganyika, and Nigeria become independent.

1962–1973 United States is involved in Vietnam War.

1967 Gabriel García Márquez writes *One Hundred Years of Solitude*.

1970 Derek Walcott publishes *Dream on Monkey Mountain*; Márquez brings out *Death Constant Beyond Love*.

1972 Ingeborg Bachmann writes *Three Paths to the Lake*, which includes *The Barking*.

1975 Wole Soyinka publishes *Death and the King's Horseman*.

1980 Mahasweta Devi writes *Breast-Giver*; Anita Desai brings out *Clear Light of Day*.

1990 East and West Germany are united.

1991 The Soviet Union collapses amid economic chaos and nationalist unrest.

1993 The World Wide Web is made accessible.

1999 A European common currency, the "euro," is issued.

2000 Anita Desai publishes *Diamond Dust*, which includes *The Rooftop Dwellers*.

non-hierarchical and non-linear fashion, to write multi-layered and closely interwoven works that could be bewildering but sometimes virtuosic in their use of language and imagery. These "literary" works, largely novels and short stories, have been perhaps more discussed than read and, at least in the world of academia, they have overshadowed a huge publishing industry that thrives on directly-told narratives that focus on people's everyday life experiences, romance, or fast-paced thrillers. It is arguable that these works are far more influential, and writers such as Nick Hornby (*b*. 1957; *Fever Pitch*, 1992, and *High Fidelity*, 1995), Robert Ludlum (b. 1927; most famous for the "Bourne Trilogy"), and Helen Fielding (*b*. 1958; *Bridget Jones's Diary*, 1996) may be seen as more reflective of their time. It is no coincidence that many of these works have been made into successful movies, giving them wider exposure and ensuring that more people read the original books.

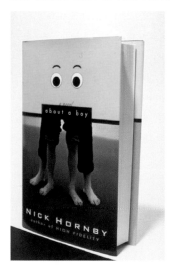

NICK HORNBY'S *ABOUT A BOY*

POST-WAR FRANCE

Although suffering from the after-effects of invasion during World War II, and having to side-step some of the more unsavory aspects of collaboration, the post-war center of European culture and intellectual life was undoubtedly France, more particularly Paris, which was still presided over by its pre-war cultural élite, including such luminaries of the Left Bank as Jean-Paul Sartre and Jean Cocteau.

Both Sartre and Cocteau promoted a new generation of cutting-edge thinkers and writers, including one of the most original writers of post-war France, Jean Genet (1910–1986). After a rather scandalous early life, working as a prostitute and petty thief, he began to write poetry, and wrote his first influential novel *Notre Dame des Fleurs* (1944) while in prison. After Sartre and Cocteau petitioned for his release, Genet went on to write several more novels, the central themes drawn on his own experiences of the gay underworld and criminality, as well as some notable plays. During the last 20 years or so of his life, he adopted a far more political stance and became a left-wing activist, writing on issues such as the attempted 1968 revolution in France and the Israeli massacres at the Palestinian refugee camps of Sabra and Shatila.

SAMUEL BECKETT

LEFT: *WAITING FOR GODOT,* 18 July 2005,
At Theatre Royal, Bath.

Famously described as a "play in which nothing
happens," *Waiting for Godot* consists of two
characters, Vladimir and Estragon, who are waiting for a third, Godot, who never arrives. Bleak
and with a cruel sense of humor, the play was
heralded as a new vision for theater.

Although Genet was not associated with the *nouveau roman* ("new novel"), those writers who became the main exponents of the style were also the darlings of Paris's Left Bank. Chief among these was Alain Robbe-Grillet (1922–2008) whose 1963 essay *Pour un Nouveau Roman* argued for a constant reinvention of the form, one in which narrative and character are given a lesser role in favor of descriptions of objects and place. Robbe-Grillet also wrote a number of screenplays for movies, notably *L'Année dernière à Marienbad* (1961) for Alain Resnais, continuing the close collaboration between writers of the *nouveau roman* and *nouvelle vague* ("new wave") French cinema. Two writers whose work is associated with that of the *nouveau roman,* but who both resisted the label are Michel Butor (*b.* 1926) and Marguerite Duras (1914–1996). Duras's novels, such as *Moderato Cantabile* (1952) and *L'Amant* (1984), are close in spirit to the *nouveau roman* and much of the text has an air of ambiguity. The work of Michel Butor is a little different, being more poetic and with a greater sense of overall form than that of other experimental French novelists.

Taking their key from the ideas of the *nouvelle vague* and *nouveau roman* the Oulipo Group consisted of writers such as Georges Perec (1936–1982) and Raymond Queneau (1903–1976), as well as the movement's two founders Jacques Roubaud (*b.* 1932) and François Le Lionnais (1901–1984). Founded in 1960, the acronym Oulipo stands for *Ouvroir de littérature potentielle* or "workshop of potential literature." The aim of the group was to devise explicitly new methods of writing novels. Many of these experiments involved repetition, either of situations from many different points of view or in style, or through spatial organization of the text that allows multiple readings of a narrative.

Because of its status as the pre-eminent cultural city in Europe, Paris attracted writers from abroad, including the playwrights Samuel Beckett (1906–1989) and Eugène Ionesco (1909–1994). Both Beckett and Ionesco wrote much of their work in French even though it was not their first language. While some may have come merely because they could, for others it became a place of refuge. The Romanian writer Ionesco found himself in France, trapped by the battles of World War II, and remained in the country for the rest of his life. He is known as the most important figure of the "Theater of the Absurd," using his works to turn language into the central act of the drama where, especially in his early works such as *La Cantatrice chauve* (1950), the structure of the language itself, using repetition, rhythm, and rhyme, provides the "plot". His most famous work is *Rhinocéros* (1959), which attacks the conformism that Ionesco saw permeating contemporary life. Irish by birth, Beckett also used absurd elements in his writing, and sought to portray what he saw as the essential alienation of the modern human condition. In many ways Beckett is the link between modernism and the ideas of post-modernism.

Ionesco and Beckett were not the only foreign writers to live in the city. The Argentine writer Julio Cortázar (1914–1984) moved to France because of his opposition to the government of Perón during the 1950s. His novels and short stories draw on a range of techniques, from the stream of consciousness of modernist writers to the elements of the absurd and the experiments of the *nouveau roman* and Oulipo, especially his novel *Rayuela* (*Hopscotch*, 1963) that has an open-ended structure. The African American writer James Baldwin (1924–1987) also found himself living in exile in Paris, in his case to avoid both the racial discrimination and homophobia of the times prevalent in his native country. Themes of racial and sexual identity dominate his writing, and his novels, including *Giovanni's Room* (1956) and *Tell Me How Long the Train's Been Gone* (1968), are often explicitly homoerotic.

The tradition of writers going into exile also worked for the French author Michel Houellebecq (*b.* 1958) who left France to live in Ireland and Spain. His disturbing and self-obsessed novels, especially *Les particules élémentaires* (*Atomised*, 1998), have proved to be controversial, not least because of their unremittingly bleak view of human nature.

POST-WAR GERMANY AND AUSTRIA

As the defeated nations after 1945, and with having to come to terms with the horrifying consequences of the Nazi-run concentration camps, it is not surprising that post-war literature from Germany and Austria is dominated by the themes of war, suffering, and guilt as writers struggled to cope with their countries' past. In Germany the two foremost writers, both Nobel Prize winners (in 1972 and 1999 respectively), who dealt with this theme were Heinrich Böll (1917–1985) and Günter Grass (*b.* 1927). Böll was born and lived much of his life in the city of Cologne and its near complete destruction from Allied bombing during World War II affected him greatly, so much so that his writing is often referred to as *Trümmerliteratur*, or "'literature of the rubble." In his books, from *Der Zug war pünktlich* (*The Train was on Time*, 1949) to *Ansichten eines Clowns* (*The Clown*, 1963) and *Die verlorene Ehre der Katharina Blum* (*The Lost Honor of Katharina Blum*, 1974), he attacks the status quo and figures of established authority (from politicians to members of the church) while finding valor in the actions of the dispossessed and those who are victims of discrimination. Born and raised in Danzig (now Gdansk in Poland), Günter Grass uses elements of fantasy—verging on magic realism—in his coruscating dissections of Germany during the Third Reich. His

---

ANNE FRANK

The young Jewish girl's diary, describing the two years she spent in hiding with her family during the German occupation of the Netherlands, became a classic of war literature. It has been translated into more than 50 languages and is probably the best known work of the Holocaust.

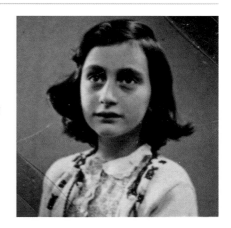

home town is the setting for his three most famous works, *Die Blechtrommel* (*The Tin Drum*, 1959; made into a memorable movie in 1979), *Katz und Maus* (*Cat and Mouse*, 1961), and *Hundejahre* (*Dog Years*, 1963), which chart the rise of Nazi Germany and the fate of Danzig and its inhabitants.

Both Böll and Grass were members of Gruppe 47, a rather loose federation of writers founded in 1947 (hence its name) with the aim of reinventing and encouraging new German literature in the aftermath of World War II. Other important members of the group who took part in its seminars and discussions were the Austrian poet Ingeborg Bachmann (1926–1973), whose work was deeply philosophical in nature, and the Jewish-Viennese writer Ilse Aichinger (*b.* 1921), who drew on her experiences of persecution under the Nazi regime. However, the most famous of the chroniclers of the Holocaust was the German poet and playwright Nelly Sachs (1891–1970). Her intensely personal work is often mystical and conflated with other elements of her life, such as a doomed love affair. For a long time she was closely associated with the Romanian-Jewish poet and translator Paul Celan (1920–1970), much of whose work details his life while incarcerated in the concentration camp of Auschwitz. The Italian-Jewish writer Primo Levi (1919–1987) was also imprisoned in Auschwitz and described the experience in *Se questo è un uomo* (*If This is a Man*, 1947). Anne Frank (1929–1945) is probably the best-known of Holocaust victims, whose diary, which published as *The Diary of a Young Girl* (1947), is the most widely read diary of the Holocaust.

If Böll and Grass are harsh in their view of the historical record of Germany, they pale into insignificance next to the views of the Austrian writer Thomas Bernhard (1931–1989) on his compatriots. In his plays and novels, such as *Heldenplatz* (1988) or *Ein Fest für Boris* (*A Party for Boris*, 1968), he attacks the post-war Austrian state and its inhabitants for their complacency and dubious relationship with history with a zest that was always controversial

"WOLKEN.HEIM. UND DANN NACH HAUSE" BY ELFRIDE JELINEK

The play blends short quotes from writers of the German Romantic period, from Hölderlin and Kleist to philosophers Fichte and Hegel. These are mixed with references to Martin Heidegger and RAF terrorist Meinhoff, and relate to political movements such as Nazism and, somewhat surprisingly, the environmental movement

and at times led to calls for his works to be banned. A similar contempt, or concern, for the Austrian state and its institutions can be found in the work of novelist and poet Elfriede Jelinek (*b.* 1946) who was awarded the Nobel Prize in 2004. Besides having a deeply political critique of contemporary Austria and its recent history, her work, such as *Die Klavierspielerin* (*The Piano Teacher*, 1983) and *Die Liebhaberinnen* (*Women as Lovers*, 1975), often deals with female sexuality, sometimes of a sado-masochistic or pornographic nature.

POST-WAR POETRY

The spirit of experimentation that suffused the post-war world was nowhere more evident than in the sphere of poetry. Less linear and narrative in nature than the texts of novelists and playwrights, poems, following the example of pre-war poets, such as E.E. Cummings, and Ezra Pound, lent themselves to a greater play on grammatical structure, vocabulary, and even typesetting. Many of these experiments were carried out by

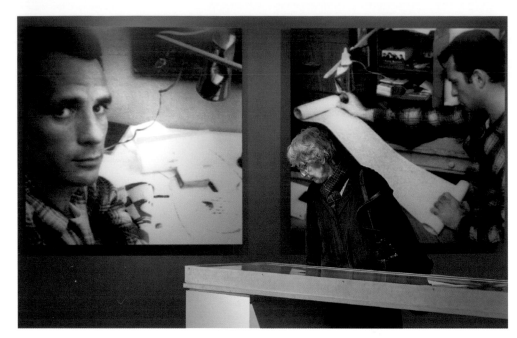

poets living and working in the United States and much of their work was brought to the attention of a wider audience through the publication in 1960 of the anthology *The New American Poetry 1945-60*, edited by Donald Allen, which identified three broad groups of poets, known as the Black Mountain Poets, the New York Poets, and the poets of the San Francisco Renaissance. Chief of these, and with a huge influence on the San Francisco and Black Mountain Poets, are New York-born Allen Ginsberg (1926-1997) and, also from the East Coast, Jack Kerouac (1922-1969). Along with the novelist William Burroughs (1914-1997), they are the main representatives of the "Beat Generation."

With a huge effect on the so-called "counter culture" of the 1960s, these three writers symbolized rebellion against the social mores of their time and their work is often tied up with the use of drugs and sexual experimentation. Not all of the work of the Beats was poetry (although distinctions between genres often seem to break down in their work) but the first major work by any of the three main figures was the poetic collection

Howl (1956) by Ginsberg. *Howl* has a highly fragmentary style that glorifies those far from the mainstream of contemporary society. It also, in common with much work of the Beats, contains highly graphic sexual imagery, and there were moves to try and ban the collection under anti-obscenity laws. The poem thus achieved a certain notoriety, which contributed significantly to its subsequent fame. The two other major early works of the Beat movement are *On the Road* (1957), a travelog by Jack Kerouac, and *Naked Lunch* (1959), a novel by William Burroughs.

Following the experiments of the Black Mountain, New York, and San Francisco groups, as well as the Modernist Objectivists (Williams and Pound), were the experiments of the L=A=N=G=U=A=G=E poets. Starting in the 1970s, the movement takes its name from a New York magazine that published highly experimental works that, on the fringes, moved away from the very idea of language as a communicative medium. Both the Beats and the L=A=N=G=U=A=G=E poets were to have a considerable influence on the revitalized British poetry scene of the 1960s and 1970s. This "British Poetry Revival," characterized by writers like Iain Sinclair (b. 1943) and Eric Mottram (1924–1995), sought to move away from the work of English poets of the immediate post-war period whom they considered to be too traditional. These earlier writers, known as "The Movement" after a review that labelled the group as such, included Kingsley Amis (1922–1995) and Philip Larkin (1922–1985).

Harder to place in a category, and without any affiliation to a particular movement, is British Poet Laureate Ted Hughes (1930–1998). Inspired by nature, his works often seek to show the skull beneath the skin, giving much of his poetry, such as *Crow* (1970) and *Wolfwatching* (1989), a hard, brilliant quality. Hughes also made a notable translation of the *Oresteia* by Aeschylus, and translation has also been a preoccupation of Ireland's most important post-war poet Seamus Heaney (b. 1939), who was awarded the Nobel Prize in 1995. Besides translating *Beowulf*—Anglo Saxon poetry has had a great effect on his work—Heaney has produced a large body of poetic works, many of which deal with life in Northern Ireland.

POST-WAR THEATER IN ENGLISH

Like the Theater of the Absurd that was being explored in Paris, and as in much modern poetry, drama being written in English was also extending boundaries. These tended, however, to be social boundaries of class rather than those of technique and language, and sought to deliver a gritty realism as opposed to the rarefied but bleak nihilism of Beckett and Ionesco. In England, this style was dubbed "kitchen sink drama" after the description given to the plays of John Osborne (1929–1994). His most outstanding work was *Look Back in Anger* (1958). Using themes of social and political alienation, the works of Osborne, Arnold Wesker (b. 1932), and Harold Pinter (1930–2008) are steeped in the politics of the left and the ideal of class struggle, although much of their writing reflects many of the playwrights' middle-class backgrounds. A

A STREETCAR NAMED DESIRE, British actor Vivien Leigh as Blanche and American actor Marlon Brando as Stanley in a still from the movie, Directed by Elia Kazan in 1951

Tennessee Williams received the Pulitzer Prize for Drama in 1947 for this play. In this and other works, Williams wrote about family relations and conflict (in part brought on by broading on issues such as gay relationships) and the clash between traditional ideals and the intrusion of the modern world.

notable aspect of this move to social realism was its crossover into cinema and television, where movies such as *Saturday Night and Sunday Morning* (1960, from the 1958 novel by Alan Sillitoe, b. 1928), *A Taste of Honey* (1961), and *Cathy Come Home* (1966) were far more effective at bringing home the social realist message than those works for the stage.

In the United States, playwrights were similarly concerned with social themes. Among the most celebrated is Tennessee Williams (1911–1983), whose plays, such as *Cat on a Hot Tin Roof* (1955) and *A Streetcar Named Desire* (1948), are drawn on his upbringing in the Southern United States. Arthur Miller (1915–2005) might be seen in chronicling the northern experience in the same way as Williams did for the south. One of his most famous works, *The Crucible* (1953), is about the Salem witch trials and is a not-so-veiled attack on the witch-hunts of the McCarthy era (Miller himself appeared before the House Un-American Activities Committee). Of his other works, *Death of a Salesman* (1949) can be read as an indictment of American capitalism.

THE NOVEL IN ENGLISH

The novel had by the 20th century become the dominant literary form and that was a trend that was to continue after World War II, if anything, achieving an even greater hegemony over other forms such as drama, poetry, and the short story. Writers who had been active before the war initially remained dominant on the literary scene in Britain, especially those with a long writing career such as Evelyn Waugh (1903–1966) and Graham Greene (1904–1991). Of those British novelists who came to prominence in the post-war years, among the first were William Golding (1911–1993) and Kingsley Amis. Golding's work is often mythic in feel, dealing with essential struggles between peaceful co-existence and violence, especially as exemplified in his books *Lord of the Flies* (1954), his most famous work, and *The Inheritors* (1955). Amis was the first British writer to delve into his own experience of teaching at a university for a setting for a novel. The result, *Lucky Jim* (1954), was to spawn a whole series of "campus novels"—books somewhat narcissistically located in the academic world that had a faintly comic flavor—by other writers. Of these, the two most prominent authors are Malcolm Bradbury (1932–2000; *The History Man*, 1975), and David Lodge (*b.* 1935; *Small World*, 1984, *Nice Work*, 1988).

In some ways carrying on the tradition of combining travel writing and fiction exemplified by Graham Greene and Somerset Maugham, Lawrence Durrell (1912–1990) spent much of his life outside of Britain—in Greece, Egypt, and France—and his work deals almost exclusively with these locations. His most famous novels are the four books of the *Alexandria Quartet* (*Justine*, 1957, *Balthazar*, 1958, *Mountolive*, 1958, and *Clea*, 1960), all of which are blessed with a powerful sense of place and tinge of eroticism. An exploration of a slightly different kind is found in the books of Anthony Burgess (1917–1993). Now best known for his dystopian novel *A Clockwork Orange* (1962), made into a controversial movie by Stanley Kubrick in 1971, he also falls into

A CLOCKWORK ORANGE, British actor Malcolm McDowell finds himself in prison in this still from the movie, 1971

the same tradition as Greene and Durrell with his first published books comprising a "Malayan trilogy" (*Time for a Tiger*, 1956, *The Enemy in the Blanket*, 1958, and *Beds in the East*, 1959).

With the coming of the 1980s a new generation of British writers began to emerge. These were dubbed the "young British novelists" after a list published in the literary magazine *Granta* in 1983, and many of the names that have appeared in *Granta* have continued to dominate the British literary scene. The first wave of authors, including Martin Amis (*b.* 1949, and son of the writer Kingsley Amis), Julian Barnes (*b.* 1946), Ian McEwan (*b.* 1948), and William Boyd (*b.* 1952), all seem to veer toward a more harshly condescending and superior tone.

More subtle in their writing, and with a longer perspective, are some of the post-war British women writers. Doris Lessing (*b.* 1919), awarded the Nobel Prize in 2007, is perhaps unusual as she is well-known for her science fiction writing (particularly the *Canopus* series, 1979–1983) although her early work was greatly inspired by her communist beliefs, critically explored in one of her greatest novels *The Golden Notebook* (1962). A writer who has tried to peel back the veneer of civility of middle-class British life, rather than explore worlds of the imagination, is Iris Murdoch (1919–1999). In novels such as *The Black Prince* (1973) and the Booker Prize-winning *The Sea, the Sea* (1978), she presents a finely honed exploration of power and sex, very little of it flattering to the characters involved. More quirky and imaginative—and perhaps the best British writer of magic realism—Angela Carter (1940–1992) also wrote science fiction works and was more overtly "feminist" than the preceding two writers. Drawing on myth and fairy tales, her novels, such as *Wise Children* (1991) and *Nights at the Circus* (1984), as well as short stories and dramas, lead you into a fantastic and eclectic world of plot and characters.

Post-war writing in the United States took a somewhat different path, tending toward large, sweeping narratives that attempt—at times in vain—to describe the experience of living in such a vast and disparate nation. This might be best characterized as the on-going search for "the great American novel," itself the title of a 1973 book by Philip Roth (*b.* 1933) and a label that has been applied to numerous titles over the last 100 years or so (possibly implying that chasing the one "great American novel" could be futile).

Among the greatest and most influential of the writers whose work the title might be applied to is Saul Bellow (1915–2005). Wide in breadth, the vast majority of his novels, among them *The Adventures of Augie March* (1953), a homage to Cervantes, *Herzog* (1964), and *Humboldt's Gift* (1975), are set in Chicago and, through their inclusion of a socially wide variety of characters, seek to portray the diversity that lies at the heart of the American experience. Similarly influential is the writer Norman Mailer (1923–2007). His contribution to the development American literature, along with Truman Capote, was through the so-called "non-fiction novel," a journalistic approach to narrative that

uses real events as the basis for literary works. Mailer's works are often long and difficult, and required large amounts of research in their writing (especially *Ancient Evenings*, 1983, set in Ancient Egypt). A constant theme has been politics and political institutions, from *Barbary Shore* (1951) to *Harlot's Ghost* (1991), both of which dealt with different aspects of Northern America during the Cold War. Writers associated with Mailer and his journalistic style include Hunter S. Thompson (1937–2005; *Fear and Loathing in Las Vegas*, 1971), and Tom Wolfe (*b.* 1931; *The Kandy-Kolored Tangerine-Flake Streamline Baby*, 1965; *The Electric Kool-Aid Acid Test*, 1968; *Bonfire of the Vanities*, 1987).

Another author who has attacked the political direction of neo-liberal America is Gore Vidal (b. 1925). A great campaigning

TRUMAN CAPOTE

Capote rose to fame with the writing of his semi-autobiographical and controversial novel *Other Voices, Other Rooms* (1948). He is perhaps best remembered, however, for his 1958 short work *Breakfast at Tiffany's* and the "non-fiction novel" *In Cold Blood* (1966), which records his visits to a convicted murderer.

writer he has portrayed both Roosevelt and Nixon as well as gay relationships in his work, Vidal is also known for his outspoken attacks on the American establishment. Vidal's great rival was the colorful Truman Capote (1924–1984), one of the instigators of the "non-fiction novel."

Two of the most widely read American authors, however, are known for only one book apiece and subsequently wrote very little else. The first, Harper Lee (b. 1926), was a close friend of Capote and is responsible for the 1960 novel To Kill a Mockingbird, about racial discrimination in the Deep South. J.D. Salinger's (b. 1919) Catcher in the Rye (1952) records another side of the American experience, the loneliness of the big city, told through the exploration of New York by a run-away boy. Vladimir Nabokov (1899–1977) although he wrote and translated many other works—including a number of early novels in Russian—is, in terms of American literature, also known for one work, the controversial novel Lolita (1955), which was written while the author was living in the United States.

More recently the writer Don DeLillo (b. 1936) has attempted to pull the great sweep of American life into his substantial novels, starting with Americana in 1971 but reaching its apotheosis with the monumental Underworld (1997). DeLillo's work is broadly post-modern, relying on multiple narrators and viewpoints to try and portray such a large sway of experience. A different take on the American experience has come from the literary "brat pack" of younger writers. Chief among these is Bret Easton Ellis (b. 1964), whose novel American Psycho (1991) parodies crime fiction, yet caused outrage for its extreme portrayal of violence.

J.D. SALINGER'S _CATCHER IN THE RYE_, First edition, 1981

POST-COLONIAL LITERATURE

Outside of Europe it was not only in the United States of America that writers addressed ideas of identity and nationhood. Much of what has been written in the last 60 to 70 years by authors, poets, and playwrights from Africa, the Middle East, South Asia, the Caribbean, and parts of South America is often placed under the rubric of "post-colonial literature." This broad term seeks to encapsulate all literature written since the dissolution of the European empires after World War II. Specifically, it deals with the experience of the colonized and seeks to view the world from their perspective. In many ways it can be seen as the written history of the previously ignored, or the underdog. The term itself is often attacked for being too vast and for relegating all cultural endeavor in previously colonized parts of the world as a reaction to the colonial experience, an obvious over-simplification, but it remains a handy catch-all term that academics seem loath to give up.

Dominant Western ideologies had relegated the status of the indigenous inhabitants to those of an illegitimate counterforce to what the colonial power regarded as its, often God-given, rights. Writers during the period of struggle for independence and, especially, once the countries had been decolonized began to redress the balance by casting indigenous peoples as victims of colonial aggression and by the (re)discovery of local histories and culture that helped to assert a local identity over that bequeathed by the colonial power. Obviously much ended up being retained—not least English or French as the dominant languages of post-colonial discourse—and the mixing, at times verging on a positive synthesis, of institutions and cultures has given rise to some of the most interesting examples of writing from the non-European world.

Post-colonial writing has not been devoid of theory and polemic that have served to provide both a justification and driving force for some writers; indeed the area has at times seemed to suffer from a surfeit of theory. However, certain writers have proved immensely influential, chief among them the *Négritude* French writers, Frantz Fanon (1925–1961) and Edward Saïd (1935–2003). *Négritude* grew out of the ideas and writings of a group of French-African intellectuals, notably Aimé Césaire (1913–2008) from Martinique, the Senagalese Léopold Sédar Senghor (1906–2001) who became president of independent Senegal, and Léon Damas (1912–78) from French Guiana. Their idea of a pan-Black (or African) culture separate from that of

the West was instrumental in opposing racist attitudes and gave a theoretical basis to emerging anti-colonial struggles. This was explored to an even more far-reaching extent in the writings of Fanon, especially *Peau noire, masques blancs* (*Black Skin, White Masks*, 1952) and *Les damnés de la terre* (*The Wretched of the Earth*, 1961), texts that were highly influential on the anti-colonial movement in Africa. The Palestinian writer Edward Saïd was to bring the scrutiny of post-colonial theory on the West's relationship with the Middle East and South Asia in his major work *Orientalism* (1978).

Influenced greatly by the *Négritude* movement, Black African writers were to emerge during the 1950s and with the publication of the Nigerian writer Chinua Achebe's (*b*. 1930) *Things Fall Apart* in 1958, it began to achieve prominence on

LOLITA, Dominique Swain as Lolita and Jeremy Irons as Humbert in director Adrian Lyne's movie version of Vladimir Nabokov's novel

Humbert, the 45-year-old angst-ridden college professor, falls in love with Lolita, the 12-year-old daughter of a rooming house owner, whom Humbert later marries.

the world stage. Achebe's fellow Nigerian playwright and poet Wole Soyinka (b. 1934) became the first African writer to be awarded the Nobel Prize for Literature in 1986. While both Achebe and Soyinka write in English, there began to be calls for works in local languages and to move away from the language of the colonial powers. The most prominent writer to adopt this stance is the Kenyan Ngugi wa Thiong'o (b. 1938), who now writes exclusively in his local language Kikuyu.

The journalist and political activist from Trinidad, C.L.R. James (1901–1989) produced one of the first Caribbean novels with *Minty Alley* (1936) and soon other authors began to explore the particular issues facing their identity as West Indians. Also from Trinidad, the caustic novelist and commentator V.S. Naipaul (b. 1932) rose to prominence with works such as *A House for Mr Biswas* (1961); he was also awarded the Booker Prize in 1971 and the Nobel Prize in 2001. Another Nobel Prize winner (in 1992) from the region is the poet Derek Walcott (b. 1930), whose long narrative *Omeros* (1990), loosely based on Homer, explores ideas of travel and relocation.

AKINWANDE OLUWOLE "WOLE" SOYINKA, First African writer to be awarded the Nobel Prize for Literature.

MAGIC REALISM

A slightly different take on the Caribbean experience is given by the Guyanese author Wilson Harris (b. 1921) whose *Guyana Quartet* (*Palace of the Peacock*, 1960, *The Far Journey of Oudin*, 1961, *The Whole Armour*, 1962, and *The Secret Ladder*, 1963) takes the reader on a mythic journey along the rivers of his native land, imbuing the topography and characters with significance that is equally baffling and seductive. Harris's writing in the *Quartet* verges on a process often described as "magic realism"—a label, like "postcolonialism," from which authors are often keen to disassociate themselves. The most famous exponent of this is the Colombian writer Gabriel García Márquez (b. 1927) whose 1967 novel *One Hundred Years of Solitude* is often credited with introducing the genre. Magic realism uses the technique of introducing fantastic, "magical," elements into a narrative set in the concrete world. This can involve the use of spirits, dream sequences, shifts to parallel and differing narratives, and imaginary histories.

Márquez is often viewed as the *éminence grise* of the genre, using the technique in a string of works including *Chronicle of a Death Foretold* (1981), *Love in the Time of Cholera* (1985), and *The General in his Labryinth* (1989). However, another earlier South American writer, the Argentinian Jorge Luis Borges (1899–1986), had already explored similar techniques in his writings—especially short stories—with the use of invented worlds in which to set his often fantastic narratives. An even more explicit early use of magical realism is found in the works of Cuban writer Alejo Carpentier (1904–1980). In his novel *The Kingdom of this World* (1949), he refers to "*lo real maraviloso*" (literally "*magic realism*") as the only way of describing the South American experience.

The technique is not limited, however, to writers from South America. The Portuguese author José de Sousa Saramago

(b. 1922), who received the Nobel Prize for Literature in 1998, besides experimenting with grammatical construction and punctuation, often uses fantastically-inspired narratives to present a coruscating critique of the state of his native land, causing great controversy for his 1991 book *The Gospel According to Jesus Christ*.

Outside of Europe, the Nigerian writer Ben Okri (b. 1959), although he eschews the label of magic realist, has woven a fantastic net of indigenous myth and legend around the narratives of works such as the novel *The Famished Road* (1991). Perhaps the most prominent of all writers using magic realist techniques outside of South America though is the Mumbai-born author Salman Rushdie (b. 1947; also one of the 1983 "young British authors"). It was his 1981 novel *Midnight's Children* that first brought him to international attention, winning the Booker Prize the same year (it was later voted, in 2008, the best novel in the 40 years of the prize). The story follows a child born at midnight on 15 August 1947 (the exact moment India gained independence

from British rule) and takes in much of the subsequent history of the newly independent state. This was followed by *Shame* (1983), which explored the politics of Pakistan, but it was his subsequent novel, *The Satanic Verses* (1988), that brought him fame of an entirely different kind. The novel's treatment of Islam and the Prophet Muhammad was deemed by some Muslims to be offensive and when the spiritual leader of Iran, the Ayatollah Khomeini, issued a death sentence against the author, Rushdie went into hiding for several years. He continued to write, however, publishing a stream of novels that were still broadly magic realist in character, including *The Moor's Last Sigh* (1995), *Shalimar the Clown* (2005), and *The Enchantress of Florence* (2008).

INDIAN LITERATURE

While Rushdie's work greatly influenced numerous Indian authors, the tradition of publishing in South Asia stretches back much further and the sub-continent has a long history

Cow, 1936) is considered one of the most important works of all Indian literature.

Many writers, including Rao and Anand, were caught up in the Indian independence movement, and fell especially under the influence of M.K. Gandhi (1869–1948), and the struggle in turn influenced Indian literature from around the middle of the century, with the horrors of Partition forming a particularly important background to much writing, including Khushwant Singh's (*b.* 1915) *Train to Pakistan* (1956). A different side to the departure of the British is given in Nirad C. Chaudhuri's (1897–1999) work *The Autobiography of an Unknown Indian* (1951) that laments the passing of the British Empire, making Chaudhuri a controversial figure in South Asia. The idea of a predominantly rural India, however, one that was dear to Gandhi's heart, was continued by R.K. Narayan (1906–2001). With many of his stories set in and around the fictional South Indian village of Malgudi, he became the chronicler of the trials and tribulations of every day life in India for much of the 20th century. Besides notable popular versions of the great epics *Mahabharata* and *Ramayana*, his novels include *Waiting for the Mahatma* (1955), *The Man-Eater of Malgudi* (1961), and *The English Teacher* (1945).

RABINDRANATH TAGORE

Tagore was the first Asian to win the Nobel Prize for Literature in 1913. He wrote novels, short stories, songs, dance-dramas, and essays on political and personal topics. *Gitanjali* (*Song Offerings*), *Gora* (*Fair-Faced*), and *Ghare-Baire* (*The Home and the World*) are among his best-known works.

of writing, both in English and local languages. In the 20th century, writing in English began to receive attention following the work of the Bengali poet Rabindranath Tagore (1861–1941), who was awarded the Nobel Prize for Literature in 1913. Early novels in English include *Untouchable* (1935) by Mulk Raj Anand (1905–2004) and *Kanthapura* (1938) by the South Indian writer Raja Rao (1908–2006). The themes of these early books are concerned with life in India's myriad villages, especially the harsh conditions suffered by those at the bottom of the social structure. In this, both Anand and Rao follow the example of the great Hindi-Urdu writer Munshi Premchand (1880–1936) whose novel *Godan* (*The Gift of a*

From the 1980s onward, a new generation of writers emerged, and basking to a certain extent in the reflected glory of Rushdie, they began to put Indian literature in English into the international limelight. Of these, one of the most talented is Vikram Chandra (*b.* 1961) who came to prominence with his magical realist novel *Red Earth and Pouring Rain* (1995), followed by the tour-de-force of *Sacred Games* (2006), a detective story set in the underworld of Mumbai. Arundhati Roy, born in the same year, was to achieve a similar level of success with her first novel *The God of Small Things* (1997), for which she won the Booker Prize. A worthy challenger to Rushdie as the chronicler of post-independence India is

Vikram Seth (*b.* 1952), whose monumental *A Suitable Boy* (1993) charts the search by a mother for a husband for her daughter set against the changes of the early years of independence. The past and future have been explored by Amitav Ghosh (*b.* 1956) in *The Calcutta Chromosome* (1995) and *The Glass Palace* (2000), and he returned to a historical theme for his recent novel *Sea of Poppies* (2008), while the beautifully crafted work of Anita Desai (*b.* 1936) often explores the role of women in Indian society, including the near-autobiographical *Clear Light of Day* (1980). In the recent past, Kiran Desai (*b.* 1971, daughter of Anita Desai) won the 2006 Man Booker Prize for her novel *The Inheritance of Loss*, and Aravind Adiga (*b.* 1974) made his mark with his debut novel *The White Tiger,* a story of a man's journey from Indian village life to entrepreneurial success, for which he won the 2008 Man Booker Prize.

SOUTH AFRICA, AUSTRALIA, AND CANADA

The colonial experience of countries such as Australia and Canada was very different to that of most African and Asian nations. The ruling class differed very little from the country's status as a colony to that of independence, in that it is was white, largely descended from inhabitants of the British Isles, and native English-speaking. The Australian experience of colonialism and its aftermath has perhaps been most cogently dealt with by the writer Peter Carey (*b.* 1943). His works almost build up a literary historical survey of the settler experience from the freewheeling narrative of a confidence trickster in the *Illywacker* (1985), to trails and tribulations in the outback in both *Oscar and Lucinda* (1988) and the almost "non-fiction novel" of the *True History of the Kelly Gang* (2000). It might be imagined that given the almost equally vast and wild nature of

AMITAV GHOSH

Indian author Amitav Ghosh with his book *Sea of Poppies.* Ghosh was one of six authors shortlisted for the 2008 Booker Prize.

PETER CAREY

New York-based Australian author Peter Carey wins the Booker Prize for his book *True History of the Kelly Gang* on October 17, 2001.

the landscape, Canadian literature would be similar in scope and theme to that of Australia. In reality, there is little that appears to unite post-war Canadian writers, of whom the most prominent is the feminist Margaret Atwood (b. 1939), perhaps best known for her science fiction writing.

The situation in South Africa reflects a very different reality, where writers had, and have had, to come to terms with the racist apartheid regime that dominated the country between 1948 and 1994. One of the first writers to confront this was Alan Paton (1903–1988), whose novel *Cry, the Beloved Country* (1948) prefigures the racial and social divisions that were to be put in place by the Nationalist Party, themes that were to dominate his subsequent writings. Following on from Paton came South Africa's two Nobel Prize winners, Nadime Gordimer (b. 1923, prize winner in 1991) and J.M. Coetzee (b. 1940, prize winner in 2003), both noted for their brave critiques of the ruling apartheid regime. Since the fall of apartheid more black writers

have come to the fore, many writing in regional languages. In addition, the focus has shifted from battling a powerful ruling class to dealing with the more complex and nuanced problems of the new country.

Although coming from outside of the countries usually associated with post-colonial literature, other writers from non-English-language traditions have achieved prominence due to both the quality of their writing and the skillful translations. Writers from Japan have achieved world-wide recognition; both Yukio Mishima (1925–1970) and Haruki Murakami (b. 1949) have been widely translated, although they present very different literary faces to the world. Mishima's writing is steeped in traditional Japanese culture, including works for the Noh and Kabuki theaters, while that of Murakami inhabits a post-modern, magic realist Japan, often with a haunting atmosphere. The beautifully wrought texts of the Nobel Prize-winning Turkish author Orhan Pamuk (b. 1952) chronicle both contemporary and historical Turkey in a very similar way to those of the

Egyptian Nobel Prize winner Naguib Mahfouz (1911–2006) do for Egypt. Pamuk's *Cevdet Bey ve Ogullari* (*Mr Cevdet and his Sons*, 1982) follows the fortunes of a family living in Istanbul while Mahfouz's exceptional *Cairo Trilogy* (1956–1957) does the same for Cairo.

POST-MODERNISM IN LITERATURE

Post-colonial writers have to a certain extent been influenced by, and have themselves made contributions to the development of, the contentious area of post-modernism. Notoriously hard to define, the movement takes its cue from the ideas of largely French philosophers and writers, in particular Jacques Derrida (1930–2004), Jacques Lacan (1901–1981), and Jean-François Lyotard (1924–1998), and moves away from the modernist conception of order within complexity to the notion that there is no underlying order and that the artist (in this case the writer) should revel in the play and multiple interpretations that then open up. In order to achieve this, writers adopted a plethora of techniques to present a bewildering and chaotic world. These include: the widespread use of multiple voices and viewpoints within a text, often using elements of literary pastiche and even quotation (known as "intertextuality"); a stressing of the artificiality of the text itself (the "artifice" of the "art") by making the literary technique obvious; ironic or disturbing juxtapositions of unrelated subjects, characters, plots, or devices to break up the narrative and create disorder; and, playing with the temporal flow of the narrative, so that it does not move—as we have come to expect—in a linear way. It might be argued that none of these techniques, or even the combination of them, is new (c.f. *Tristram Shandy* by Laurence Sterne written in the 18th century) and the whole idea of a post-modern literature has fierce supporters and critics alike.

The Italian writers Umberto Eco (*b.* 1932) and Italo Calvino (1923–1985) have both produced works that play with these ideas. In the case of Eco *Il nome della rosa* (*The Name of the Rose*, 1980) and *Il pendolo di Foucault* (*Foucault's Pendulum*, 1988) both play with history, conspiracy (another post-modern preoccupation), and multiple voices, and the latter makes a play on the name of Michel Foucault (1926–1984), another French thinker associated with post-modernism. Calvino, by contrast, moved from his early social realist novels toward a style akin to that of magic realism, using ideas of myth and fantasy in works such as *Cosmicomiche* (1965) and *Se una notte d'inverno un viaggiatore* (*If on a Winter's Night a Traveller*, 1979). The ironic and detached style of

UMBERTO ECO

Bestselling Italian author Umberto Eco signs his book, *The Mysterious Flame of Queen Loana*, during a book reading tour in 2004. Eco's suspenseful books play with history, conspiracy, and multiple voices.

the Czech writer Milan Kundera (*b.* 1929) also seems to contain elements of post-modern thought, particularly in *Nesnesitelná lehkost bytí* (*The Unbearable Lightness of Being*, 1984), although it is doubtful that the author himself would accept the label.

Perhaps more representative would be the writings of American authors Kurt Vonnegut (1922–2007) and Thomas Pynchon (*b.* 1937). Vonnegut has worked within a number of genres, although he is best known for his science fiction works. In his writing he plays with time, especially in *Slaughterhouse Five* (1969), and brings the artifice of the writing to the fore, including himself as a character in *Breakfast of Champions* (1973). The works of Pynchon are some of the more difficult American novels to have been written since World War II, with very dense and closely structured texts. His two most famous books, *The Crying of Lot 49* (1966) and *Gravity's Rainbow* (1973), bring in elements of popular culture, science, and conspiracy as well as intertextuality and multiple narrators.

An intriguing extension of the idea of multiple narrators has now been provided with the development of on-line writing, specifically "hypertext" fiction. With these works, the reader is free to decide where to jumpback and forth by using hypertext links within the text. This is still in its infancy and it remains to be seen whether readers are willing to abandon the traditional format of the printed book. However, the plethora of work by younger writers, be it in the form of fan fiction (works written using favorite characters invented by other authors) or science-fiction inspired cyberpunk (dystopian, technologically inspired futuristic writing) that is now being published, often for free on the Internet, suggests that a generational shift may be taking place.

SCIENCE FICTION AND FANTASY

The scientific advances of the 19th century had soon found their way into literature and, coupled with the sense of the fantastic

2001: A SPACE ODYSSEY

A shot from Stanley Kubrick's film based on the novel *2001: A Space Odyssey* by science fiction writer Arthur C. Clarke.

already explored in books such as Shelley's *Frankenstein*, a new genre of scientific adventure stories came into being. Although earlier writers had dealt with scientific themes in their work two authors, Jules Verne (1828–1905) and H.G. Wells (1866–1946) popularized the scientific narrative as a separate genre. However, it was the mid-20th century that saw an explosion of speculative (or predictive) narrative, usually novels, that had a technological focus. Not all of these imagined worlds were utopian, although some tended that way, and one of the earliest and most influential science fiction novels, *We* (1920–1921), by the Russian writer Yevgeny Zamyatin (1884–1937) was set in a dystopian future and was acknowledged by George Orwell as a model for his novel *1984* (1949).

Among the most popular science fiction writers following World War II were Isaac Asimov (1920–1992; *Nightfall*, 1941; *I, Robot*, 1950; and the *Foundation Trilogy*, 1951–1953), Arthur C. Clarke (1917–2008; *The City and the Stars*, 1956; *Rendezvous with Rama*, 1972; and *Childhood's End*, 1953), Robert A.

Heinlein (1907–1988; *Starship Troopers*, 1959; and *Stranger in a Strange Land*, 1961), and, one of the most cerebral of all science fiction authors, Stanislaw Lem (1921–2006; *Solaris*, 1961). Their novels often dealt with questions of how humans would evolve and react to the use of new technologies (for instance as in Asimov's Three Laws of Robotics), as well as predicting what those technologies might be. Some of these have now come to pass, such as Arthur C. Clarke's idea of using geostationary satellites as communication hubs, or are under consideration, again his idea that rockets might become outdated by the use of lifts linked to geostationary space platforms.

Like other popular genres of 20th-century writing, many science fiction novels have been made into movies, among the most celebrated being Stanley Kubrick's adaption of Arthur C. Clarke's *2001: A Space Odyssey* (1968), which was written in parallel to the movie script, and *Blade Runner* (1982) adapted from *Do Androids Dream of Electric Sheep?* (1968) by Philip K. Dick (1928–1982). Cinema and television have equally fed back into the world of science fiction writing, with movies such as *Star Wars* and television series like *Star Trek* spawning spin-off books and giving new life to the sub-genre of science fiction epics.

Linked to science fiction—with a similar sense of the unworldly and imagination—was the rise of fantasy literature. Often difficult to separate as distinct genres, fantasy is often held to be distinct in that it deals with the "impossible," usually achieved through the invocation of magic and the supernatural. The overwhelming importance of a setting akin to the medieval world in fantasy literature might be traced back to the Gothic fantasies of the Romantics, and especially the later works of Richard Wagner, but it was the post-World War II works of J.R.R. Tolkien that firmly established this as the dominant sense of place in fantasy writing.

Tolkien wrote *The Hobbit* in 1937, however, its follow-up *The Lord of Rings* (1954–1955) tapped into a post-war longing for an escape from the trauma of bombings, genocide, and the Cold War into an imagined past or heroic world of knights and elves and clear-cut stories of good versus evil. A morally ambiguous counter-balance to this was provided by the works of Mervyn Peake (1911–1968), whose dark Gothic vision of the rambling castle of Gormenghast was played out in three novels (*Titus Groan*, 1946; *Gormenghast*, 1950; and *Titus Alone*, 1959). Closer to Tolkien perhaps is the work of his friend C.S. Lewis (1898–1963) whose Narnia stories, while inhabiting a fantastic world of lions, witches, and magical wardrobes, espouse a Christian world view.

LORD OF THE RINGS MUSICAL, A production at the Theatre Royal, London, 18 June 2007, of the epic fantasy novel *Lord of the Rings* by J.R.R. Tolkien, the English writer who was also a professor of philology.

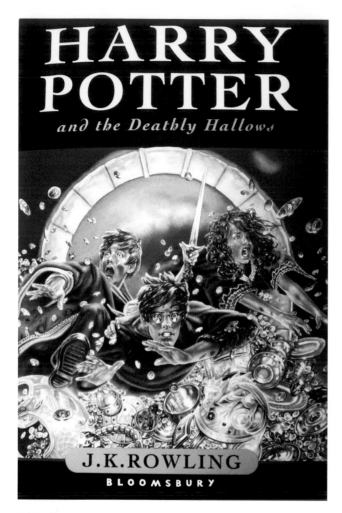

HARRY POTTER AND THE DEATHLY HALLOWS, By J.K. Rowling. This is the 7th and final novel of the Harry Potter series.

Both genres, science fiction and fantasy, have now developed numerous sub-genres that at times blur the distinction between each other, with plots taking place within dystopian cities or themes generally associated with fantasy transplanted to distant planets and alien worlds. Science fiction has also notably been used by writers exploring feminist themes to explore the constructs of gender and power; particularly fine examples include *The Left Hand of Darkness* (1969) by Ursula K. Le Guin (*b.* 1929) and Margaret Atwood's *The Handmaid's Tale* (1985).

Fantasy has also stayed into the realm of horror, a modern-day continuation of the Gothic tradition of writers such as Edgar Allan Poe and H.P. Lovecraft (1890–1937), with a number of contemporary authors achieving immense popularity including the American writer Stephen King (*b.* 1947).

The two genres of fantasy and science fiction—and institutions from the real world—have been affectionately subverted and lampooned by Terry Pratchett (1948) in his Discworld series, attracting a loyal fan base. Nobody, however, has come close to the popularity enjoyed by J.K. Rowling (*b.* 1965). Her seven books charting the adventures of the boy wizard Harry Potter who battles against the evil Lord Voldemort were written between 1990 and 2007, and have become some of the best- and fastest-selling titles in the world. Her skill in creating a world that exists within and parallel to our own—and that retains many of the more cosy elements of children's literature as well as adventure—prompted a global passion for the books, with translations into many languages and a series of movies that made the young actors almost as famous as the author herself. While some have criticized her work as being overly conservative (the books are set in a magical boarding school, echoing the vast majority of earlier children's books where the lead characters are drawn from a small and privileged social class), Rowling has also been credited with sparking a renaissance in children's reading.

CHILDREN'S FICTION

The works of J.K. Rowling have proved to be almost as popular with adults as children. In fact, throughout the 20th century children's literature developed into one of the most vibrant and interesting areas of writing. Books have been explicitly written for children—and been popular with adults alike—since the 19th century: in Germany works by Heinrich Hoffmann (1809–1894; *Der Struwwelpeter*, 1845–1858) and

Wilhelm Busch (1832–1908; *Max und Moritz*); in Italy with *Pinocchio* (1883) by Carlo Collodi (1826–1890); and in Britain, from *Alice's Adventures in Wonderland* and *Through the Looking Glass and What Alice Found There* (1865 and 1871) by Lewis Carroll to *Wind in the Willows* (by Kenneth Grahame, 1908) and *Winnie-the-Pooh* (A.A. Milne, 1926–1928), or the many illustrated works by Beatrix Potter (1866–1943). While these books dealt either with a fantastic imaginary world (as in the Alice novels) or the anthropomorphized stories of animals and toys (as in the latter books), one of the most successful children's authors of the 20th century, Enid Blyton (1897–1968), set most of her books in a comfortably upper middle-class England with straight-forward plots that usually involved a group of children (on the side of good) uncovering and foiling the dastardly deeds of ne'er-do-wells, who are often minorities. While very conservative, her works have proved enduringly popular with children and her *Famous Five, Secret Seven,* and *Adventure series* continue to be among the most translated and best-selling children's books in the world.

A similar, although more wholesome and sophisticated, flavor of adventure can be found in the books of Arthur Ransome (1884–1967). His stories of the "Swallows and Amazons" (two families of children after which the first of his books is named), published between 1930 and 1947, mostly take place in the Lake District and Norfolk Broads. The tales of camping, sailing, and invented adventure are the epitome of idyllic school holidays. Ransome's books are located within the real world of the 1920s and 1930s, but another of the more thoughtful children's authors, Phillip Pullman (*b.* 1946), set his most famous books, including *His Dark Materials* (*Northern Lights*, 1995; *The Subtle Knife*, 1997; *The Amber Spyglass*, 2000) in a series of fantastic parallel worlds. His books have been seen as an atheist response to those of C.S. Lewis and J.K. Rowling that draw heavily on Christian ideas of good versus evil.

Another popular idea within children's fiction is that of the anti-hero, the young anarchist who rebels against the seemingly stupid rules of the adult world, often with highly comic results. One of the first examples of this is found in the adventures of Max and Moritz, although they come to sticky end. More benign—especially in their final results—are the escapades indulged in by William Brown and his gang in the books by Richmal Crompton (1890–1969), and these bear close relation to the *Le Petit Nicolas* series by the French writer René Goscinny (1925–1977) and illustrator Jean-Jacques Sempé (*b.* 1932). A rather darker vision of childhood transgressions was given by the British author Roald Dahl (1916–1990) in a string of books

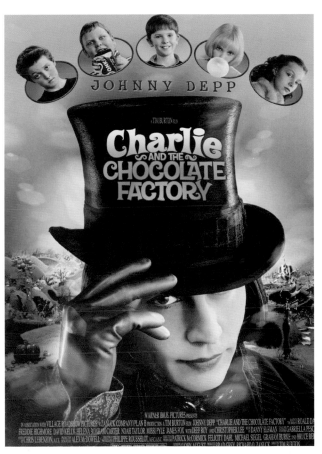

CHARLIE AND THE CHOCOLATE FACTORY, Poster at the Planet Hollywood restaurant in New York City, NY

that have now become classic examples of writing for children, including *Charlie and the Chocolate Factory* (1964), *Danny, Champion of the World* (1975), and *The Witches* (1983).

SPY FICTION AND THRILLERS

While the English writers Somerset Maugham (1874–1965) and John Buchan (1874–1940) had written political and adventure novels about World War I that included spying, building on the "great game" narrative of Kipling's *Kim* (1901), it was the onset of the Cold War between the USA and USSR that really brought the genre into its own. Graham Greene drew on his wartime experiences during his travels in a range of novels from the early-1950s onward, setting spy narratives in a variety of exotic locations (Cuba, Vietnam, and the Congo).

While glamorous far-flung settings became part of the defining element of the genre, some of the very best spy fiction of the era was, of necessity, set along the "Iron Curtain" between Eastern and Western Europe. Of these works, the exceptional novels of John le Carré (*b*. 1931) perhaps best capture the spirit of the age, especially through his beautifully drawn central character of George Smiley in a string of novels including *The Spy Who Came in from the Cold* (1963), *Tinker, Tailor, Soldier, Spy* (1974), and *Smiley's People* (1979).

The very opposite of Smiley and the drab, morally compromised world that le Carré invokes is the derring-do of Ian Fleming's (1908–1964) hero James Bond. Violent, womanizing, hard-drinking, and a great movie character, Bond is now better known through the movies loosely based on the books than from the books themselves, but his appearance introduced a more misogynistic element into the spy genre, which has been hard to shake off. Besides Robert Ludlum (1927–2001), other writers of spy fiction include Len Deighton (*b*. 1929) and Robert Harris (*b*. 1957).

These latter three authors might also be described as writing "thrillers," a more loose definition that covers a number of genres, including spy fiction, crime writing, and even science fiction. Very similar to spy novels that depend on the idea of a "cliffhanger" to keep the readers' interest, thrillers usually pit a central heroic figure against an often shadowy band of enemies. Some of these writers have achieved extraordinary sales, such as John Grisham (*b*. 1955), who specializes in stories based around the legal profession, and Dan Brown (*b*. 1964), best known for his bestseller *The Da Vinci Code* (2003), and *The Lost Symbol* (2009).

ROMANCE FICTION

One of the most overlooked and under-researched, at least in the academic world, areas of fiction, but one that is phenomenally popular, putting the sales of many other genres firmly in the shade, is that of romance literature. Often derided by more haughty commentators, romance is nonetheless an important literary genre with a large and disparate fan base. While romance has always formed a central theme in Western literature, modern mass-market romance fiction began in earnest when the publishing house Mills & Boon turned its attention to producing cheap, relatively short, and easily read romances in the 1930s. These proved to be very popular, and with authors writing to a formula, a number of new titles could be produced every month. At first the books were fairly coy in their depiction of intimacy between people, but as social attitudes changed, so did the degree to which sex could be graphically portrayed. There are an almost limitless number of sub-genres to romance fiction, taking in medical, historical, erotic, work-place, and science fiction plots. All, however, seem to be predicated on a happy ending.

FOR YOUR EYES ONLY: IAN FLEMING & JAMES BOND PRESS VIEW, Imperial War Museum, 16 April 2008, London, England.

While those working to formulas for mass-market publishers have tended to remain anonymous, some romance authors have achieved considerable fame. Of these Danielle Steele (*b.* 1947) is known for her racy depictions of glamorous people in far-flung locations, the highly prolific Barbara Cartland (1901–2000) was initially rather controversial, but her long writing career ensured that by the end of her life she even seemed mildly outdated, while the books by Catherine Cookson (1906–1998) are often historical and deal with the difficult lives of working people. Romance has been criticized for its often traditional depiction of the role of women in society and their expectations, but a related genre—dubbed "chick lit" and aimed at younger, aspirational women—arose during the 1990s. The central characters, while not exactly bra-burning feminists, do tend to be professional young women, and the writing is often sexually explicit.

GLOSSARY
LITERARY TERMS

Alliteration The use of the same letter or sound, usually at the beginning, in consecutive words.

Allusion The technique of conjuring up an idea or situation without explicitly mentioning it.

Autobiography A self-authored life story.

Automatic Writing A technique of unconscious writing (i.e. one not governed by explicit thought) used by the surrealists.

Ballad Initially a type of song and also applied to narrative poetry written in stanzas.

Bard An early poet working in an oral tradition.

Beat Literature Writings associated with American poets, travel writers, and novelists of the counter-culture of the late-1950s and 1960s.

Bildungsroman A novel that deals with a coming-of-age or education of the central character.

Biography A text, generally laid out chronologically, that describes someone's life.

Blank Verse Poetry written in unrhymed iambic pentameters.

Book The main artefact used in the dissemination of literature, consisting of printed or written pages bound into a whole. Also the libretto and dialogue of a musical.

Campus Novel Post-war British narrative, often comic, set within academia.

Canon A controversial concept that identifies a generally accepted, or proposed, selection of the finest and most representative works of a body of literature, music or of the visual arts, often excluding minority viewpoints and/or works that are politically radical.

Catharsis A term derived from Ancient Greek drama where the release of emotion is said to psychologically cleanse.

Chick Lit A sub-genre of romance fiction aimed at younger women, often with an element of sexually explicit writing.

Chivalry The social code of the Middle Ages that incorporates knightly behavior and courtly love.

Chorus In Ancient Greek drama a group of actors who speak in unison, commentating on the action of the play.

Colloquial Informal, everyday language.

Comedy Initially a work with a happy ending but also now with a connotation of being amusing.

Commedia dell'Arte A popular Italian dramatic form using stock characters from which pantomime derives.

Commentary A work that discusses another, usually religious.

Couplet In poetry two lines of verse usually of the same length and rhyme.

Cyber Punk A sub-genre of fantasy and science fiction that is urban, dystopian, and with a focus on technology.

Dactyl In verse, a stressed or long syllable followed by two unstressed or short syllables.

Dialogue A written, imagined discussion, often philosophical, between two characters.

Discourse A discussion or debate.

Drama A play.

Dramatic Personae The characters within a play.

Dystopia The opposite of a utopia, an imagined world where everything is bad.

Elegy Either an Ancient Greek poetic form written in couplets or a serious poem that may take the form of a lament.

Empfindsamkeit A sentimental German literary movement of the 18th century.

Epic A narrative poem, often deriving from an oral source, that describes the actions of a heroic central figure.

Epic Theater Largely associated with Bertold Brecht, a drama that reinforces the sense of a story being retold, thus enhancing the artificial nature of the drama.

Epigram A short witty or amusing aside or saying.

Epistolatory A form in which letters, arranged and read chronologically, are used to tell a story.

Essay A short non-fiction work that explores a particular idea.

Fable A story that illustrates moral behavior.

Fairy Tale A simple story, usually aimed at children and derived from oral sources, with fantastic elements and sometimes with a moral aim.

Fan Fiction Works written by amateur admirers of an author using favorite characters from that author's work.

Fantasy A genre akin to science fiction that is speculative but with elements of magic and, commonly, a medieval setting.

Fiction Written prose that describes the actions of imaginary characters.

Fourth Wall A term devised by Diderot to describe the boundary between the actors and audience in a theater.

Free Verse In poetry, writing that does not conform to a set system of line length, rhyme or structure.

Galant A term derived from music that refers to a work that is charming and light.

Genre A type or style of writing, music, painting or sculpture.

Grammar The rules that govern the workings of a language.

Hagiography A description of the lives of the saints or a biographical work that is obsequious in its treatment of the main subject.

Half-Rhyme The rhyming of the last consonants of successive lines of verse.

Hero An exemplary male figure at the center of a narrative, usually an epic.

Heroine The female equivalent of a hero.

Hexameter In poetry, a line with six metrical components.

History A written account, or the study of, the past.

Hymn A religious song of praise.

Hypertext Fiction Works published on-line that allow the reader to jump between different sections and versions of the text, often by multiple authors.

Iambic Pentameter A line of verse with five iambs, a metrical device consisting of one unstressed/short syllable followed by a stressed/long one.

Iconography The study of visual representation.

Intertextuality Quotation from, or allusion to, another work, especially in post-modern literature.

Irony The use of statements meaning the exact opposite, often for comic effect.

Jongleur An itinerant poet of the middle ages.

Kitchen Sink Drama Realist play of the 1950s that sought to portray the difficult lives or ordinary people.

Künstlerroman A novel that depicts an artist's coming-of-age.

Legend A historical story, often an epic, that is generally held to have an element of truth.

Letter A written communication.

Libretto The text of a dramatic musical work.

Lyric Either an emotional poetic work or the text of a song.

Magic Realism A prose form, usually a novel, that employs elements of the fantastic.

Meter The rhythmic pattern of a line of poetry.

Minnesanger Medieval German court poets.

Monologue A passage recited by one actor in a play or an entire work that is given over to the thoughts and speech of a single character.

Monophonic Where the action of a narrative is seen from one perspective, often that of the narrator.

Mystery Play A medieval morality play on a Christian theme.

Myth A historical story, often an epic, that is not generally held to have a basis in fact, commonly describing the actions of deities and supernatural figures.

Narrative A story or written account of an event.

Narrator The person who tells a story.

Neologism A new word.

Non-Fiction Novel A 20th-century genre that used elements of real life and reportage as well as fiction.

Nouveau Roman In post-war France, the 'new novel' that experimented with the form relying to greater extent on description than development of plot and character.

Novel A long work of prose fiction, generally with a strong narrative.

Novella A shorter version of the novel.

Ode A lyric poem originating from the sung poems, or odes, of Ancient Greece and Rome.

Old English The spoken and written language of Anglo-Saxon England (c. 450-1150).

Oral History A historical narrative passed on by word of mouth without being written down.

Oral Literature Epics, stories, myths and legends passed on by word of mouth without being written down.

Panegyric A spoken of written work of praise.

Parable A story, sometimes religious, that illustrates a moral position.

Parody An imitation that is often grotesque or exaggerated for comic effect.

Parrhesia To speak the truth.

Pastoral A work that describes a rural idyll or is set in an idealized rural landscape.

Periodical A publication, such as a newspaper, that is brought out at regular intervals.

Picaresque A fictional work written in episodes.

Pièces à Theses French plays of the 19th century with a moral or philosophical message.

Play A written work of drama intended for performance on the stage.

Plot The main elements of a narrative.

Poem A broad category of writing that involves the discussion or description of a place, emotion or narrative in a non-prose form, often with the use of specific techniques of meter, rhyme and structure.

Poetry Either a synonym of poem or the overall genre of poems.

Polyphony Literally 'many voices', where the plot of a novel unfolds through the viewpoint of a number of a different characters.

Post-Colonial Literature Works, usually in English and French, dealing with the experience of colonization, by writers from countries that were previously under colonial, especially British, rule.

Prose Written text that is akin to everyday language, usually without the poetic techniques of meter and rhyme.

Protagonist The main character of a narrative.

Punctuation Elements of written language, aside from the actual words, that help to clarify a text.

Rhetoric Derived from Ancient Greece and Rome, the art of persuasion and argument using specific techniques of repetition, sentence construction, and questioning.

Rhyme The use of the similar sounds of different words to create a structure, often at the end of successive lines of poetry.

Rhythm In poetry, patterns of stress and length of syllables, often repeatitive.

Ritterdrama An offshoot of Sturm und Drang that located narratives in an imagined medieval past.

Romance Either a genre of literature concerned with romantic love, usually with a happy ending, or medieval stories of courtly love and later works that take these as their model or theme.

Roundel A poem with three stanzas of three lines, with alternate rhymes and repeated first words.

Saga Literally 'story', Icelandic and Norse narratives of which there are three types, heroic, royal and family sagas.

Samizdat Literature Works published clandestinely.

Satire A work in which irony, parody and comic effect is used to attack and criticize an idea or person.

Scholasticism A theological movement of the middle ages that sought to find a rational basis for Christian thought and doctrine.

Science Fiction Prose narratives that are speculative, often based in the future with an emphasis on technology.

Script The written text for a play or film.

Sensibility An ideal popular in the 18th century of a heightened emotional and aesthetic response to situation.

Serialization A narrative presented in successive parts, often in a periodical.

Short Story A written prose narrative that is complete within itself, but which is shorter than a novel.

Skaldic Verse A complex set of poetic rules used by Norse poets of the 10th and 11th centuries.

Social Realism The attempted depiction of real life in as truthful a way as possible, often with a political or social aim.

Soliloquy In a play when a character talks aloud to his- or herself, expressing inner thoughts.

Sonnet A poem with fourteen lines, often of ten syllables each.

Spy Fiction Works of narrative prose that take espionage as their central theme, largely inspired by the cold war.

Stanza In poetry, a group of lines that form a unit, often setting the metrical form.

Stepped Triadic Line A poetic form used by William Carlos Williams,

Story An imaginary narrative.

Stream of Consciousness A narrative written in such a way that the reader experiences everything through the eyes, and mind, of the narrator in a continuous and often non-linear fashion.

Sturm und Drang Literally 'storm and stress', a German literary movement of the 18th century that sought to portray emotional turbulence as a counterfoil to Neoclassical ideals.

Syntax The satisfactory and grammatically correct arrangement of words in a sentence.

Tale A story.

Tetralogy A series of four works that are linked in some fashion.

Text A written artefact.

Theater Either the place where plays are performed or the totality of the activity surrounding the production of a play.

Theater of Cruelty Drama that sets out to shock the audience into a realization of the futility of existence.

Theater of the Absurd A 20th-century movement, strong in France, that broke down dramatic conventions to portray the futility of existence.

Theology The study of religion and religious belief.

Thriller A fast moving and exciting novel often using conspiracy, twists of plot, and cliffhangers to maintain the momentum.

Time-Shift Where a narrative moves from one historical period to another.

Tragedy Derived from Ancient Greek drama, a narrative that has an unhappy ending often with the downfall of the central character.

Translation The act of rewriting a text from one language into another.

Travalog A prose work that describes a journey.

Treatise A formal prose work that expounds upon a particular subject or activity.

Trilogy A series of three works that are linked by common elements or themes.

Troubadour A Provençal singer and poet of the medieval courts.

Trouvère A northern French singer and poet of the medieval courts.

Trümmerliteratur 'Literature of the rubble', a description of the post-war works of German writer Heinrich Böll.

Typography The art and appearance of printed text.

Variable Foot A poetic meter devised by William Carlos Williams divided poetic lines in an approximation of American vernacular speech.

Verismo A late-19th century and early-20th century Italian realist movement.

Vernacular Everyday, ordinary language and speech

Verse Poetry arranged using a metrical pattern and usually with rhyme.

Weimar Classicism A German literary movement, named after the town in Saxony, of the late-18th and early-19th centuries whose main figures were Goethe and Schiller.

AUTHORS INDEX

Pope, Alexander 13, 87, 88

Potter, Beatrix 207

Pound, Ezra 157, 159, 171, 172, 173, 191

Pratchett, Terry 206

Premchand, Munshi 200

Prešeren, France 110

Proust, Marcel 157, 158, 161, 163, 169

Prus, Bolesław 140

Pullman, Philip 207

Pushkin, Aleksandr Sergeyevich 112, 113

Pynchon, Thomas 204

Queneau, Raymond 189

Quevedo, Francisco de 63

Rabelais, François 50, 51

Racine, Jean 65, 67, 117

Radcliffe, Anne 107

Ransome, Arthur 207

Rao, Raja 200

Rhys, Jean 108

Richardson, Samuel 82, 89, 90, 91

Richelieu (pseudonym of Armand Jean du Plessis de) 63, 64, 65

Rilke, Rainer Maria 82

Rimbaud, Arthur 124, 157, 158, 159

Robbe-Grillet, Alain 189

Roche, Sophie de la 82

Rochefoucauld, La 49, 66

Ronsard, Pierre de 51, 52

Rossetti, Christina 129

Rossetti, Dante Gabriel 106, 129

Roth, Philip 195

Roubaud, Jacques 189

Rousseau, Jean-Jacques 77, 78, 80, 83, 100, 115

Rowling, J.K. 206

Roy, Arundhati 200

Rushdie, Salman 7, 92, 199, 200

Ruskin, John 163

Sachs, Nelly 191

Sade, Marquis de (title and pen name of Donatien-Alphonese-François, comte de Sade) 100, 107

Saïd, Edward 197

Saint-Pierre, Jacques-Henri-Bernardin de 100

Salinger, J.D. 196

Sand, George 103

Sappho 14

Saramago, José de Sousa 198

Sartre, Jean-Paul 183, 188

Sassoon, Siegfried 161, 165

Sayers, Dorothy 153

Scève, Maurice 52, 53

Schiller, Johann Christoph Friedrich von 83, 84, 85, 86, 87, 95

Schlegel, August Wilhelm von 96

Schlegel, Friedrich von 96

Schwitters, Kurt 180

Scott, Walter 109, 111

Seneca 20, 47, 63

Senghor, Léopold Sédar 197

Seth, Vikram 201

Shakespeare, William 19, 41, 47, 48, 62, 72, 83, 84, 85, 87, 101, 103, 105, 117, 122, 132, 169, 174

Shaw, George Bernard 130, 131

Shelley, Mary 107, 204

Shelley, Percy Bysshe 105

Sholokhov, Mikhail 185

Sidney, Philip 42

Sillitoe, Alan 193

Sinclair, Iain 193

Singh, Khushwant 200

Skram, Amalie 145

Sládkovic, Andrej (born Andrej Braxatoris) 111

Socrates 18

Sophocles 17, 95

Sophrony, Bishop 110

Soyinka, Wole 198

Spender, Stephen 184

Spenser, Edmund 45, 46, 73

St. Adomnan 29

St. Aldhelm 29

St. Anselm 31

St. Athanasius 29

St. Augustine 29, 65

St. Gregory I 29

Staël, Mme de 101

Stanislavsky, Konstantin 143

Steele, Danielle 209

Steinbeck, John 172, 174, 178

Stendhal (born Henri Marie Beyle) 117, 118

Sterne, Laurence 77, 82, 90, 91, 92, 111, 113, 203

Stevens, Wallace 157, 174

Stevenson, Robert Louis 108

Stoker, Bram 108

Storm, Theodor 137

Strindberg, August 141, 144, 145

Štúr, Ľudovít 110

Sturluson, Snorri 22, 23

Svetlá, Karolína 141

Swift, Jonathan 78, 88

Swinburne, Algernon Charles 106, 129

Tacitus 21

Tagore, Rabindranath 200

Tasso, Torquato 56, 69, 85

Tennyson, Alfred 106, 128

Terence 18, 66

Thackeray, William Makepeace 126

Thiong'o, Ngugi wa 198

Thompson, Hunter S. 195

Thoreau, Henry David 148

Thucydides 14, 15

Tibullus 68

Tieck, Ludwig 96

Tocqueville, Alexis de 147

Tolkien, J.R.R. 205

Tolstoy, Leo 62, 131, 132, 133, 134, 143, 148

Turgenev, Ivan 133, 134, 143

Turner, Frederick Jackson 147

Twain, Mark 150

Tzara, Tristan 182, 184

Valéry, Paul 158, 160

Valla, Lorenzo 42

Van Dine, S.S. 153

Vega, Lope de 62, 63

Verga, Giovanni 138, 139

Verlaine, Paul 124, 158, 159

Verne, Jules 204

Vidal, Gore 196

Vigny, Alfred-Victor, comte de 102

Virgil 14, 19, 39, 46, 57, 66, 73, 87

Voltaire (pseudonym of François-Marie Arouet) 77, 78, 79

Vondel, Joost Van Den 75

Vonnegut, Kurt 204

Walcott, Derek 198

Waller, Edmund 73

Walpole, Horace 107

Waugh, Evelyn 194

Wells, H.G. 204

Wesker, Arnold 193

West, Rebecca 173

Whitman, Walt 151, 172

Wilde, Oscar 108, 130

William of Malmesbury 32

William of Ockham 31

Williams, Tennessee 193

Williams, William Carlos 172

Winckelmann, Johann Joachim 87

Wolfe, Tom 195

Wollstonecraft, Mary 104

Woolf, Virginia 91, 158, 163, 164, 168, 169

Wordsworth, William 84, 105, 128

Wycliffe, John 31, 44

Yeats, William Butler 17, 52, 105, 106, 164, 168, 169, 170, 173, 185

Zamyatin, Yevgeny 204

Zeno 18

Zhukovsky, Vasily 112

Zola, Émile 121, 122, 123

PICTURE CREDITS

a-above, b-below, l-left, r-right, m-middle

COVER ILLUSTRATIONS
far left: Miguel de Cervantes Saavedra (1547-1616); AKG Images
left middle: Johann Wolfgang von Goethe (1749-1832); Bridgeman Art Library
right middle: Simone de Beauvoir (1908-1986); Getty Images
far right: Joanne Rowling (*1965) ©picture-alliance/dpa-Report

ASSOCIATED PRESS
5m, 5r, 83r, 144b, 157, 171b, 180, 187, 191, 199, 201l, 202, 203

GETTY IMAGES
4a/m, 4b, 7a, 12, 13, 14, 18, 19r, 21, 22a, 24a, 25b, 26, 28, 33, 35r, 38, 40, 43, 44, 47, 48, 51r, 53, 54b, 55l, 57, 58, 59, 63b, 64r, 66, 67, 71, 73r, 74, 75l, 76, 79l, 80l, 81, 84l, 87, 88, 90, 91a, 92, 93a, 94, 95, 97r, 99, 106, 107, 109, 112, 114, 116l, 117, 118r, 119, 120b, 122l, 125, 127r, 129, 130b, 133, 134, 137l, 138, 140b, 143, 145r, 146, 147, 148, 158, 159b, 160, 161a/r, 162l, 163, 165a, 166, 167, 168, 169, 170, 172, 174, 175r, 176, 177, 178, 181, 182, 183, 184, 186, 188, 189l, 190, 192, 193, 194, 195, 196, 197, 198, 200, 201r, 204, 205, 206, 207, 209

MARY EVANS PICTURE LIBRARY
4a/l, 4a/r, 5l, 6, 7b, 8, 9, 10, 11, 15, 16, 17, 19l, 20, 22b, 23, 24b, 25a, 27, 29, 30, 31, 34, 35l, 36, 37, 39, 41, 42, 45, 46, 49, 50, 51l, 52, 54a, 55r, 56, 61, 62, 63a, 64l, 65, 68, 69, 70, 72, 73l, 75r, 77, 78, 79r, 80r, 82, 83l, 84r, 85, 86, 89, 91b, 93b, 96, 97l, 98, 100, 101, 102, 103, 104, 108, 110, 113, 115, 116r, 118l, 120a, 121, 122r, 123, 124, 126, 127l, 128, 130a, 131, 132, 135, 136, 137r, 139, 140a, 141, 142, 144a, 145l, 149, 150, 151, 152, 153, 154, 155, 156, 159a, 161a/l, 161b, 162m, 162r, 164, 165b, 171a, 173, 175l, 179, 185, 189r